KU-021-743

# SOPHIE GRIGSON'S

# INGREDIENTS BOOK

To Paul,

with best wishes

Sophie Grigson x

# SOPHIE GRIGSON'S INGREDIENTS BOOK

PHOTOGRAPHY BY JESS KOPPEL

PYRAMID BOOKS

For Dominic Owens and Mary Hatchwell,
too small a token of appreciation.

It seems a very long time since my initial meeting with Isabel Moore and Janice Anderson of Paul Hamlyn Publishing to discuss writing a book of ingredients. Indeed, it was a long time ago, and I have not only to thank them for the idea itself, but also for their extraordinary patience. They must often have wondered if they would ever see a completed manuscript.

I was thrilled that they both agreed with me over the choice of photographer. I met Jess Koppel when we were both setting out on our careers. We share a passion for food, particularly eating it, and became firm friends. I know of no other photographer whose work could illustrate my words so appositely and so beautifully. Food stylist and home economist, Lyn Rutherford has worked closely with her, tracking down obscure items and preparing dishes for photography. Not always an easy or enviable task.

I have turned to so many authors, some in person, for information and advice that it would be impossible to name them all. The bibliography provides a fuller list, but I would especially like to thank Claudia Roden, Sri Owen, Frances Bissell, Carolyn Heal, Michael Allsop, and the late Tom Stobart, whose books I have referred to frequently.

Many companies and tourist authorities have made it possible for me to travel to countries I would otherwise never have reached. They are gambling their money since they know well that I may never mention their product in print. I have pestered retailers and suppliers for information which they have provided willingly where possible. I am particularly grateful to local shopkeepers who have answered endless streams of questions, the answers to which must frequently have appeared startlingly obvious.

Puff Fairclough has spent hours testing recipes, as well as sustaining me with a constant flow of encouragement, enthusiasm, tea and coffee. Numerous friends have bravely tasted a succession of unlikely sounding dishes, and made constructive comments where necessary. Both friends and family, especially the Hatchwells, have been infinitely supportive when the going was rough. Finally, I would like to thank my grandmother for a piece of advice she gave my mother, and my mother for passing it on to me: "If there's something on the menu you haven't tried, order it!".

Photographic stylist: Marian Price
Photography assistant: Jeremy Hopley
Home economy assistant: Jacqueline Gibson
Design: Paul Welti

This edition published in 1991 by Pyramid Books,
an imprint of Reed International Books,
Michelin House, 81 Fulham Road, London SW3 6RB

Text © Sophie Grigson, 1991
Illustrations and design © Reed International
Books Ltd, 1991

ISBN 1 855 100 762

Produced by Mandarin Offset – printed in Singapore

## USING THE RECIPES

Recipes should be treated as guidelines, not authoritarian sets of rules. The proper degree of seasoning is a matter only to be decided by the cook him- or herself, and only as they cook. However, it is wise, especially when cooking with unfamiliar ingredients for the first time, to adhere to a couple of basic conventions. Use either imperial or metric measurements, not a mish-mash of both. Unless otherwise stated, spoonfuls are rounded, not heaped or levelled.

Precise oven temperatures can be vitally important when, for instance, cooking soufflés or baking cakes (though even here a degree or two either way will not prove a disaster), but by and large there is some degree of latitude. Oven-technology is not sophisticated enough to ensure perfect uniformity. In other words, it is quite possible that your gas oven's Mark 6 will be a couple of degrees hotter or colder than my electric oven's 200°C. As a result, it is impossible to give exact cooking times. Similarly, the width and depth of a pan, and the interpretation of such phrases as "over a low heat" affects cooking times on the hob. Ultimately, it is the responsibility of the cook to check and adjust timings as they judge fit.

# CONTENTS

# INTRODUCTION

When friends have asked me what I have been working on, I have described this as a self-indulgent book, part jokingly, part seriously. It has given me the opportunity to indulge wholeheartedly in two of my favourite pastimes. The first is shopping, for which I need little excuse. I can never resist the temptations of strange and intriguing food shops, here or abroad, and inevitably return home loaded with the spoils. The second is experimenting and playing with new ingredients, discovering how to use them as they are meant to be used, and then seeing how they will slot into other dishes, giving new twists to familiar recipes.

Not that all the items on these pages are out of the ordinary or hard to find. Far from it. In amongst the more recherché ingredients are a fair number that may seem surprisingly commonplace, even mundane, and others which fall somewhere between the two extremes. The choice has been dictated by certain set parameters which, nonetheless, allowed for a considerable degree of subjective interpretation.

All the ingredients included are special in some way, and are at the very least worth looking for and, in many cases, worth making special trips to track down. Cost was no criterion; some are encouragingly cheap, others frighteningly expensive, whilst the majority are neither one nor the other. In the end, it is culinary virtue alone that made them worthy of inclusion. For instance, canned truffles, at least those I have sampled, are a complete waste of money, bought out of one upmanship rather than for flavour – out. Fresh truffles, on the other hand, are worth their weight in gold (just as well, really, because that is more or less what you have to pay) – in. In the exotic fruit and veg range, babaco and colocassi have pretty names but little flavour, whereas sapodillas and sweet potatoes may not look up to much, but taste wonderful. I have also included a handful of everyday items which have been debased by misuse. The two that spring instantly to mind are beetroot and kiwifruit. Both inspire a missionary zeal in me. Treated respectfully, they are every bit as delicious as many more highly rated fruit and vegetables. They desperately need re-instating.

The selection is a highly personal one. I have made no attempt to be comprehensive, which some readers may find annoying. That cannot be helped. The ingredients are all ones which I have had the opportunity to use, and I can say with absolute honesty that I think every one worth trying. You may not always agree. You may wonder why I have omitted something that you think quite sensational. Tastes differ and there is no getting round that. During the course of writing, I have come across new things that I would have liked to include, but the line had to be drawn somewhere if the book was ever to be completed.

I hope that reading what follows will open up new avenues, and give you the confidence to explore them. Eating is one of life's few true necessities. Make the most of it, make it as interesting and enjoyable as you can. Commonsense, not self-indulgence.

SOPHIE GRIGSON
LONDON, 1990

# HERBS
# & SPICES

Herbs and spices are the fine details of the art of cooking, small additions in terms of volume, but what a difference they make. Anyone can learn to cook competently, but using spices well requires both experience and a natural flair. It is, I think, what makes the difference between an average cook, a good cook and a sensational cook. Most people can reach stage two if they really want to, but there are not many who can be counted as stage three-ers. I know a few (and I would not include myself amongst their ranks), some of them chefs, a couple of food writers and others who cook merely for pleasure. They just have an instinctive understanding of how to balance flavours to perfection.

For the rest of us, experience and a willingness to experiment are the keys. When using herbs or spices, familiar or unfamiliar, learning to trust one's own judgment is essential, and in the end a far better guide than the exact quantities given in recipes. It is impossible for me or any other food writer to tell you how much of this or that herb or spice to use. Any one herb or spice will vary in strength according to provenance and to strain.

As a general rule, herbs or spices grown in hot climates, imported maybe from Italy or further afield, will be stronger than ones grown in a greenhouse in the Channel Islands or your own windowbox or garden. I happen to like fairly strongly flavoured foods, you may prefer a more subtle approach. So any quantities I mention can only indicate roughly how much you could use.

Recent years have seen an increasingly wide range of herbs and spices sold in ordinary supermarkets and grocery shops. The more exotic ones tend to carry correspondingly exotic price tags, a sad but not inevitable fact of life. If you are prepared to spend a little more time on your shopping, you will often find that smaller shops catering to local ethnic communities offer the same flavourings in more generous quantity and at a lower price. Middle Eastern and Indian shops are rich sources of aromatic leaves and spices, fresh and dried.

Look around the shelves while you are there, and you are bound to notice a host of other spices, some of which you may never have encountered before. Most of them are worth trying, though admittedly I have come across some which seem so dull as to be totally pointless. Perhaps I have just not found the right way to use them yet. Anyway, the point I want to make is that trying out new spices or herbs is exciting and fun, and can lead to the discovery of wonderful flavours that can be adapted to fit in very well with your style of cooking.

## Using Herbs

With a few exceptions, fresh is best. Fresh herbs have a lively, green zest that is inevitably lost when dried. Some herbs lose not only their liveliness but also virtually their entire flavour when dried – prime examples are basil and coriander – and all you are left with is a musty echo of their former selves. And, of course, dried herbs are for the most part only of any use when cooked. A final sprinkling of dried hay over your delicious stew is hardly going to do much for its taste or for its visual appeal.

Although more fresh herbs than ever are available in shops, the supplies are erratic and still limited. The answer is to grow your own whenever possible, in windowboxes, in the garden, or in pots on the windowsill – a ready supply always at hand. If you are growing your own, do not be mean-spirited. Plant half a dozen plants (or more if you are particularly taken with them) of those herbs which do not grow into huge, solid clumps. One basil or coriander plant, for instance, is not going to take you very far. Once established, a single plant of lovage, sweet cicely, thyme or rosemary will flourish and should be enough to keep you going. Look out in garden centres for the more unusual herbs. Seed merchants, and mail-order herb specialists will fill most gaps. If you buy 'cut' herbs, you may often find that they come with root attached, so try popping them into a small pot of earth to see if they take.

Naturally, there are times when you will have no choice but to settle for dried herbs. As a rough guideline, those that dry well are the strongly flavoured ones, often, but not always, those with more robust, thicker leaves – bay leaves, kaffir lime leaves, curry leaves, rosemary, thyme, lemon grass, fenugreek. They need a good soak to release their flavour, and lose their dryness, either in the cooking pot, or in a dressing, or in some cases in warm water before use. Remember, last minute sprinklings are a no-no.

If you are faced with a surfeit of fresh herbs, freeze them. Pack the cleaned herbs loosely into plastic bags, put them into the freezer and, once they are solid, crush them with a rolling pin so that they can be stashed into smaller containers in the freezer, ready to use.

## Using Spices

Spices are the seeds, fruit, and roots of aromatic plants. That definition means that garlic, horseradish, and fresh ginger should all be classed as spices, although my natural instinct is to think of them as herbs, if they have to be classified at all. I know the derivation of this instinct – spices are usually dried, herbs should be fresh. It does make me wonder what those dried spices would taste like if I ever had the chance to try them fresh. Growing my own coriander introduced me to the exquisite taste of green coriander seeds which harbour both the taste of the fresh leaf and the dried seed. In most instances, however, I doubt that the opportunity will ever arise.

Unlike most herbs, dried spices retain a concentrated aromatic scent. The aromatic quality is contributed by the volatile oils that are captured as they dry. From the moment a whole spice is ground, the volatile oils begin to waft off into their surroundings, released from imprisonment, hopefully to imbue some food with their scent. A newly opened tub of ground spice will release a superb aroma, but once it has been opened and closed half a dozen times or more, most of the volatile oils will have had a chance to float away into the air, and the powder will have lost a good deal of its power. Moral: whenever possible buy whole spices and grind them yourself (in an electric coffee grinder or a mortar). For the fullest flavour, dry-fry the spices first. The difference is remarkable.

**Dry-frying:** Recipes will often tell you to toast or roast spices before use. Rather confusing terms, since what they usually mean is neither toasting nor roasting in the

# HERBS

ANGELICA

LOVAGE

conventional sense. Dry-frying is much more descriptive. Use a small, heavy frying pan, and shake or stir the whole spices in it, over a moderate to high heat, with no oil, until they give off a heady scent of incense, and begin to turn a shade darker. They may also start jumping, so do not be surprised as one or two leap athletically out of the pan. Tip them into a bowl before they get anywhere near burning, and cool them. Not only does dry-frying bring out a superb flavour, but it also crisps up the spices, making them more brittle, and easier to grind to a fine powder.

## ANGELICA

There is a steep and twisting path down to the Devil's Hole on the wilder north coast of Jersey. In late spring and early summer the verges on either side of the path are crowded with bright green ferny umbellifers: not cow parsley as I imagined at first glance, but a sea of angelica run wild. Nobody seems to take much notice of it, which is no doubt why it grows in such profusion.

Fresh angelica is little known; even the delicious, emerald green candied angelica is becoming harder to find. Fresh, it has a delightful musky, sweet scent. The leaves and stalks can be used in savoury dishes, but are really better fit for puddings, sweets and jams. A handful of angelica leaves stewed with plums or rhubarb dampens down their acidity, reducing the need for sugar. Though candying angelica is a protracted process, bottling in syrup is an easy way of preserving it. Cut large stalks into suitable lengths, boil them in water until just tender, then drain and strip off the outer skin. Boil them again in fresh water until a good green. Strain and cool. Make a thick sugar syrup, add the angelica and simmer for 5 minutes. Pack the angelica into sterilized preserving jars, cover with the syrup and seal tightly.

The stalks can be eaten like celery, plainly steamed or boiled and dished up with a large knob of butter.

## LOVAGE

An old English pot-herb that has, for some unfathomable reason, fallen into neglect. Even I, with my far from green fingers, have no problem growing it. It pushes out its celery-like stalks with no encouragement apart from an occasional splash of water in very hot weather.

Lovage leaves have a powerful flavour, an aromatic blend of celery and citrus. Lovage and potato soup is a classic, but it can be added, cautiously since it can be overpowering, to all manner of meat and vegetable (particularly root vegetable) dishes. The leaves are good in salads, or with cream or cottage cheese. The stems can be candied, like angelica.

Gather and dry the seeds which have a similar celery-like flavour.

SWEET CICELY

SALAD BURNET

THAI BASIL

## SWEET CICELY
(Sweet chervil)

A pretty plant with a pretty name. Sweet cicely has lacey, fern-like leaves, with a sweetish flavour, aniseedy and reminiscent of lovage. I love it in salads, marinades and cream cheese, but with its sweetish taste, its natural role is in sweet dishes. Like angelica, it not only imparts flavour but reduces the tartness of stewed or baked fruits. It is a good addition to fresh fruit salads. Though I have never tried it, nor come across any reference, I see no reason why the thicker stems should not be candied or preserved in syrup. Apparently the roots may be boiled to serve hot as a vegetable, or cold as a salad.

SUMMER SAVORY

## SALAD BURNET

The pretty little tooth-edged leaves of salad burnet have a cucumberish scent, and the flavour is again cucumberish and slightly bitter. As the name suggests, the leaves are often added to salads (pick the smaller ones before they get toughened by age), and are occasionally included in the bunches of young salad leaves sold in Italian markets. Not that this is the sole purpose of salad burnet. Chopped up, it is good in sauces, especially cold ones, such as a vinaigrette, or mayonnaise-based sauces, and soups. The leaves are also used to flavour vinegar, or floated on top of chilled summer drinks.

## SAVORY

Summer and winter savory have similar flavours, reminiscent of thyme with an underlying notion of rosemary, and a bitter edge. Savory is a strong herb and needs to be used with care, but in the right place and right quantity it is a gem. The rightest place of all is with pulses — butterbeans, haricot beans, peas, lentils. It also has a place in rich meaty stews, and stuffings, always used judiciously. A herb for robust, comforting dishes.

## BASIL

Holidays in Italy and the south of France have revived the British love of basil; it was a better known plant in Tudor England than it is today. Sweet basil and bush basil, with its tiny leaves, are the most familiar of the many forms of basil, which include cinnamon, lemon, liquorice and ginger basils. They all, however, originated in the tropics, and most of them in India. All types have marvellously aromatic, spicy scents, at their most powerful when grown in hot climates. Sweet basil grown in Italy has a dramatic peppery, clovish smell, which my much-appreciated home-grown basil just cannot compete with. Bear this in mind when using any type of basil flown in from Asia.

**Purple- or Opal-leaved basil** This is frightfully chic. You can occasionally buy plants of it from garden centres, and many specialist seed companies offer the seeds. The leaves are a dark bronzed purple, and look quite beautiful on a tomato salad. The flavour is well-nigh the same as that of sweet or bush basil, though possibly a tinge muted. Use it wherever the colour will show to advantage. Pesto made with purple-leaved basil looks muddy and murky . . . not a good idea at all.

PURPLE BASIL

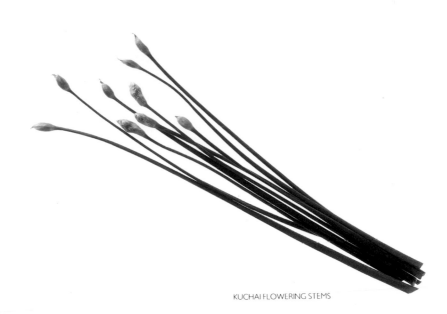

KUCHAI FLOWERING STEMS

**Holy basil** Usually flown in from Thailand, Holy basil has large, dark green leaves, sometimes streaked with purple. It has a strong aniseed and pepper flavour and is every bit as beguiling as sweet basil. Do not restrict it to South-East Asian cooking, but use as sweet basil in Mediterranean dishes, remembering that you may need a little less. I have found that it actually works out cheaper than basil bought in those plastic-wrapped trays in supermarkets. Shops specializing in Chinese, Indonesian, Thai or Malaysian produce will often stock it. Plants and seeds can be bought from some garden centres and seed companies specializing in herbs.

## KU CHAI
(Cuchay, Garlic chives, Chinese chives, Flowering Chinese chives)

The leaves and the flowering stems of ku chai are usually sold separately in Chinese and Oriental food shops. Both are similar to chives in taste, but stronger and with a hint of garlic. The leaves are long and flat, about 5mm (¼ inch) wide, like a floppier version of the green part of spring onions. The flowering stems are round, crisp and juicy, tipped with a pale tight bud. Pretty though they may be when the bud has opened to reveal the flowers, this indicates that the plant was older when picked, and therefore likely to be tougher and more fibrous. Unless you want the flowers purely as an edible decoration, do not be tempted.

The stems, wrapped in a plastic bag, keep happily for up to a week in the vegetable drawer of the refrigerator, whilst the leaves are rather less hardy, and will last for little more than 3 or 4 days.

Leaves and stems can be used as ordinary chives, bearing in mind that they have a comparatively forceful flavour. They are delicious in omelettes, on salads, or chopped into thick yoghurt or soured cream (particularly good with smoked fish, or beetroot). Both can be used in stir-fries, retaining colour and texture. Stems and leaves are sometimes stir-fried or braised on their own to be used as a vegetable side dish.

## FILE POWDER
(Filet powder)

Filé powder is the dried, powdered leaf of the sassafras. It is mainly used in Louisiana, in Creole dishes, above all in gumbos, big hearty, earthy stews of shellfish and/or poultry, as an alternative or sometimes alongside okra. Like okra, it has a distinct mucilaginous quality which gives the stew its characteristic smoothness. Add to that a light, spicy flavour and you have a herb that is worth experimenting with in other dishes besides gumbo. Try stirring a tablespoon or so into your own soups or stews, 5–10 minutes before cooking time is up.

## CORIANDER
(Chinese parsley, Cilantro)

Coriander and basil are the two herbs I love best. Although they both have powerful flavours, there are few foods they clash with. In fact, off hand I cannot think of any savoury foodstuff that I would not partner them with. Perhaps if I set my mind to it I would come up with something but it hardly seems worth the bother.

A passion for coriander is one that creeps up on you slowly. At first, the flavour is strange, but quite pleasant, then little by little the appeal grows and you find yourself using it in abundance. My introduction to coriander came with my first dabblings in Oriental cooking. It is widely used, too, in the Middle East and South America. On holiday in Portugal, I was surprised to find it chopped into butter, and then in other dishes. It is not a herb I had connected with European food (though the seeds are used all around the Mediterranean), except perhaps that of Greece and Turkey. The penny dropped – the Portuguese have adopted coriander from their old Indian colonies.

The possibilities for using fresh green coriander are so wide that it is hard to pick only a few suggestions. It makes a good addition to salads, green or tomato, or others. It is superb with fish, shellfish or chicken, in marinades, sauces or stuffings. Butter flavoured with chopped coriander, lemon juice, and garlic, is delicious with grilled fish, lamb or poultry. Coriander is excellent with root vegetables. Add it to sauces and "dips" – mayonnaise, plain yoghurt, hummus. And the list rolls on and on.

Fresh coriander is easy enough to buy now. If you have the choice, ignore the expensive and mean-portioned supermarket packets, and buy it from a Middle Eastern, Greek or Indian shops, where they sell it in generous big bunches. Unless you are going to use it all straight away, cut off any roots and stand the stems

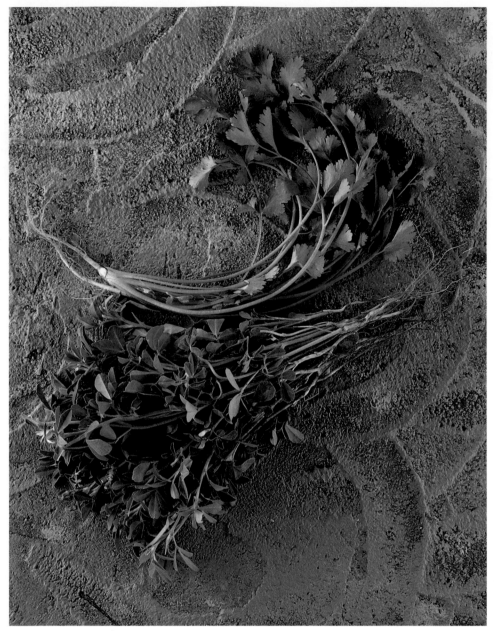

TOP: CORIANDER; BOTTOM: FENUGREEK

in water to keep the coriander perky for several days. But do not throw out the roots. They are used in Thai cooking, finely chopped, to flavour curries, and there is no reason why they should not be used in other ways. Wash, then wrap in paper and store in the refrigerator. Dried coriander, which I have recently seen for the first time, is a disaster and not worth buying.

Coriander grows easily. In theory you can just plant the seeds from your spice

rack, although I have had more success with small plants brought from the garden centre. One of the great joys of having the plant growing in your own garden is that you will get to taste the fresh green seeds. In this state, they bridge the difference between leaf and dried seed, carrying both the greenness of the herb and the orangey aroma of the spice. Use them while you can, picked straight from the plant, in salads, crushed in marinades and sauces.

## FRESH FENUGREEK
(Methi)

Fenugreek seeds are an essential part of many curry powders, but the green leaves are also widely used in Indian cookery. I have bought fresh fenugreek from Indian groceries, and Greek Cypriot ones too. The flowers smell of curry, but the leaves have a delicious bitterness, which makes them too strong to use as a vegetable on their own, but a delight when mixed with starchy vegetables (particularly potatoes, and pulses) and aromatic spices. Dried methi is sold in most Indian shops and is a good substitute for fresh. Try adding either one to stews and soups, or spiced vegetable dishes.

## CURRY LEAVES

Curry leaves look a little like reduced bay leaves, shiny and dark green though not half as tough. They can be found fresh or dried in Indian food shops. Fresh ones can be dried at home, or frozen. Just as the name implies, they have a curryish scent and flavour (minus the chilli content), and are used whole, chopped, or pounded to a paste in all kinds of curries. They adapt well to Western styles of cooking, again in marinades, dressings, soups or stews, giving a warm but subtle scent of curry, without actually turning the dish into a full-blooded Eastern masterpiece.

CURRY LEAVES

KAFFIR LIME LEAVES

## KAFFIR LIME LEAVES

These leaves, glossy and dark green, curving in and out like hourglass-shaped bay leaves, are indeed the leaves of a variety of lime and give a sharp aromatic citrus flavour. They are often sold fresh in Indian shops, but, if not, you should be able to lay your hands on dried leaves. When you do get fresh ones, usually still on the branch, hang what you are not using in a cool airy place to dry. They can also be frozen.

Do not confuse them when buying with curry leaves (see above). If you are not sure which is which, tear a small piece off a leaf and have a sniff; there is no similarity between the citrus scent of lime leaves and the curryish scent of curry leaves.

The leaves are used like bay leaves, torn up and thrown into soups, marinades, curries, or whatever, and fished out, if you can be bothered, before serving. The fruit of the Kaffir lime is small, green and

gnarled, strangely beautiful. Only the zest is used. One friend, food writer Alan Davidson, always includes a few kaffir limes along with the Seville oranges when making marmalade — and extremely good marmalade it is, too.

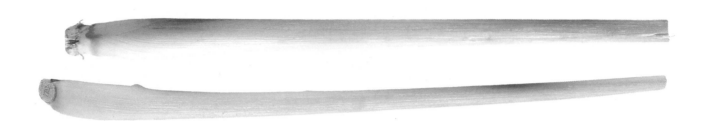

LEMON GRASS

## LEMON GRASS
(Citronella, Sereh)

The exquisite flavour of lemon grass is the key note of South-East Asian cooking. Aromatic, citrusy, grassy, faintly gingery, quite blissful. The tapering stalks are now more easily available in the West, in Oriental food shops and even, from time to time, in some supermarkets. It keeps well for several weeks, wrapped in newspaper, in the vegetable drawer of the refrigerator.

How you use it depends on the recipe. Where the lemon grass is used as a flavouring to be removed at the end of cooking, rather like a bay leaf, the whole stem, cut into 4 cm (1½ inch) lengths, can be used. Where the lemon grass is to be finely chopped, or ground to a paste, the lower, thicker 10-12 cm (4-5 inches) or so of the stem is the bit you want. Remove the toughest outer layer, then bruise the stem with a mallet, or by pressing it down with the flat side of a knife blade. Then chop or slice as needed. Do not throw out the fibrous top half, but use it to flavour stocks, or soups. It can also be bruised and used to brush oil over meats, fish or vegetables that are to be grilled, imparting a delicate trace of its own scent.

Dried lemon grass, sliced or powdered can be substituted for fresh. Sliced, it needs to be soaked for an hour before use. Powdered lemon grass can be added straight to the pan as any other spice. It is often suggested that a strip of lemon zest is an adequate substitute for lemon grass. It isn't, but on the other hand, it will be better than nothing if push comes to shove.

## PERILLA
(Shiso, Beefsteak plant, Japanese basil)

Japanese perilla belongs to the same family as mint and basil, though its scent is less aromatic and pungent. Green perilla leaves, some 5-7.5 cm (2-3 inches) wide with jagged edges, are sometimes available in Japanese food shops. They are used as a garnish, deep-fried in tempura batter, or chopped as any ordinary herb might be.

I have never seen fresh red perilla leaves (from a different species) in this country, and suspect that they are, if not totally unavailable, at least extremely rare. They wilt speedily after picking, which no doubt explains their absence. Pickled red perilla leaves are a different matter, as they are available either on their own in vacuum-packed plastic bags, or mixed in with pickled umeboshi plums.

## PANDANUS
(Screwpine, Daun pandan, Kewra, Kevda)

Of the many types of pandanus plant that grow in tropical Asia, two are cultivated for culinary purposes. The male flowers of *Pandarus tectorius* have an exquisite sweet perfume, captured by distillation. Kewra, or kevda, water is used to flavour many sweet dishes and syrups. It is sold in some Indian foodstores under one or other name. The essence is highly concentrated, and should be added a drop at a time.

Fresh screwpine leaves, long fibrous and elegant, come from *Pandanus odorus*. Though the scent is less dramatic, it is still exotic, musky, and grassy. You may be able to buy them fresh or dried from shops specializing in Indonesian or Thai provisions. To use, cut into 7.5 cm (3 inch) lengths, and simmer or infuse in sugar syrups, milk or cream for puddings of all sorts, using four or five pieces to a pint or so of liquid – pandanus-scented baked custards and bavarois are heavenly. In some parts of Asia pandanus leaves are also employed in savoury dishes, from boiled rice to curries. To make a delicately fragrant tea, brew a few pieces of leaf along with light China tea.

# SCENTED LEAVES AND FLOWERS

PINEAPPLE SAGE

BLACKCURRANT LEAVES

## PINEAPPLE SAGE

I was so bowled over by my first sniff of the sweet true pineapple scent of this plant that I rushed out and bought one for my garden the very next day. I have never found the smell of the variously pineapple, apple, ginger or other scented mints or sages anywhere near as wonderful as that of pineapple sage. My small plant, less than 30 cm (12 inches) tall when I planted it, grew to a great bush some 120 cm (4 feet) high within a year, and I often stand in the garden rubbing the leaves for the pure pleasure of their fragrance.

In culinary terms, their use is limited, but not negligible. I add the leaves, torn in half, to fruit salads and salsas, infuse them in syrups to use for drinks, or for poaching fruit, and to add a delicate scent to cakes (see the recipe for Elderflower Cake on page 36). Other than that, their use in *casa Grigson* has been purely decorative, tucked in around puddings, or as a bed for scoops of ice cream or sorbet.

## PEACH LEAVES

The peach tree in my garden has never shown any inclination to produce fruit. Well, it is not very tall, so maybe there is time for that yet. Nonetheless, it is not without culinary merit. It had never

occurred to me to use the leaves until I worked with Joyce Molyneux, chef and owner of the Carved Angel Restaurant in Dartmouth, Devon. She infuses them in milk and cream to make a delicious thin *crème anglaise*, with a subtle, bitter almond flavour. A leaf or two can be added to all kinds of milk or cream-based puddings – baked in with a rice pudding, infused in the cream for a baked custard, ice cream or a bavarois. They can be used to line the base of a cake tin, sending their delicate flavour up into the cake as it bakes. If you have a tree, whether it fruits or not, take advantage of it.

## SCENTED GERANIUM LEAVES AND BLACKCURRANT LEAVES

Both of these can be used in the same way as peach leaves, though the flavours are different, not so much almondy, but more fragrant in the case of geranium leaves; there are rose, lemon, cinnamon, nutmeg, orange geraniums and others. The leaves can also be used to scent jellies and jams, ice creams and sorbets, or mixed with the fruit for fruit pies or crumbles.

## ROSES

I admit it, I have stolen roses on more than one occasion. I do not have the right type for cooking in my garden. They need to be the big, dark red, highly scented sort, and all I have got are dainty little numbers with a comparatively muted fragrance. So, yes, there have been occasions when I've been unable to resist leaning across a wall and snitching a couple of glamorous blooms, but only from rose bushes covered in a mass of flowers so the owners probably never noticed.

Whatever the provenance of the roses, they need to be used quickly before their scent fades. The petals should be separated from the stem, and in theory, the white "heel" needs to be removed. In forgetful moments I have neglected this last part, and have not noticed any terrible reaction as a result. Choose roses that have not, to your knowledge, been sprayed with a hundred and one ghastly chemicals (that is the big disadvantage of stealing them from unknown gardens – you cannot be sure of their life history). Rinse the petals in cold water and dry on kitchen paper or a clean tea towel before using.

If I do not have any particular destiny in mind for them, I will either make up a jar of rose syrup, or quickly liquidize them with

CLOCKWISE FROM TOP LEFT: ROSE, LAVENDER, GERANIUM LEAVES, NASTURTIUM FLOWERS AND LEAVES

lemon juice, to preserve the colour (minus lemon, they turn a murky brown), and a little icing sugar to make a purée which can be frozen in small batches. Both of these can be used at a later date to flavour creams and ices. Clean dry petals (or dried rose buds) can be layered with sugar in a jar to give rose-scented sugar.

The petals may be infused in white wine

vinegar, or added directly to jams and jellies. Rose petal scented raspberry or strawberry jam is excellent, and the petals give a wonderful fragrance to apple, quince, or redcurrant jellies. I have now found a source of ready-made rose petal preserve, with a heavenly scent, sold in small cans, made in Pakistan. If you happen to have a generous supply of rose petals, you can make your own – simmer a good 450 g/1 lb rose petals in 300 ml/1 pint of water for 3 minutes. Draw off the heat, add 450 g/1 lb sugar and the juice of 2 large lemons and stir until dissolved, then simmer until the syrup is good and thick – the preserve will not gel like ordinary jam as there is no pectin in the petals.

Cookery writer Frances Bissell suggests scenting fresh unsalted butter, by wrapping it in muslin and burying it in a bowl of petals, covering and leaving for 12 hours in a cool place. The delightfully scented butter is delicious on toasted brioche, or warm scones. Other scented flower petals or leaves can be used instead or as well.

## LAVENDER

Lavender water, sachets of lavender in the underwear drawer, lavender in pot pourri, but lavender in cooking? At first it may seem a bizarre notion, but used with restraint, lavender can add an elegant fragrance to both savoury and sweet foods. The flowers are more appropriate for the sweet end of the range, a few sprigs infused in cream or milk for ice creams, or other creamy puddings. They can be used to flavour sugar syrups, for drinks or poaching fruit. Finely chopped, they can be added directly to cakes and biscuits. In *Cooking with Herbs* by Emelie Tolley & Chris Mead (Sidgwick & Jackson), they give a recipe for a lavender praline, made as an ordinary praline, using an equal volume of fresh lavender flowers to sugar.

Both flowers and leaves, used in small quantities, give a subtle scent to rabbit, or

lamb, tucked around them as they roast, or slipped into the pot when braising. Personally, I do not care much for lavender with fish, though I have come across recipes which pair the two. However you choose to use the lavender, go easy at the first attempts. Remember that dried lavender is stronger than fresh. It is as powerful a flavouring as rosemary, if not more so, and too much of a good thing is, in this case, far from enjoyable.

## NASTURTIUM FLOWERS AND LEAVES

Nasturtiums are such cheerful plants, tumbling happily through the garden with their bright splashes of orange and yellow flowers. Both leaves and flowers are edible. The flowers have a scented peppery flavour, the leaves a stronger peppery flavour. I often set a large posy of them in the centre of the dinner table, to be whisked away, to the consternation of guests, after the main course, reappearing in the salad, leaves mixed in with the other greenery, flowers perched on top. Nasturtiums with variegated leaves make a particularly pretty addition to salads.

Both parts can be chopped to add to cream cheese, scrambled eggs or omelettes, pasta, sauces, butters and soups, or used with shellfish, or poultry. Nasturtium ice cream is surprisingly delicious – add finely chopped nasturtium flowers to a basic vanilla ice cream mixture to make a pretty ice cream speckled with yellow and orange. Both buds and seed pods can be pickled like capers.

## ELDERFLOWERS

Every year, from the beginning of May onwards, I monitor the elderbushes near my house, impatiently watching as the flower buds form. Once they open to reveal the creamy white flowers, I have a

couple of weeks to revel in the heady, muscat scent of elderflowers.

My mother used to make elderflower fritters for pudding every year, dipping the flowers into a batter lightened with whisked egg whites, frying them stem upwards, snipping off the stalks once the batter had set, flipping them over to brown the second side. We would eat them hot from the pan dusted with sugar, sharpened with a squeeze of lemon juice. The other pudding we would eagerly look forward to was creamy gooseberry fool, flavoured with elderflower, only possible when gooseberry and elderflower seasons coincide. Later on, she was given a recipe for elderflower cordial, which became an established family favourite.

Following on her lead, I have experimented widely and successfully with elderflowers, using them to flavour sorbets, ice creams, baked custards, bavarois, jellies, and cakes. The method is usually much the same – the heads of elderflower are simmered or infused in a syrup, which may or may not be sharpened with lemon juice, or milk or cream. Once the flavour is extracted the liquid is strained and then used as usual. Scenting cakes requires a different approach, so I have given a full recipe later in this chapter. To make elderflower vinegar, delightful in dressings, or to deglaze a pan after cooking chicken, fill a preserving jar loosely with flowers and cover with good white wine or rice vinegar. Seal tightly, and leave for a couple of weeks or longer before opening.

When picking elderflowers, begin by finding a bush that is far away from the pollution of the road as possible. Snip off the flowers that are newly opened and at their finest; give each umbel a gentle shake – if you are caught in a poetic shower of white flowerlets, move on to another one. Use the flowers as soon as possible, certainly the same day. The scent fades swiftly. Never wash the flowers, but give them a shake to dislodge any insect life.

# SPICES

## PEPPERCORNS – Black, white and green

Black, white and green peppercorns are all berries of the climbing vine, *Piper Nigrum.* Despite the apparent disparities in flavour, black peppercorns are no more than dried green peppercorns, picked when they are still unripe. Left on the vine, the corns mature to a bright red. At this stage the outer skin is easily stripped off, to expose what we know as white peppercorns.

White pepper is used in white sauces, or wherever specks of black pepper would mar the purity of colour; however, it contributes little but heat. The aromatic flavour of pepper resides largely in the skin, so unless you feel strongly about the impropriety of black specks in an otherwise virginal white sauce, it hardly seems worth bothering about laying up stocks of white pepper.

I have no time, either, for ready-ground black pepper. A total waste of money, if you ask me. Once you have opened your tub of ground pepper a couple of times, it will be reduced to a rather dull powder and you might as well throw it out. Far better to invest in a good pepper mill which can be refilled regularly with whole black peppercorns.

The labels on most packets or tubs of black peppercorns give little prominence to the country or area of origin, with one exception – Tellicherry (or Jellicherry) pepper from Kerala in southern India. Snap

TOP: GREEN PEPPERCORNS, WHITE PEPPERCORNS; BOTTOM: BLACK PEPPERCORNS, SZECHUAN PEPPERCORNS

it up if you get the opportunity. It has quite the most superior flavour of all peppers, wonderfully aromatic and sensuous.

Green peppercorns are preserved either in brine or by freeze-drying. I tend to opt for the latter, finding them more useful as they can be crushed to a powder like any other spice. If necessary, they can also be reconstituted by soaking for a few minutes in hot water.

## PINK PEPPERCORNS

Pink peppercorns are not related at all to black peppercorns. They just happen to be about the same size. They are not even particularly peppery either, having an aromatic, pine flavour. There has been considerable debate about how safe they are. It seems that in generous quantity they can be toxic. Unless you develop a rampant passion for pink peppercorns this is unlikely to prove a problem in day to day cooking. I have never experienced any side-effects, nor have I met anyone else who has suffered as a result of eating pink peppercorns. Not proof absolute, I agree, but enough to assuage my personal doubts. I shall keep on using them, every now and then, sometimes mixed with green and black peppercorns in sauces, or added to fish, meat or cheese dishes for their own glamorous colour and taste.

## SZECHUAN PEPPER
(Chinese pepper, Anise pepper)

Szechuan pepper is no relation to ordinary black pepper, and though peppery, it is tingly rather than straight hot. It is also headily aromatic and I would be tempted to dry-fry a few grains for the smell alone. Although it is predominantly used in Chinese cooking, particularly in the province of Szechuan, it slips happily into many a Western dish. Always dry-fry the rust-red berries and crush or grind them before using.

The Chinese make a condiment of ground roasted Szechuan pepper, mixed with salt (5 parts spice to 1 part salt) to sprinkle over cooked foods, an idea worth appropriating.

HORSERADISH

## HORSERADISH

Next time you reach for a jar of creamed horseradish in the supermarket, read the ingredients list before you slip it into your basket. It winds on and on, and includes a host of things that I would really rather not have in my creamed horseradish. There are exceptions, of course, a few small brands which stick to the essential ingredients, omitting the host of artificial sweeteners, emulsifiers, etc. etc. but you do have to search them out.

Dried powdered and flaked horseradish is infinitely preferable, requiring only the addition of water to reconstitute. Fresh horseradish is naturally best of all. This often muddy yellowish root is not a regular at the greengrocers, more's the pity. You are most likely to find it in areas with a large Jewish population, around the time of the Passover in late March or April, when it may be served as part of the ritual Seder meal, symbolizing the bitterness of the Jews in slavery.

Horseradish is easy to grow. Rather too easy perhaps, as it tends to spread with gusto and is difficult to get rid of. The horseradish in my garden has always proved a disappointment with thin, tough stringy roots, impossible to grate, but maybe I am just unlucky.

When buying fresh horseradish choose roots that are firm and fat. They keep for several weeks in the salad drawer of the refrigerator. To use, scrub them vigorously, divide into three or four pieces, then grate as much as you need of the outer part. The inner core is as tough as old boots and comparatively weak on flavour. Throw it out when you get down to it. Grated horseradish loses its pungency if kept hanging around, so freeze any that you are not using straight away. If you like your seasonings pungent and tear-jerking, mix the horseradish with nothing more than white wine or cider vinegar and sugar. For a subtler sauce, use it to flavour soured cream, crème fraîche, thick yoghurt, or whipped cream (half whipped cream half thick yoghurt is excellent), adding a little sugar, salt and a dash of lemon juice to balance the flavours. Chopped walnuts, and/or chives are a good addition too. Serve with roast beef, of course, or fish, particularly smoked fish, eggs or chicken. Horseradish is wonderful with beetroot, or in apple sauce.

The volatile oils that give flavour and pungency are extremely susceptible to heat. By all means warm a horseradish sauce, but never let it get anywhere near boiling point. Add the horseradish at the last possible moment.

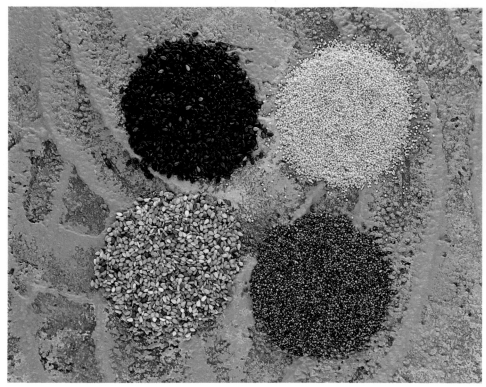

LEFT, BLACK AND WHITE SESAME SEEDS; RIGHT, WHITE AND BLACK POPPY SEEDS

Black or white, sesame seeds are much improved by dry-frying until they jump vigorously. This brings out a deep nutty flavour, imperative if you are going to sprinkle them over salads or other cooked dishes as a final garnish. Of course, if they are baked on or in bread etc. there is no need to toast them first. Dry-fried sesame seeds, ground to a thick powdery paste with an electric grinder, or in a mortar, make a good basis for a thick dressing or dip, or a sauce. Black sesame seeds will give a very dramatic colour in this case, white a more conventional and some might say, acceptable, nut brown hue.

## STAR ANISE

The name gives an idea of both the shape and flavour of this Chinese spice. Star-shaped, flower-shaped, with five to ten "petals", actually the seed pods, hard and woody. Inside each one is a shiny brown seed. The flavour is similar to aniseed, but stronger and a touch bitter.

Star anise can be used whole, divided up into segments, or ground to a powder, and is essential in many Chinese dishes, marrying particularly well with fattier meats such as duck or pork. It is one of the spices that make up Chinese five-spice. Use it to flavour stocks, soups, stews and any number of savoury dishes. It sits well, in moderation, with anything from eggs, through fish and all kinds of meat. Always dry-fry before grinding. In its whole state, star anise keeps remarkably well.

STAR ANISE

## POPPYSEEDS – Black (or blue) and white

Like sesame seeds, poppyseeds come in two opposing shades. Unlike sesame seeds, it is the slate black poppyseed, which may also be referred to as blue, that is the most widely available in the West. Indian poppyseed is almost invariably white.

The seed comes from the opium poppy, but do not imagine that a generous helping of poppyseed strudel last thing at night is going to induce hallucinogenic dreams. Opium is derived from the white latex that seeps out of the unripe seed pods when cut. The ripe seeds contain none of the opium alkaloids.

German and Eastern European poppyseed cakes, buns, tarts and strudels can be heavenly confections when well prepared. The ones I like best have a filling of crushed poppyseeds, mixed with a small amount of plain chocolate, but there are many variations. For these sweetmeats the

poppyseeds may either be softened by soaking in water for an hour or so, or toasted and crushed to bring out their full nutty, sweet taste which seems the better bet to me. Poppyseeds, like sesame, are good sprinkled over breads and biscuits. In India, white poppyseeds may be used to thicken sauces as well as add flavour.

## SESAME SEEDS – Black and White

White sesame seeds are well known but black ones are less common. They taste the same, so the reason for opting for black rather than white comes down to looks alone. Sprinkled on to breads, cakes and biscuits, or mixed in with the dough, they have considerably more visual impact than the white sort. Substitute them or a mixture of the two wherever appropriate. Reference books tell me that sesame seeds also come in red, but these seem to be even harder to come by than black.

TAMARIND

VANILLA PODS

## TAMARIND
(Indian date)

The brown bean pods of the tamarind tree hide a sticky pulp wrapped around black, shiny seeds. The pulp is the important part, with a high tartaric acid content giving it a concentrated sourness. Tamarind is used as a souring agent, like lemon juice or vinegar, with an added fruitiness.

You may occasionally come across whole tamarind pods, but far more common are the sticky black-brown blocks of crushed pods, pulp and seeds, sold in most Asian food shops. To use, simply break off a small piece, around the size of a large quail's egg, squeeze flat, then soak in a few spoonfuls of hot water for 15-30 minutes or so. Strain off the tamarind water, pressing some of the pulp through the sieve, and discard the debris. One ounce of tamarind makes around 300 ml (½ pint) of thin tamarind water (which is what you will usually need), or 150 ml (¼ pint) of thick tamarind water. Fully dried slices of tamarind are soaked in the same way, but require at least 30 minutes' soaking, if not more, to extract the juice.

Ready-prepared tamarind syrup is sold in bottles and can be used as is, allowing for the fact that it is probably stronger than thin tamarind water and should be used in small quantity, adding more if needs be.

Tamarind has a high pectin content, so is useful in jams and jellies, particularly those made with fruit with a low pectin content (e.g. pears or peaches) which can be most temperamental. It is widely used in pickles and chutneys, makes a wonderful marinade for fish and poultry, and is delicious in salad dressings. Incidentally, it is also a laxative, so don't go overboard!

## VANILLA PODS

The vanilla pod is the fruit of a climbing orchid, *Vanilla planifolia*, from the rain forests of tropical America. The flower itself, I am told, is no great beauty, but the pods have been valued for centuries, a secret of the Aztecs long before the Spanish first set foot in the New World.

Vanilla is such a common-place flavouring that it may seem odd to include it amongst this selection of more unusual spices. It is here partly because in its real form it is one of the most exquisite of all the "sweet" spices, and more importantly because the use of crude synthetic vanillin has become so widespread that the subtlety of true vanilla risks being devalued.

Although vanilla essence is useful, I prefer to use either the pod itself or vanilla sugar in cooking. The essence is powerful stuff, and a few drops too much can overwhelm. It is all too easy to be deceived into buying synthetic vanillin. Take time when shopping to read the label – anything with the words "flavouring" or "flavoured" printed, often in small type, between or near the word "vanilla" is fake.

A vanilla pod, on the other hand, is a vanilla pod and no two ways about it. They may seem expensive, but they last for ages and can be used again and again. Store vanilla pods in an airtight jar of sugar, and within a few days the sugar will be imbued with the scent of vanilla, and you will have an ample supply of vanilla sugar as well. As the sugar level drops, top it up with more sugar. Whenever you use a pod, simply rinse it well, dry thoroughly and tuck it back into the sugar.

CLOCKWISE, FROM TOP LEFT: SAFFRON, GROUND ANNATTO, ASAFOETIDA, AMCHUR, WASABI

## SAFFRON

The most expensive spice in the world. The fine red yellow threads are the stamens of the saffron crocus. In the plains of La Mancha, in Spain, where much of the best saffron is grown, great fields of purple flowers stretch out into the distance every autumn. For a few weeks everyone prays for good weather; heavy rain or even one violent storm can decimate the crop. The flowers are picked by hand, the stamens are plucked out a flower at a time. The price is not unjustified.

Luckily for us, the power of those stamens is considerable. A generous pinch of threads is all you will need to release the strange, delicious, almost metallic flavour through most dishes. Although it can be bought in powdered form, it is safer to stick with the whole stamens. Fakery is rife (never be tempted by cheap saffron because the one thing it will not be is pure saffron) and it is far easier to adulterate the powder. Guard, too, against being duped into buying dried marigold petals, which will provide a yellow colour but not the exquisite flavour.

There is no substitute for real saffron – that other yellow spice, turmeric, like marigold petals, changes the nature of a dish. Do not expect real saffron to colour a dish bright shocking yellow. Unless it is used in ferocious quantity, it will give a paler primrose yellow. To use saffron, either soak the threads in a small amount of warm water for 10-15 minutes to loosen the colour, or crush to a powder in a mortar (dry-frying for a few seconds makes this easier). As well as classic dishes like Risotto alla milanese and Paella, saffron adds a good flavour to tomato sauces, is a natural partner with shellfish, and is delicious in sweet cakes (such as Cornish Saffron cake), breads and puddings.

## AMCHUR
(Amchoor, Mango powder)

Amchur is no more than dried green mangoes, crushed to a dull fawn powder. Like sumac and dried lime, it has a sensational, fruity sharpness, distinguished from the other two by the lingering scent of pine wood. Amchur belongs to the Indian continent, finding its place as a souring agent in curries, pickles, chutneys, marinades, with vegetables and more. It is best, I find, with only brief heating, added towards the final part of the cooking period, though it does need some amount of cooking or blending into a dish. The texture is too powdery to use as a straight condiment. It is excellent, however, in marinades, particularly for fish and poultry, where it not only imparts flavour but tenderizes too.

## ASAFOETIDA

I have mixed feelings about asafoetida. Used in small quantities it adds an oniony flavour to foods, and is much used in Indian vegetarian cooking, especially by those religious sects to whom onions are prohibited. So far so good. The big drawback is the appalling stink of the stuff. *Foetida* is derived from the same Latin root as fetid, and that is exactly what it is. The foul smell is destroyed in cooking, so it will not actually affect the appetite, but once ground to a powder, asafoetida must be kept in a tightly sealed airtight container.

Asafoetida is the dried gum of a species of giant fennel. In theory, it can be bought in lump form, when it is comparatively odourless. In practice, you will probably have to settle for powdered asafoetida and companion smell. Powdered asafoetida is nearly always adulterated with flour and may be dyed, so you may find that you have to use slightly larger quantities than stipulated in some recipes. Go cautiously at first, and only increase the quantity once you are accustomed to the taste.

## WASABI
(Japanese horseradish, Green horseradish)

While you are unlikely to come across fresh wasabi root outside Japan, even the meanest of Japanese stockists abroad is sure to sell cans of powdered wasabi, and maybe tubes of wasabi paste. Mind you, powdered wasabi has a seemingly endless shelf-life, and all you need do is add water, just as if it were English powdered mustard, so choose cans rather than tubes.

Wasabi is like a very pungent purée of horseradish, dyed in a gay pale green. It should be used soon after it is made up, in the Japanese manner, as an accompaniment to sushi and sashimi, or mixed with plenty of soy sauce as a dipping sauce. Go easy at first as it packs a really powerful punch.

It can serve as an alternative to ordinary horseradish, often a better bet than the much adulterated bottles of "creamed horseradish sauce". Stir a small amount of made-up wasabi (you can add more later) into whipped cream (or whipped cream mixed with thick Greek yoghurt), along with a dash of lemon and a pinch of sugar, to serve with roast beef, fish, and particularly smoked fish.

## ANNATTO
(Achiote, Bija, Bijol)

You may have noticed those packets of bright orange-brown smoked mackerel, quite obviously dyed, which proudly proclaim on the label that they include no artificial additives or colourings. The dye is, to be fair, perfectly natural, although it seems to me to be totally unnecessary. What is wrong with smoked mackerel-coloured smoked mackerel? Gripe over and done with. The orangey-yellow dye is usually derived from annatto seeds. The same dye has long been used to colour cheeses such as Red Leicester and Cheshire.

This powerful colouring ability eclipses the fact that annatto seeds also have a very pleasing mildly peppery, pine-fragrant flavour. They are used in the Caribbean, parts of Latin America and in the Philippines both for taste and colour. If you can lay your hands on annatto seeds (they are sold occasionally in shops supplying West Indian or Filipino provisions) try adding them to rice as it cooks, or gently frying the seeds, maybe with a few chillies, for 4-5 minutes in plenty of oil, covering the pan if they start to jump, then leaving them to cool, to give a spiced orange oil for flavouring. The seeds can also be ground, to use directly in marinades, say, or with fish, vegetables or white meats.

## NIGELLA
(Black onion seed, Black cumin)

The blue flowers of love-in-the-mist were one of the pleasures of the small garden of the house in France where my family spent a large part of each year. Nigella seeds come from a less decorative relation of the same plant. The seeds are tiny and black, with a striking resemblance to onion seeds, hence their alternative name. In some parts of India they may also be known as black cumin, though they have nothing to do with real black cumin, either botanically, or in any culinary sense.

The small crunchy seeds have a peppery, mildly bitter taste, and are used in stir-fried vegetable dishes, some curries and with dals. Two other Indian applications which can be transposed to Western dishes, are in pickles and on breads. Add nigella seeds to pickling spices, for anything from pickled onions to sweet and sharp chutneys. I have mixed them with poppyseeds, sesame seeds and/or sunflower seeds for seed breads, or for sprinkling over cheese biscuits.

## DRIED LIMES

Quite self-explanatory. You can buy small dried limes, about 4 cm (1 ½ inches) in length from Middle Eastern shops, or dry them yourself. It will take a couple of months for an ordinary lime to dry out until it is as light as air and hollow inside, but you can give them a helping hand by sitting them in a sunny windowsill, the airing cupboard or on the radiator.

Bought or home-dried, they are a wonderful addition to a spice collection. They provide a sharp, aromatic citrus flavour, delicious in stews and soups, or ground down to flavour butters or marinades. To use, crack the lime (one is sufficient for a fairly generous stew) into pieces with a hammer, or in a mortar. The pieces can then be used as they are, or ground to a powder.

## SUMAC
(Sumaq)

Although you could make your own sumac powder from the fruit of some varieties of garden sumac, it is not that advisable as several of them are poisonous (they belong to the same family as poison ivy). Better to buy the spice ready-prepared in Middle Eastern and Turkish shops when you can be sure that what you are getting is the dried and ground fruit of the wild Mediterranean or Elm-leaved sumac.

The coarse, almost crystalline deep rust-red powder has a marvellous astringent, fruity flavour, and once you taste it you will no doubt come up with all kinds of possibilities for use. It is employed as a souring agent throughout the Middle East, especially in the Lebanon, often in place of lemon or vinegar. I often sprinkle it on to salads, or over cold cooked dishes as a condiment, but that is only the beginning.

Add it to marinades for fish or poultry, or simply rub into the flesh before grilling. It can be added straight to stews or casseroles, or mixed into salad dressings too. Yoghurt or lebne sharpened with sumac is served as a sauce alongside grilled and fried dishes.

## MAHLEB
(Mahlab)

The tiny pale tan grains of mahleb are the kernels of the fruit of a wild cherry that thrives in parts of the Mediterranean and the Middle East. Until recently I have only been able to buy mahleb in tiny packets from Greek and Cypriot shops, but a new Moroccan shop near my home sells comparatively large bagfuls at a more than reasonable price.

These kernels have the characteristic almondy and slightly bitter taste of all *Prunus* kernels. Think of the taste of amaretti biscuits, made with apricot kernels, and you will be getting close. Unlike many of the *Prunus* kernels, it harbours no prussic acid, and so can be eaten safely, raw or cooked (heat drives off the toxins in apricot kernels so there is no cause for apprehension when you are next faced with amaretti).

Mahleb can be used, ground to a powder, in pastries, cakes and biscuits in much the same way as ground almonds, though in rather smaller quantity as it has a more dominant flavour, or to add a pleasing bitter almond note to milk puddings. Grind the mahleb to a powder only when needed as the flavour soon evaporates.

## ROOT GINGER
(Fresh or Green ginger)

Root ginger is no longer an unusual sight in our shops, but beware of retailers who try to palm off elderly, drying out lumps of far from fresh ginger on unsuspecting customers. Unfortunately, this is a fairly common occurrence – I have often noticed wrinkling, softening roots for sale – due, I hope, to ignorance rather than sharp-practice.

In fact, fresh root ginger keeps fairly well for several weeks in the salad drawer of the refrigerator. You can preserve the roots in sherry, but although the gingered sherry and the root themselves can still be used as flavourings, they are never as good as truly fresh ginger. Since the price is low, it hardly seems worth it. Do not be alarmed if your ginger begins to sprout; the sprouts can be used as a mildly gingery green herb, chopped over salads and other dishes.

Fresh ginger, chilli and garlic are the ubiquitous Oriental trio of fundamental flavourings, and it is impossible to imagine the foods of the East without them. The trio resurface again in the West Indies. Incidentally, dried ground ginger is no substitute for fresh, and should be treated as a completely separate spice. There is no need to confine the use of fresh ginger to exotic creations. Add it, finely chopped, or grated, to a fresh tomato sauce (fry gently along with the onions), excellent with shellfish, or to add a gingery spike to vegetable soups, or stews, or in marinades. To give the taste of ginger to dressings minus the fibrous lumps, grate then squeeze to extract the juice. Mix in a teaspoonful at a time until you hit the right balance.

ROOT GINGER

GALINGALE

## GALINGALE
(Galangal, Laos, Lengkuas, Siamese ginger)

Both greater and lesser galingale are used in the Far East, particularly in Indonesia, but the one that appears to be most favoured is the greater galingale (*Alpina galanga*), known as laos in Indonesia, and as lengkuas in Malaysia. It is also the only one of the pair that you are likely to come across in the West, so assume that references to galingale in cookery books written for the English speaking market, and in this book from now on, imply greater galingale.

At a quick glance, galingale might well be mistaken for root ginger, but it is actually rather more elegant and svelte. The ivory-coloured roots are partially covered in a brown-reddish skin, and if it is very young and in prime condition, may have charming pink buds. The flavour is allied to ginger, but there is a predominant pine and citrus scent to it. Altogether a very seductive combination.

It is used in much the same way as ginger, thinly sliced or chopped. I love the flavour of galingale in clear soups, maybe with a few noodles added for good measure – warm, comforting, and reviving. Dried galingale, in pieces (which should be soaked in cold water before use), and powdered galingale are also available in Oriental stores, but have far less appeal.

## MASTIC

Next time you pass by a Greek or Middle Eastern shop, stop and ask if they have any mastic. It does not look too promising, small chunks of solidified resin (from the acacia tree), dustily translucent like pieces of glass washed up on the shore. It does not smell of anything much, either. Chew on a piece and it soon becomes elastic and gummy (it is used as a form of chewing gum), but offers no inkling of its real delight. This only appears when the mastic is pounded and heated, forcing it to yield up its exotic, resinous incense.

It is used in the Middle East, Turkey and Greece to scent and thicken milky, or creamy puddings, fruit compotes, ice creams, and some breads and biscuits, as well as the occasional savoury dish. A small quantity, a quarter to half a teaspoon, is quite enough to flavour a pudding for four to six people. It is also used in Turkish delight, and in greater quantity to make highly scented "spoon sweets", where its gluiness is used to set the sweet syrup.

Try adding it to more traditional European puddings, a bavarois, perhaps, or a cold soufflé. To use, grind the mastic to a powder with sugar (1 teaspoon sugar to ¼ teaspoon mastic lumps) with a mortar and pestle, or a small, electric coffee grinder. Add to whatever it is that is to be flavoured, while it is simmering and hot towards the last minute or so. You might, for instance, add the powdered mastic to milk that is being scalded for a custard, just before it reaches boiling point.

## CHILLIES

When Columbus brought the first capsicums back to Europe in 1493, he can hardly have foreseen the results. Within a hundred years chilli peppers had swept across Asia. Today, chillies – hot capsicums – are the most widely grown and used spice in the world.

Not only do they provide heat, but they also impart distinct flavour. Different varieties of chillies, at different stages of maturity (from green through to ripe post-box red, or in some cases dark mahogany brown) will vary wildly in intensity and taste.

Most of the fresh and dried chillies sold in Britain are imported from Africa or Asia. The chillies of Mexico and South America are a rare commodity, despite being widely available in North America, and theoretically easy enough to import.

The pungency of chillies is rated in Scoville Heat units. Sweet bell peppers score nought, whilst bird and tabasco chillies (used almost exclusively for Tabasco pepper sauce) rate a massive 30,000 or more. The general rule of thumb is that the smaller the fruit, the hotter it is. Red chillies are simply ripened green chillies, and have a sweet, rounded flavour, compared to the fresh, clean taste of immature chillies (think of the difference between green and red bell peppers). Red chillies may often seem milder since the sweetness balances the pungency. Unused green chillies, left lying around in a warm kitchen, will soon turn bright red. Unfortunately, they also begin to dry out and wrinkle, losing some of the charm of fresh chillies.

CHILLIES

## Using Chillies

The pungency of chillies is derived from a substance called *capsaicin*, extremely powerful lingering stuff. Certain precautions should be strictly observed when preparing chillies. Always, always, wash your hands thoroughly with soap and water as soon as you have finished. Above all, do not rub your eyes, or pat the dog absent-mindedly before you do so. If you have very sensitive skin, wear plastic gloves. Chopping boards should be scrubbed, knives well washed and rinsed straight away. Change the water before you do any more washing up.

*Capsaicin* is most concentrated in the seeds. Recipes will usually instruct you to seed chillies, unless an unusually fiery preparation is in hand. Ignore this advice at your peril. Dried chillies are often hotter than fresh ones. If you are using them as a substitute, reduce the quantity initially, and add more later if the "burn" is too weak.

Chillies keep for several weeks in the vegetable drawer of the refrigerator. There are several ways of preserving them. They can be frozen, but need 3 minutes' blanching first. Alternatively, thread them on to string and hang up to dry in a cool airy place.

More interesting is to submerge them in some useful liquid which can later be used in cooking. The method is the same for dried and fresh chillies, quantities adaptable. Place chillies in a glass jar, or wide-necked bottle. Halved garlic cloves, sprigs of herbs, or bruised spices can be added, too. Cover generously with a) wine or cider vinegar, b) oil, either a tasteless one, or a light olive oil, c) alcohol e.g. dry or medium sweet sherry, vodka, gin, brandy, rum (and no garlic, please). Store in a cool dark place. Leave for at least three days before using, and top up with the relevant liquid as the level drops, ensuring that the chillies are completely submerged. Both the liquid and the marinated chillies can be used, although you may find that fresh chillies turn slimey after a few months. At this point, it is best to strain off the liquid and discard the chillies.

Use chilli oil and vinegar as condiments, in dressings, and sprinkled over cooked dishes (try tossing pasta with chillied olive oil, garlic, parsley, and Parmesan). The alcoholic versions can be added to sauces, soups, casseroles, etc. A few drops in a Bloody Mary, or a Dry Martini launches the cocktail hour with a bang.

## Chilli Roll-call

Identifying chillies is more complicated than you might imagine. Even the most up-to-date botanical reference books often disagree, whilst suppliers can rarely tell you more than country of origin. This list provides exact names wherever possible, and the closest chilli-type where there is some doubt.

### Fresh:

**Scotch Bonnet**  Extremely hot West Indian chilli, round and lumpen, yellow through to letter-box red, 2.5-4 cm (1-1 ½ inches) in diameter. Closely related to the Mexican *habanero*.

**Bird or Birdseye Chillies**  Powerfully hot, tiny chillies from the Far East, usually Thailand. Small and spindly, dark bottle green, ripening to orange-red.

**Cayenne**  Hot. Dark bottle green, ripening to red. Thin-walled slightly lumpen.

**Fresno**  Medium-hot, usually grown in Kenya or Zambia, and widely available from supermarkets, these are 4-7.5 cm (1 ½-3 inches) long, and cone-shaped. Glossy, smooth, light green, ripening through orange to red. Fresnos are thick-walled chillies, suitable for grilling and stuffing – if you can take the heat.

SCOTCH BONNET CHILLIES

BIRD CHILLIES

JALAPENO CHILLIES

**Jalapeño**  Hot, green chillies, available in cans from specialist shops, occasionally fresh from supermarkets. Easily confused with fresnos, but slightly smaller, darker green, with sloping shoulders. Thick-walled, jalapeños cannot be dried in the normal way, but must be smoked dry, which makes them *chipotle* peppers.

**Westlandse Langa**  Medium-hot. Perfect, smooth, glossy red chillies, tapering elegantly to a point. Developed and grown in Holland.

**Annaheim-type**  Medium-hot to mild. Light olive-green, curved and tapering to a point. Grows up to 20 cm (8 inches) long and 5 cm (2 inches) wide.

**Pepperoncini-type**  Medium-hot to mild, slimmer than Annaheim-type.

**Dried:**

**Rat dropping chillies (also known as Bird chillies)**  Extremely hot, tiny red chillies from the Far East. Usually imported from Thailand or India.

**Sannam Chillies**  Long, thin rich red chillies from India, very hot. The dried chillies sold in supermarkets are often Sannam chillies.

**Cascabel**  Very hot, round Mexican pepper, usually dried. Dark reddish-brown, glossy. Larger than cherry peppers.

**Cherry-type**  Small, hot Chinese chillies, round, dark black-red, 1 cm (½ inch) or so in diameter.

**Chipotle**  Smoke-dried Jalapeño chillies, with a wonderful intense smoky flavour. Chipotles are widely used in Mexico. They are often canned, sometimes *en escabeche*, i.e. in a sauce which takes on the chipotle flavour. Hot.

MEXICAN DRIED CHILLIES, FROM THE LEFT: MULATO, GREEN SANDIAS, PEGUIN, CHIPOTLE

**Ancho (Poblano)**  Poblano is the name given to many rather similar green chillies, widely used in Mexico. Ancho usually refers to the dried pods of one particular kind of poblano, pickled and dried when ripe, giving a dark brick-red colour. Anchos range from relatively mild to hot.

**Mulato (Poblano)**  Like the ancho, a dried variety of green poblano. Looks similar to the ancho, though with a blacker colour, tougher skin and a sweeter flavour.

**Pasilla**  This long, slender South American chilli has a distinctive dark rust-brown colour when fully ripe which deepens to a shiny black when dried. Fresh pasillas are uncommon outside Mexico, and it is usually the dried chilli that is used. Pasillas are relatively mild in flavour.

DRIED CHILLIES

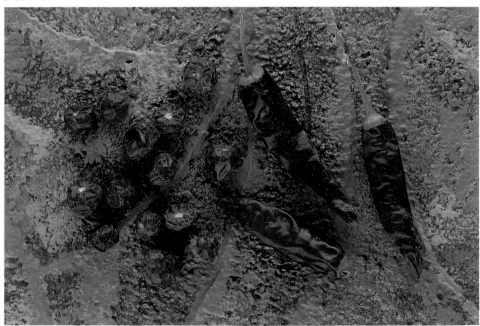

## SPICE MIXTURES

Most countries have their own special blends of spices and herbs, the hallmarks of their style of cooking. In Britain, mixed spice (equal parts of allspice, cinnamon, ginger, nutmeg and cloves) is our most commonly used spice mixture, used in cakes and pastries, with rarely a thought to its particular constituents.

Like our mixed spice, many spice mixtures are bought ready-prepared in their country of origin, and are often available here in specialist shops. Though they may be delightfully fragrant when the packet is first opened, like any ground spice, they soon dull to a pale shadow of their former selves. Whenever possible it is better to make up your own from whole seeds and herbs in small quantity, when needed. It does not take long, and home-made, with newly roasted and ground spices, they will, in most instances, be infinitely preferable to even the highest quality bought preparation. You also have the added pleasure of being able to jiggle with quantities to create a balanced flavour unique to yourself. Few spice mixture formulas are set in stone, so as long as you keep more or less to the basic ingredients, you can please yourself without stepping far out of the bounds of authenticity.

The handful of spice mixtures I give here are ones that I have a particular fondness for, but such a limited collection is no more than the tip of the iceberg.

## ZATHAR

A Middle Eastern blend of dried thyme and sumac (2 parts thyme to 1 part sumac) which may be spread over flat breads before they cook, or into which the hot, freshly-baked bread may simply be dipped. It is excellent, too, with hard-boiled eggs, perhaps quail's eggs, or simple crudités. Toasted sesame seeds are sometimes added. I occasionally use oregano instead of thyme, which I like even better.

## DUKKAH

A marvellous Egyptian mixture of toasted nuts and spices, which varies from one household to another, leaving plenty of room for improvization. It can be served as a "dip" for crudités, hard-boiled quail's or hen's eggs, or warm bread – provide a bowl of olive oil and bowl of dukkah, and dip first into the oil, then the dukkah. I also sprinkle it over grilled meats, salads of raw or cooked vegetables and anything else that takes my fancy.

4 tablespoons sesame seeds
2 tablespoons coriander seeds
1½ tablespoons cumin seeds
½ tablespoon black peppercorns
2 teaspoons ground cinnamon
25 g (1 oz) toasted hazelnuts, roughly chopped
½ tablespoon salt

Dry-fry the sesame, coriander, cumin and peppercorns. Cool and grind to a coarse powder. Crush the hazelnuts separately, whizzing briefly in an electric grinder so that they are not reduced to an oily paste. Mix all the ingredients together and store in an airtight jar.

## CHINESE FIVE-SPICE

This blend of spices gives an instant Chinese flavour. It is used in all manner of Chinese dishes, but perhaps most importantly with pork. The five spices in question are star anise, cloves, Szechuan pepper, fennel seeds, and cassia or cinnamon, in equal quantities, ground to a fine powder. The pepper gives a mild tingly heat, cloves and cinnamon or cassia a warm aroma, star anise and fennel seeds a liquorice flavour. Liquorice-haters should not be put off; I loathe liquorice in its straight form, but love the balanced flavour of Chinese five-spice. You can grind your own five-spice at home, but the small cans of made-up spice have a fine flavour as long as they are replaced frequently.

## QUATRES-EPICES

Four spices, that ought to be clear enough, though, illogical as it may sound, this mixture may sometimes contain five or six spices. Which particular four or more spices depends on country of origin. French quatres-épices, used mainly in charcuterie, for flavouring sausages, pâtés and other cooked pork dishes, is usually made up of pepper (white or black) and/or allspice, nutmeg, cloves, cinnamon or ginger. I tend to stick with my mother's formula given in *Charcuterie and French Pork Cookery* (Michael Joseph/Penguin) – 7 parts pepper to 1 part each of nutmeg, cinnamon, and cloves, finely ground together in an electric coffee grinder – but there is ample room for variation.

Tunisian quatres-épices is made up of dried rose buds, pepper, paprika and cinnamon.

DRIED CHILLIES

## JAPANESE SEVEN-SPICE SEASONING
(Schichimi togarashi)

A hot mixture of coarsely ground spices used primarily as a condiment. The seven "spices" are chilli, hemp seeds (or mustard or rape seeds), poppyseeds, nori seaweed, sansho leaves, sesame seeds and dried mandarin peel. You would be hard put to find several of those, so making the real thing yourself is out of the question. Seven-spice seasoning is sold in small tubs in most Japanese food shops.

I make an anglicized version which is extremely good and aromatic, even if not the real McCoy:

the peel of 2 tangerines, dried
3 tablespoons sesame seeds, dry-fried and
    cooled
1/2 tablespoon poppyseeds
3 tablespoons black peppercorns
1 tablespoon mustard seeds
1 tablespoon freeze-dried green
    peppercorns
4 tablespoons red chilli flakes

Mix all the ingredients, and grind to a coarse powder in an electric coffee grinder, or pound in a mortar. Store in an air-tight jar.

## GARAM MASALA

Garam masala is an Indian blend of spices, usually added towards the end of cooking, or sprinkled over food as a condiment. There are hundreds of different recipes, varying from region to region, cook to cook. This is one spice mixture I always make for myself, dry-frying the seeds first and grinding them in an electric coffee mill. Since it is barely cooked or not at all, it is important that the mixture retains its full aroma, and I cannot bear the often dusty taste of ready-made mixtures. Most Indian cookery books will suggest at least one, probably more, formulas. This is the basic one I use, though I vary it wildly according to whim and mood.

8 green cardamom pods
1 tablespoon whole coriander seeds
1 tablespoon whole cumin seeds
1 cinnamon stick, broken into pieces
1 teaspoon whole cloves
1/2 tablespoon black peppercorns
2 bay leaves, broken into small pieces
1/4 teaspoon freshly grated nutmeg

Slit the cardamom pods and extract the black seeds. Mix seeds with all the remaining spices, except the nutmeg. Dry-fry, then cool and grind to a fine powder, with the nutmeg, in an electric coffee mill. Store in a screw-top jar in a cool, dry place.

## RAS-EL-HANOUT

Ras-el-hanout is a wonderfully exotic blend of spices from North Africa, most closely associated with Moroccan food. There is no one recipe. Spice merchants and grocers pride themselves on their personal blends, which may contain anything from ten ingredients right up to a round one hundred! It is used in tagines and other meaty stews, rice and couscous dishes. Paula Woolfert in her marvellous book *Good Food From Morocco* (John Murray), analyzes one ras-el-hanout mixture, containing twenty-six constituents, amongst them orris root, tiger nuts, cubeb and melegueta peppers, galingale, Spanish fly and deadly nightshade! The basic, standard list is nutmeg, cinnamon, rose buds, ginger, cloves, peppers, cumin, and cayenne, perhaps with the addition of mace, aniseed, lavender, allspice, and white, green or black cardamom.

In theory, you could run up your own version at home, but in practice it is easier to buy it ready ground. Look out for it in Middle Eastern shops. The one drawback I have found is that it is often sold in large packets, and unless you use it day in day out for six months, it is going to lose most of its flavour before you have even got quarter of the way through. Store in an airtight jar once the packet is open, and be strong minded and throw out the un-used powder when the scent starts to fade noticeably.

BLACK PEPPERCORNS

# ACHIOTE & CHILLI OIL

*A Latin-American flavoured oil that can be used in marinades, stews and salads, to dress rice, or noodles, or even to flavour and colour a mayonnaise (use 1 tablespoon to 150 ml/¼ pint oil).*

**2 tablespoons annato seeds (achiote)**
**1–2 dried red chillies, seeded and crumbled**
**4 tablespoons light olive or vegetable oil**

Heat the annato seeds, chillies and oil in a small pan over a moderate heat, stirring occasionally. Once the seeds begin to pop, cover the pan and cook for a minute or so more, until the popping quietens down. By now the oil should have taken on a glorious golden-orange colour. Strain, cool and store until needed.

# ACHIOTE OIL MARINADE FOR FISH OR CHICKEN

**2 tablespoons achiotte and chilli oil (see above)**
**juice of 2 Seville oranges, or juice of 1 sweet orange and 1 lemon**
**½ teaspoon ground cumin**
**½ teaspoon dried oregano**
**1 small onion, chopped**
**1 garlic clove, chopped**
**pinch of salt**

Mix all the ingredients, and use as a marinade for chicken or firm white fish.

# CHICKEN OR DUCK BROTH WITH NOODLES

*A reviving soup, that can be adapted to fit whatever herbs and spices you have to hand. The essentials are good stock and noodles. Second most important, lemon grass, ginger, chilli, garlic and coriander. The others all combine together to enhance the soup, but are not all absolutely necessary.*

**Serves 4**

**1.75 litres (3 pints) good chicken or duck stock**
**1 onion, roughly chopped**
**3 stems lemon grass, cut into 2.5 cm (1 inch) pieces and bruised**
**3 curry leaves**
**2 kaffir lime leaves, torn up**
**3 garlic cloves, chopped**
**2 green or red chillies, seeded and chopped**
**1 × 2.5 cm (1 inch) piece galingale, chopped**
**1 × 2.5 cm (1 inch) piece of fresh root ginger, chopped**
**1 tablespoon light muscovado sugar**
**juice of ½ a lemon**
**salt**
**100 g (4 oz) Chinese egg thread noodles**
**3 tablespoons roughly chopped coriander, or a mixture of coriander and holy basil**
**soy sauce**

Place all the ingredients, except the noodles, coriander or basil and soy sauce, in a pan and bring to the boil. Simmer for 20 minutes. Taste, and adjust the seasonings. Strain and return to the pan. Bring back to the boil, and add the noodles. Cook for a few minutes until the noodles are just *al dente*, then throw in the coriander and a shake of soy sauce. Serve immediately.

# CHEESES MARINATED WITH HERBS

*This is based on a northern Italian dish of marinated cheeses, but given a new direction with a mixture of English and Eastern herbs. It is superb served as a first course, or instead of a selection of cheeses. Provide plenty of good country bread to mop up the marinade.*

**Serves 6**

**Either 3 × 100 g (4 oz) young soft cheeses, or 350 g (12 oz) cream cheese, or 175 g (6 oz) ricotta mixed with 175 g (6 oz) cream cheese**
**20 g (¾ oz) roughly chopped fresh parsley**
**6 sprigs salad burnet, roughly chopped**
**5 large holy basil leaves, chopped**
**2 sprigs sweet cicely**
**½ tablespoon roughly chopped marjoram**
**1–2 garlic cloves, chopped**
**2 tablespoons lemon juice**
**150 ml (¼ pint) olive oil**
**salt and pepper**

If using small cheeses, slice each in half horizontally to form two discs. If using cream cheese or cream cheese and ricotta, divide into six, and shape each into a circular patty 1–2 cm (½–¾ inch) thick. Arrange the cheeses in an oiled, shallow, close-fitting dish.

Either whizz all the remaining ingredients in a food processor until fairly smooth, or mix the roughly chopped greenery with the garlic, and chop together very finely, then beat in the lemon juice, oil, salt and pepper. Taste and adjust the seasoning (it should be fairly punchy), adding more of one or another herb, if you wish. Spoon over the cheeses, cover loosely and leave for 30 minutes at room temperature, or longer (up to 24 hours) in the refrigerator, basting occasionally. Bring back to room temperature before serving.

FROM THE LEFT: CHICKEN BROTH WITH NOODLES,
CHEESES MARINATED WITH HERBS, ROAST STUFFED CHILLIES

# ROAST STUFFED CHILLIES

*I love the combination of sweet roast chillies,
filled with cool creamy cheese, and crab or
prawn. But, be warned, this is for chilli lovers
only, and even the most hardened will be
unlikely to survive more than three chillies.
Serve as part of a mixed hors d'oeuvre, and
warn your friends before they swing a whole
stuffed chilli into their mouths.*

**Serves 4-6**

DRESSING:
**4 tablespoons olive oil**
**I tablespoon white wine vinegar**
**salt**
FILLING:
**75 g (3 oz) white crab meat**
**100 g (4 oz) young, mild goat's cheese**
**salt**
**½ tablespoon finely chopped fresh mint**

**12 jalapeno or fresno chillies (or other,**
   **larger ones with thick walls)**
**I tablespoon finely chopped green**
   **parsley**

To make the dressing, whisk the oil into the
vinegar a tablespoonful at a time. Add salt.
To make the filling, mash the crab meat with the
goat's cheese, salt and mint.

Grill the whole chillies as close as possible to
a thoroughly preheated grill, until they are
patched with black. Drop them into a plastic
bag, knot, and leave until cool enough to handle.
Strip off the skins. Make a slit from stalk to tip,
and carefully scrape out the seeds. Rinse under
the cold tap. Spread out on absorbent kitchen
paper to dry briefly, then fill each chilli
generously with the filling. Arrange in a shallow
dish, and spoon over the dressing, and half the
parsley. Cover and leave to marinate for at least
2 hours, basting frequently. Just before serving,
sprinkle with the remaining parsley.

# METHI ALOO
(NEW POTATOES WITH FRESH
FENUGREEK)

*This recipe comes from Julie Sahni's* Classic
Indian Vegetarian Cooking *(Dorling Kindersley).
By rights, it should be enough to feed four, but it
is so delicious that I ate right through half the
bowlful at one sitting.*

**Serves 4**

**100–225 g (4–8 oz) fresh fenugreek
  leaves, or 2 tablespoons dried
  fenugreek leaves
4–6 tablespoons unsalted butter
450 g (1 lb) tiny new potatoes
½ teaspoon freshly ground black pepper
½ teaspoon garam masala
½ teaspoon mango powder (amchur)
salt**

Wash the fenugreek leaves in several changes
of water, drain, and chop finely. Heat
2 tablespoons of the butter in a pan large
enough to take the potatoes in a single layer.
Add the potatoes and fry gently for 5–6
minutes until lightly browned. Add the
fenugreek and cook for a further 3 minutes until
the herb has wilted. Sprinkle on the black
pepper, add the remaining butter, 2
tablespoons water and mix well.

   Lower the heat and cook, covered, until the
potatoes are tender – about 20 minutes. Check
the pan frequently, and stir to prevent catching.
If necessary, uncover, and raise the heat to
evaporate any water. Sprinkle on the garam
masala and mango powder, raise the heat
slightly, and continue cooking the potatoes,
turning, until they are evenly coated with the
spices – a further 3–4 minutes. Serve hot,
warm, or cold.

# SALMON WITH SPICED LIME BUTTER

*A simple, flavoured butter is one of the easiest ways to add interest to plain grilled fish, but when the fish is oily like salmon, it is important that there is an element of sharpness, given here by the dried lime, if the dish is not to become overly rich.*

**Serves 4**

BUTTER:
**2 teaspoons whole cumin seeds**
**1 star anise, separated into "petals"**
**1 teaspoon black peppercorns**
**100 g (4 oz) butter, softened**
**1 dried lime, broken into pieces**

**4 salmon steaks**
**oil**
**salt and pepper**

To make the butter, dry-fry the cumin with the star anise and peppercorns in a small heavy pan until they give off a rich spicy aroma. Cool, then grind to a powder with the lime in an electric coffee grinder. Beat the butter with 2 teaspoons of the spice mixture, and chill.

Brush the salmon steaks with oil, season, and grill until just cooked through. Serve with a knob of the spice butter on each one, serving the rest separately.

# PINEAPPLE, AVOCADO & LOVAGE SALSA

*Serendipity came into play when I was testing this recipe. I was making a pineapple salsa, and noticed first the lone avocado in the fruit bowl, then a small bunch of lovage picked earlier that day. A tremendous combination as it turns out, excellent with grilled or roast duck, and other grilled meats.*

**Serves 6-8**

**1 lime**
**1 medium pineapple**
**1 avocado**
**5 lovage leaves, finely chopped**
**1 red onion, finely chopped**
**1 red chilli, seeded and finely chopped**
**salt**

Pare the zest off the lime in long strips. Blanch in boiling water for 1 minute. Drain, dry and chop. Squeeze the lime juice. Peel and core the pineapple and dice finely. Mix with the lime juice and zest. Peel and finely dice the avocado, add to the pineapple and turn quickly to coat with the juices. Add the remaining ingredients and mix. Cover and set aside for at least an hour in the refrigerator before serving. Taste and adjust the seasonings, adding a little more lovage if you think the salsa could take it.

# RACK OF LAMB WITH BASIL & PEPPER CRUST

*The crisp breadcrumb crust, flecked with holy basil and Szechuan pepper, is a perfect foil for tender, juicy lamb.*

**Serves 4-6**

**½ tablespoon Szechuan peppercorns**
**12 holy basil leaves**
**75 g (3 oz) soft breadcrumbs**
**salt**
**2 tablespoons olive oil**
**2 racks of lamb**

Dry-fry the Szechuan peppercorns in a small, heavy frying pan, shaking over a high heat until they give off a rich aromatic smell, and begin to pop. Cool, and crush coarsely. Chop the basil very finely, and mix with the crushed peppercorns, breadcrumbs, salt and olive oil.

Trim the skin and most of the fat off the outer side of the racks of lamb, leaving just a thin layer. Wrap silver foil round the tips of the bones to prevent them burning. Press the breadcrumb mixture firmly on to the outside of the racks of lamb. Lay, crust side up, in a lightly oiled baking tray.

Roast in a hot oven (220°C, 425°F, Gas Mark 7) for 30–35 minutes, depending on how well done you like your lamb. After 20 minutes or so, check that the breadcrumbs are not burning; cover them with foil, if necessary.

Turn off the oven, and open the door slightly. Leave the lamb to rest for 5 minutes. Remove the foil from the bone tips, and replace with paper cutlet frills, if you have any. Slice into cutlets to serve.

OPPOSITE, TOP: SALMON WITH SPICED LIME BUTTER; BOTTOM: METHI ALOO

# MAHLEB SHORTBREADS

*These biscuits, with their hint of bitter almond flavouring, are rich and morish with or without the final sugar coating. Mind you, I always go for the full caboodle – utterly irresistible.*

**Makes about 20 biscuits**

**75 g (3 oz) slightly salted butter**
**150 g (5 oz) flour, sifted**
**2 level teaspoons freshly ground mahleb**
**50 g (2 oz) vanilla sugar**
**icing sugar (optional)**

Melt the butter, and cool until tepid. Mix the flour with the mahleb and vanilla sugar. Add the butter and mix to a soft, crumbly dough. Roll teaspoonfuls of the mixture into balls and place on baking sheets lined with non-stick baking parchment. Bake in a cool oven (150°C, 300°F, Gas Mark 2), for 30 minutes. Let the biscuits cool on the sheets for a few minutes, then transfer them carefully to a wire tray to finish cooling.

If you wish to add a final glazing of icing sugar, take the biscuits out of the oven and let them stand for 30 seconds to begin to firm up. While they are hot, roll them in icing sugar (handle carefully as they will still be fairly crumbly), and return to the oven for 1 minute. Cool for a few minutes on the sheets, then, using a palette knife or fish slice, rather than your fingers, transfer them to a wire tray to finish cooling.

# ELDERFLOWER & ALMOND CAKE

*The elderflowers, buried at the bottom of the cake tin, gradually impart their muscat scent to the cake as it bakes. This works, not only with elderflowers, but also with lavender and rose petals, scented leaves such as peach, blackcurrant or geranium, and even pandanus leaves.*

**Makes 1 × 18 cm (7½ inch) cake**

**3 large heads of elderflower, or 6 scented**
**    leaves (see above)**
**100 g (4 oz) self-raising flour**
**pinch of salt**
**2 eggs**
**100 g (4 oz) caster sugar**
**50 g (2 oz) butter, melted and cooled**
**50 g (2 oz) ground almonds**
**icing sugar**

Line an 18 cm (7½ inch) cake tin with non-stick baking parchment, or butter and flour it. Shake the elderflowers to dislodge any unwelcome wild life, and trim off the main stem. Sit on the base of the tin, flowers upwards.

Sieve the flour with the salt. Beat the eggs with the caster sugar until pale and fluffy. Add the melted butter, and then mix in the flour and ground almonds to give a smooth batter. Pour into the cake tin.

Bake in a moderate oven (180°C, 350°F, Gas Mark 4) for 30 minutes, or until firm to the touch. Let it sit for 5 minutes, then run a knife around the edge and turn it out on to a wire tray to cool. Dust with icing sugar before serving.

# KAYA

*I bought a jar of Malaysian kaya before I had ever come across pandanus leaves or water. Kaya is similar in texture to lemon curd, very sweet, with a mysterious exotic fragrance. I could find no recipe in any of my books, so set about adapting a lemon curd recipe to the list of ingredients on the jar. The result is actually rather nicer than the prototype, the overwhelming sweetness balanced with lemon juice.*

**Makes about 300 ml (½ pint)**

**175 ml (6 fl oz) coconut milk**
**100 g (4 oz) butter**
**250 g (9 oz) light muscovado sugar, or**
**    pale palm sugar**
**4-5 pieces pandanus leaf or 1–1½**
**    teaspoons kewra water**
**juice of ½ lemon**
**4 large eggs, lightly beaten**

Place all the ingredients, except the eggs, in a bowl and set it over a pan of gently simmering water, making sure that the base of the bowl does not touch the water. Stir until the sugar has completely dissolved. Strain the eggs through a fine sieve into the mixture. Continue cooking, stirring constantly, until the mixture thickens, without letting it boil.

Pour into small clean jars, seal and store in the refrigerator for up to a month. The curd can also be frozen for up to 3 months.

# ROSE PETAL
# SYRUP

*This rosy-red syrup can be served as a drink, diluted to taste with iced water. To make an instant sherbet, fill a small glass with crushed ice, and pour syrup over the ice, right to the brim. Use also for flavouring mousses, and creams, in fruit salads, or simply poured over vanilla, peach or strawberry ice cream. It keeps for months in the refrigerator.*

**Makes about 300 ml (½ pint)**

**3 large, fragrant red roses**
**225 g (8 oz) caster sugar**
**150 ml (¼ pint) water**
**juice of ½ lemon**

Pull the petals off the roses and place in a bowl. Put the sugar, water and lemon juice in a pan, and stir over a moderate heat until the sugar has completely dissolved. Raise the heat and simmer for 5 minutes. Pour over the rose petals, and cool. Cover loosely, and leave at room temperature for 24 hours. Strain, and pour into a clean, dry bottle. Close, and store in a cool, dark place.

To serve the syrup as a drink, dilute it with iced water. To make an instant sherbet, fill a small glass with crushed ice, and pour over the ice, right to the brim. You may also use the syrup for flavouring mousses and creams.

*Variations:*
*LAVENDER SYRUP*
Make as above, substituting 8 heads of fresh lavender, or 2 tablespoons dried lavender flowers, for the rose petals.

*PINEAPPLE SAGE SYRUP*
Make as above, substituting 40 pineapple sage leaves for the rose petals.

RICE CREAM WITH MASTIC

# RICE CREAM
# WITH MASTIC

*If you cannot get the mastic, or merely fancy a change, replace with 2–3 teaspoons kewra, rosewater or orange flower water, added when the pudding is cooked, but still hot.*

**Serves 6**

**600 ml (1 pint) milk**
**6 tablespoons pudding rice**
**1 vanilla pod**
**a generous ¼ teaspoon mastic**
**40 g (1½ oz) caster sugar**
**150 ml (¼ pint) double cream**
**25 g (1 oz) toasted almonds, chopped**

Bring the milk to the boil and add the rice and vanilla pod. Stir, bring back to the boil, turn the heat down low, and cover tightly. Simmer gently for 40 minutes, stirring occasionally to prevent catching.

While the rice simmers, pound the mastic to a fine powder with ½ teaspoon of the sugar. After 40 minutes, uncover the rice, and stir in the powdered mastic and remaining sugar. Cook for a final 2 minutes. Remove the vanilla pod, and cool the rice until tepid. Whip the cream. Fold in the almonds, then the whipped cream. Serve lightly chilled, with soft summer fruit, or, in winter, with fruit poached in syrup, fresh mango, pineapple, papaya, etc.

To serve the rice cream hot, make it as above, but do not whip the cream – just stir it in once the pudding is cooked.

# OILS

The outskirts of Lucca are strangely well endowed with monkey puzzle trees. I had not noticed them on my first visit, but that time I had arrived by train, and never strayed outside the medieval walls, enthralled by the tight maze of streets, skylines pierced by slender towers, and cool, high vaults of the churches.

This second time, however, I was in Lucca for work. The pleasantest of work, too – I was here to taste olive oil, in the olive oil capital of Tuscany, perhaps of all Italy. Or even, as I am sure its inhabitants would insist, olive oil capital of the entire world.

It pleases me to imagine that these elegant, unlikely monkey puzzle trees are fashionable markers of success, owing their existence to the wealth generated by the olive orchards; wealth gathered not so much by the growers themselves as by the oil merchants, the blenders and shippers, the grandfathers of the big names in olive oil, the Bertollis, Sassos, Berios and others.

Despite the monkey puzzle trees, it is the silver-grey leaves of the olive tree which still define the countryside around Lucca, as they do in so much of the Mediterranean. Steeply terraced orchards of gnarled trunks, a dark pointed cypress or flat-top umbrella pine jutting through here and there. It is the landscape of every Renaissance painting, modernized only along the wider valley roads by the shabby concrete sprawl. And then you notice, as you drive up through the orchards, heaps of bright red and blue "wool", firmly twentieth-century colours. This is protective insulation material, ground cover, just in case hard frosts hit again next winter.

The blend of traditional method and modern refinements means we can have more olive oil and of a better quality than it would have been fifty or more years ago. In Spain, near Seville, on the plains of La Mancha, I have watched olives being picked by hand, dropped carefully into the "macaco", a curved willow-basket, slung across the body. I have followed the olives back to factories still using hefty stone wheels to crush the olives, though now encased in stainless steel drums and operated exactly by computer.

Olive oil exerts a remarkable magnetic magic. Not extraordinary, as I was about to write. Not extraordinary at all. Once you start to explore the range of tastes, of weights, the depth and heights of olive oil, it no longer seems extraordinary that you begin to use it day in, day out. It pulls newcomers into its spell and once you get the bug, it cannot be shaken off.

The realization that olive oil from Calabria in the south of Italy tastes quite different from Tuscan olive oil, that to capture the taste of a holiday in Greece, you need heavy Greek oil, that Provençal olive oil is related to but not the twin of Spanish or Portuguese olive oil, that an expensive "single orchard" oil varies from year to year, opened up for me a whole new palace of flavours. If one kind of oil

alone could give my cooking such variety, what about all the others? What could the nut oils, the grain oils do?

I would not be without five basic oils: at least two kinds of olive oil, one expensive, luxurious one, one cheaper for every day use, a toasted sesame oil, at least one nut oil, and a bland oil such as groundnut. The cheaper olive oil and the blander oil are essential, functional oils for general use. The other three, though costly enough to seem extravagant, are used in small quantities, almost as condiments, to scent and flavour dishes. Between them, they can transform one standard recipe into a multiplicity of recipes.

Mayonnaise, for a potato salad, is an obvious example. If you want a plain salad, or a very herby one, make the mayonnaise with a light salad oil, sharpened with white wine vinegar. For a more Mediterranean taste, use part olive, part plain oil, lemon juice and lots of garlic. Add a modicum of hazelnut oil, a few toasted hazelnuts, and you have something quite different. Use sesame oil instead, and a few toasted spices, and the flavour of the salad veers towards the East.

It is not often that one can have one's cake and eat it, but these wonderful oils are the exception, at least in terms of health. We know now that regular over-indulgence in saturated fats clogs our arteries, pushing us closer to untimely heart-attacks. Had I not had ample supplies of healthy mono-unsaturated olive oil, I suspect I would have found it much harder to reduce my intake of butter, in particular. As it was, it happened naturally, with never a twinge of deprivation. Most vegetable oils are high in polyunsaturates and/or mono-unsaturates, but not all. Both coconut and palm oil, for instance, are highly saturated fats, but neither are gifted with adequate flavour to justify the odd splurge.

## Storing Oils

Ideally, all oils should be kept well stoppered, in a dry, cool, dark place, preferably an old-fashioned larder. The next best thing is a nice cool cupboard in a well-ventilated kitchen. The point is that you want to prevent the oil oxidizing and developing a less-than-perfect, if not downright unpleasant, rancid taste. The three things that encourage oxidization are 1. exposure to air, 2. exposure to light, especially bright sunlight, and 3. exposure to unnecessary and constant warmth.

Short of keeping your oils in vacuum packs, and never opening them up at all, you cannot avoid some deterioration over a period of time, however good your cool cupboard or larder. An additional safeguard is to buy oils in small amounts and to use them up and replace them frequently. The horribly expensive nut oils and stunning single vineyard olive oils do tend to be sold in small quantities, which is ideal for pocket and preservation. Many will also come in opaque cans or dark glass, which is even better.

If you cannot resist hauling back some great can of the wonderful oil that laced every salad you ate on holiday, then decant it into smaller bottles as soon as you get home, and store all but one away instantly. If you do not you may find, after four or five months, that those sunny memories evoked each time you drag the can out are no longer enough to convince you that it is worth using.

Without even a decently cool cupboard, you may be reduced to keeping your oils in the refrigerator. There is some debate over the advisability of this. I used to keep my oils in the refrigerator when I lived in a two-room attic apartment, hot in the summer, chilly in the winter. They do congeal and turn cloudy and need to be brought back to a sensible room temperature to recover before being used, but I never felt they suffered deeply in terms of flavour. They just took up space.

## OLIVE OIL

The essential elements of olive oil production have barely changed over thousands of years, though the methods themselves and the equipment have been improved, cleaned up, streamlined, and in some cases computerized. The olives are picked, mostly by hand, they are crushed, the resultant oil and watery juice drained off, separated, and the oil filtered to a greater or lesser extent. That is about it, and what you end up with is first cold-pressed Virgin Olive Oil. Virgin is a denomination which raises eyebrows amongst the uninitiated, but it is eminently logical. This oil is "virgin" because it is unadulterated, untampered with, and incontrovertibly pure. It has not been heated or chemically processed.

Virgin oil varies dramatically in quality and is graded according to its acidity level – the lower the acidity the better the oil. The International Olive Oil Council, which lays down the law in these matters, defines the grades as:

Extra Virgin Olive Oil: virgin olive oil with an acidity of up to 1%;

Fine Virgin Olive Oil: virgin olive oil with an acidity of up to 1.5%;

Semi-Fine Virgin Olive Oil: virgin olive oil with an acidity of up to 3%.

In addition to this, the oils must have a fine flavour and smell to pass the test. Even so, the variation in precise taste is dramatic. Some oils are distinctly peppery and catch the back of the throat on the way down, while others may be thick with the aroma of new-mown hay. The big brand name oils, such as Bertolli, Berio, Sasso, Carbonell and Cypressa, are carefully blended to give a constant unvarying taste that is unique to that olive oil house. Oil from single groves will vary from year to year, just as wines do.

Oils that do not make it through to the top three grades will probably be refined, i.e. stripped of flavour, by chemical processes. The left-over pulp from the first

Having said all that, I shall now make the shame-faced admission that I keep most of my oils, together with vinegars and a jumble of other condiments, on the shelf about the main work surface in the kitchen. "How," you may well ask, "can you possibly justify this?" Well, I use at least one, or more, of them every day, probably to dress a salad, or hot vegetables, perhaps for frying, or to brush over fish or vegetables that I am about to cook, in a sauce, or to spice up a thick soup.

Unless I am following a specific recipe or theme, I may not decide which oil I will be using until the last second. It is a question of whim, of suitability, of imagination. I want to be able to reach out and pick the oil that is right for the exact moment. As a result, I occasionally make memorable combinations, usually pleasing ones, and an odd unwelcome disaster.

But the turnover is fast enough in most cases to keep them tolerably clean-tasting. From time to time I have to throw one away, but that means it probably was not so hot, anyway. I do keep my most prized oils (as I write this, that means a "Badia a Coltibuono" olive oil, golden and velvety, fused with fruit, and a green pistachio oil) hidden away from destructive elements.

In the end, the important thing is to get the best out of your oils, enjoying them to their utmost. Be aware of the proper storage methods and adapt them to suit your kitchen, the way you cook, and the oils you keep in the house.

LIGHT OLIVE OIL

VIRGIN OLIVE OIL

EXTRA VIRGIN OLIVE OIL

pressing will also go through one to two more extraction processes to yield up the very last drops of oil. Most of this will need to be cleaned up, too. Oils that have gone through these processes can no longer be labelled "virgin". Some will have a modicum of flavour restored by the addition of a tot of virgin oil. These were once known as "pure olive oil" but are now simply labelled "olive oil". The logic behind the terminology is less clear here. Sufficient to understand that they are oils that are lighter in flavour, and cheaper, and hence suitable for sloshing around in a carefree way.

Well, that is the theory, anyway, and it is one I used to stick to fairly rigidly. But then, a few years ago, I started to cut down on the quantity of animal fat I used in cooking, and simultaneously began to discover the sheer delight of olive oil. After a while I noticed that I was no longer using the "pure olive oil". I now use a blended extra virgin olive oil as my everyday cooking oil, because I love the taste, and find that there is little it does not go with. I use a totally bland oil such as safflower when I positively do not want the taste of olive oil or any other oil around.

And I use my special bottle of mind-numbingly expensive single-grove oil in small quantity, because that is all it takes, as a final condiment. The one exception I make to this rule is in mayonnaise. All olive oil, even pure olive oil, is just too much for me. I reckon that one-quarter to one-third extra virgin to a plain oil is just about right. Suffice it to say that one cannot lay down exact rules on these matters. In the end, it comes down to personal preference.

Olive oil and crusty bread are made for each other. An open tomato sandwich, made with bread, oil, sweet tomatoes, salt and pepper is one of life's small joys, and you can elaborate on the basic theme with thin sliced onions, olives, basil, salamis, and the rest, to your heart's content. Toast the bread, then rub with garlic and drizzle on the olive oil and you have the Italian *bruschetta*. Rub the bruschetta with a halved tomato, and it is better still. Nicest of all is bread, coated in olive oil and baked in a moderate-to-hot oven until crisp and golden brown through and through.

At the ironmonger's shop in Amalfi, I bought a crock-spouted oil pourer. Mine was the smallest size, roughly finished and as pretty as a picture. It is made to give an evenly measured trickle of oil over bread, pizzas and as the finishing touch to soups, just as you add a swirl of cream to a soup in more northerly climes. For a more pungent addition, warm the oil first with finely chopped garlic, crumbled dried red chilli, or herbs.

Dress hot pasta with the same kind of mixture and eat it straight away with freshly grated cheese, or sharpen with lemon, or wine vinegar and let it cool to make a salad. Just as quick and simple is to turn the pasta with olive oil and freshly coarsely crushed black peppercorns.

## LEMON AND OLIVE OIL

There is not much that can be done to improve on a good extra virgin olive oil, but this may be the one possibility. As the olives are pressed a sackful of fresh lemons is thrown in with them. The lemon oil from the zest, and the juice flows out along with the olive oil and juice, the juices are separated off, and what is left is the most heavenly blend of olive and citrus oils. Use it strictly as a condiment, or to make a salad dressing.

GROUNDNUT OIL       SAFFLOWER OIL       SUNFLOWER OIL       GRAPE SEED OIL

## GROUNDNUT OIL
(Peanut, Arachide oil)

All one and the same oil. This may seem obvious to anyone who is familiar with it, but it can be confusing for those who are not in the know. I once spent an age searching out the peanut oil that was stipulated in a very precise recipe book. I asked in shop after shop and nobody explained that groundnuts are peanuts. Eventually, I located a phial of Chinese peanut oil in China town. It was actually rather delicious, but not, I realized some time later, what I really needed. Nor did I realize at the time that I could just as well have used any one of the lighter, bland oils such as sunflower, safflower, or grape seed.

The common-or-garden Western groundnut oil is pleasingly ungreasy in texture, and verging on tasteless, which makes it an ideal all-purpose oil. It is *the* domestic oil in France, north of the Mediterranean olive-line, much used in salad dressing and for deep frying. I use it as a support for other flavours; neat in a vinaigrette when I want to enjoy the taste of a particularly fine ingredient with no unwanted distractions (for instance with

aged balsamic vinegar, or a handful of fresh dill); mixed with one of the powerful nut or sesame oils in a ratio of 1:4 or even 5 for vinaigrettes and 1:8 in mayonnaise. Use this or one of the other bland oils on its own for mayonnaise that is to be enhanced with herbs, spices, lightened with fromage frais or enriched with whipped cream, and so on. And, still on the subject of mayonnaise, I find that the classic olive oil mayonnaise is best made with two-thirds groundnut or sunflower, to one-third virgin or pure olive oil.

The peanut oil that you find in Oriental supermarkets is a slightly, or sometimes very, different beast, and has more in common with the chic walnut and hazelnut oils. It has a distinct taste of peanuts, and may even have a strong taste if the nuts have been toasted before the oil is extracted. Use with restraint as you would walnut or hazelnut oil.

## SAFFLOWER OIL

Again, a light all-rounder, interchangeable with groundnut and sunflower. It is extremely high in polyunsaturates.

## SUNFLOWER OIL

You have probably got this one sitting firmly in your kitchen already, and know full well that it is a good all-rounder. I find it a mite more cloying and robust than groundnut oil, but there is not a great deal in it. I like the idea that it comes from these glorious fields of smiling yellow sunflowers, and that more than makes up for any slight discrepancy.

## GRAPE SEED OIL
(Grape pip oil)

The fourth in this collection of bland oils. I suspect that my fondness for grape seed oil stems more from its connection with wine-production than with an intrinsic culinary value. It is pressed from the seeds left behind after wine-making – a satisfying instance of waste-not-want-not. I do not think I would make any detours to find a bottle of grape seed oil, but I do think it is lighter still than groundnut, sunflower or safflower. Whether I could distinguish it for sure in blind tasting is debatable.

WALNUT OIL

HAZELNUT OIL

PINE KERNEL OIL

PISTACHIO NUT OIL

ALMOND OIL

## SESAME OIL

Now we are talking. This is an oil that is worth a special trip, but with any luck that will not be necessary, since its fame is spreading and dragging it into healthfood shops and even the supermarket. There are two types of sesame oil – the pale French style, pressed from untoasted sesame seeds, with a relatively mild, raw nuttiness, and the wonderful toasted Eastern style. This latter version comes in all shades from a pretty amber colour to a deep mahogany. The colour relates directly to the degree of "toasted-ness" of the original sesame seeds and, as a result, to the depths and volume of taste. The toasting can go too far – I have tasted one murky black oil which had more than a hint of burn in it.

As with olive oil, you have to keep tasting until you find one that suits you. Bear in mind, though, that you will only be using it in very small quantities. It is an essential ingredient in Oriental cooking, used usually as a final dressing, a teaspoon or two tossed into stir-fried vegetables, warmed and trickled over steamed fish, scallops, or poultry. I often add it to marinades, or mix it with groundnut oil for

mayonnaise (1 part sesame to 5 parts groundnut) – sprinkle with toasted sesame seeds – or beat it into fromage frais, with lemon juice, whole toasted sesame seeds and fresh coriander to serve with crudités. It gives real zip to plain steamed new potatoes, noodles, or plain boiled rice, as well as keeping strands and grains separate.

## PUMPKIN SEED OIL

Pressed from roasted pumpkin seeds, this thick oil is a murky dark brown tinged with green, and has a powerful and superb nutty flavour in a similar style to sesame seed oil. My samples have all come from pumpkin seeds grown in Yugoslavia, and the importers assert that it is renowned in its home patch. That is as may be, but it ought to be better known elsewhere. Use it as sesame seed oil, not for cooking, but for flavouring, as a condiment, in salad dressings, mayonnaise (use 1 part pumpkin seed oil to 4 parts light olive or groundnut oil), or drizzled over cooked dishes in small quantities to lift them out of the ordinary. In fact, though I may be shot down for saying this, you could use it as an alternative to sesame oil in Chinese recipes.

## NUT OILS
### Walnut/Hazelnut/Pine Kernel/ Pistachio

The choice gets wider every year. I have heard whispers of a cashew nut oil, which ought to be sensational, but have yet to come across it in the shops. It occurs to me that Brazil nut oil might be rather pleasant, too, but perhaps it would turn rancid too quickly. Not that this is a major gap in the market. One or two nut oils are luxury enough in any one kitchen.

As with sesame oil, the nuts are toasted to a greater or lesser degree, and then pressed to release their oils, and what oils! Concentrated essence of nut in prime condition, with nothing lost in storage and age. I sometimes pull the bottle of walnut oil from the shelf for a mere sniff to raise the spirits. You can make the smallest of bottles last a long time that way, but as you only need to use a tablespoon or so to perfume quite an ample dish, this might appear miserly to others.

Excessive heat drives off the more volatile flavours, diminishing the power of these oils, so frying with any of them is a waste. I have occasionally made baked croûtons with cubes of bread tossed in a

CHINESE CHILLI OIL

EXTRA VIRGIN OLIVE OIL
WITH THYME AND GARLIC

LIGHT OLIVE OIL WITH ROSEMARY
AND FENNEL SEEDS

GRAPE SEED OIL WITH BLACK PEPPERCORNS,
RED CHILLIES AND GARLIC

GROUNDNUT OIL WITH
GREEN CHILLIES

mixture of groundnut and hazelnut or walnut oil, then cooked in a moderate oven until golden brown. They do retain some of the nuttiness of the original oil, but not the full strength. Even so, they are good in soups, or added to a crisp green salad dressed with the same oil. An alternative would be to toast whole pieces of the relevant nut, and add those toasted.

I have tried adding nut oil to pasta dough but it is barely detectable – better to add it to plain pasta after it has been cooked. Nut oil pastry (see page 47) turns out much better, with a short crumbly texture. It is often recommended for use in cakes and biscuits, but, to be honest, you get a much better result by adding ground or finely chopped nuts instead. It is only worth using the oil when you want a smooth-textured result. If this is what you are after, try substituting 1 tablespoon nut oil for 15 g (½ oz) butter, or multiples thereof. In the end, nut oils are put to best effect when used at room temperature or gently warmed. If you are in the happy quandary of not being sure which oil to use, ponder over which whole nut would go best. It all comes down to personal preference, but there are some classic combinations. For instance, on a bed of green salads topped

with a disc of grilled goat's cheese, use walnut oil. Toss pears and chicken in a vinaigrette or mayonnaise made with hazelnut oil. Blanched spinach takes to pine kernels like a duck to water (use both oil and toasted nuts).

## ALMOND OIL

I have separated almond oil from the bevy of nut oils above because its main uses are in puddings and confectionery. Its flavour is mild in comparison, subtly sweet, and can get drowned when used in dressings and the like. This is what makes it so useful for puddings – there is no better oil for greasing moulds for creamy mousses, charlottes, and jellies. It will not interfere, and the most that the subtlest of palates will detect is a fleeting waft of almond, and who in their right minds could possibly object to that?

## FLAVOURED OILS

The commonest of these is Chinese chilli oil, and delicious it is too. Buy it in Chinese supermarkets by all means, but since it takes all of about two minutes to make – drop a dozen or so dried chillies, broken into pieces, into a bottle of groundnut or sunflower oil – (and a couple of days to mature), it hardly seems worth it. However you come by it, use drop by drop to spice up salads, stir-fries, stews, soups and more. Other flavoured oils, with herbs and spices, are made by plain infusion, too. The one you are not likely to be making at home is the extravagant truffle oil, which is marvellous on potato salads.

# SALMORIGLIO

*This Sicilian olive oil sauce is for grilled foods. Brush fish or meat with the sauce before and during grilling, then serve the food with it afterwards.*

**Serves 6**

**I tablespoon finely chopped parsley**
**½ teaspoon dried oregano**
**approx. I teaspoon fresh rosemary
   leaves**
**I garlic clove**
**175 ml (6 fl oz) olive oil**
**3 tablespoons hot water**
**juice of I lemon**
**salt and pepper**

Pound the herbs and garlic in a mortar to release the flavours. Pour the olive oil into a warmed bowl and whisk, gradually pouring in the hot water and then the lemon juice, to give a thick sauce. Beat in the herbs, garlic and salt and pepper to taste.

# BURNT AILLADE

*This sauce is based on the walnut aillade of Toulouse and the Perigord. There, the ground walnuts replace the egg yolks of the better known aioli or garlic mayonnaise. Toasting the walnuts gives a rich, darkened sauce, softening the raw punch of the garlic.*

*I serve it with crudités, and recently it proved a tearaway success as a dressing for globe artichokes. It is tremendous with grilled poultry, duck or chicken or as a sauce for pasta. Any unused sauce can be stored in the refrigerator, well covered, for up to a week.*

**Makes 300 ml (½ pint) (enough to serve 6-8)**

**100 g (4 oz) walnut pieces**
**2 garlic cloves, chopped**
**2 tablespoons cold water**
**salt and pepper**
**85 ml (3 fl oz) walnut oil**
**85 ml (3 fl oz) tasteless, or light olive oil**
**lemon juice**
**chopped parsley or chives**

Spread the walnuts on a baking sheet and pop into a hot oven (200°C, 400°F, Gas Mark 6 or higher) for 5–10 minutes until well browned. Cool slightly. Place the walnuts, garlic, water and a pinch of salt in a food processor and grind to a paste. Keep the motor running and gradually add the oils, drop by drop at first, slowly increasing to a steady trickle, just as if you were making mayonnaise. Add lemon juice and pepper to taste. Just before serving, sprinkle the aillade with a little chopped parsley or chives.

If you want to make only half this quantity, or do not have a food processor, you will have to turn to the traditional method of pounding chopped walnuts and garlic together with a pestle and mortar, gradually working in the water to give a smooth paste. Add the oil and seasonings as above.

# HAZELNUT OIL & RED PEPPER SAUCE FOR FISH

*Another oil sauce, with a very different flavour. It has its origins in the cool of Cornwall on a damp March evening, rather than the heat of Italy. Richard Stein, chef and proprietor of the Seafood Restaurant in Padstow serves a similar warm vinaigrette with firm, fresh monkfish.*

**Serves 4-6**

**2 tablespoons sherry, balsamic or red
   wine vinegar**
**2 tablespoons water**
**salt and pepper**
**3 tablespoons hazelnut oil**
**3 tablespoons tasteless oil**
**I red pepper, seeded and finely diced**

Place the vinegar and water in a small pan, with salt and pepper to taste. Whisk in the oils, a spoonful at a time. Add the pepper and warm over a moderate heat until hot but not boiling. Taste and adjust the seasonings. Serve with grilled or steamed fish.

SCALLOP KEBABS WITH SESAME OIL MARINADE; BABY
ARTICHOKE HEARTS WITH BURNT AILLADE

# SESAME OIL
# MARINADE

*I have used this marinade, with its Eastern
flavours, for chicken, fish and even vegetables,
that are going to be grilled on the barbecue.
A favourite combination is cubed chicken breast
and scallop kebabs – a good way of making a
few fresh expensive scallops stretch around
more people than they really ought to! There is
enough marinade here for 4 chicken breasts
and 8 plump scallops. Try it, too, for aubergine
and/or courgettes.*

**Serves 4**

**1 × 1 cm (½ inch) piece fresh root ginger**
**2 spring onions, finely chopped**
**1 large garlic clove, finely chopped**
**½ teaspoon Chinese five-spice powder**
**1 tablespoon sesame oil**
**2 tablespoons tasteless oil**
**1 tablespoon lemon juice**
**2 tablespoons sake or dry sherry**

Whisk all the ingredients together and pour
over whatever you are marinating. Cover and
keep in a cool place for at least an hour, and up
to 24, stirring occasionally.

# SPANISH OLIVE OIL CAKE

## (BOLLOS DE ACEITE)

**Serves 8-10**

**225 g (8 oz) self-raising flour**
**50 g (2 oz) sugar**
**120 ml (4 fl oz) milk**
**25 ml (1 fl oz) anisette, or pernod**
**160 ml (5½ fl oz) olive oil**
**finely grated zest of 1 lemon**

Mix the flour with the sugar. Make a well in the centre and add the milk and anisette or pernod. Heat the oil and lemon zest together in a pan until very hot. Pour into the flour mixture, stirring constantly to give a smooth, sticky dough.

Spoon into a 18 cm (7 inch) cake tin, and bake in a moderate oven (180°C, 350°F, Gas Mark 4) for 45–50 minutes until golden brown and firm to the touch.

# OLIVE OIL SHERRY SHORTBREAD

**Makes approx. 15 shortbreads**

**50 g (2 oz) butter, softened**
**2 tablespoons caster sugar or vanilla**
**sugar, plus extra to finish**
**2 tablespoons oloroso sherry**
**120 ml (4 fl oz) olive oil**
**1 egg, separated**
**175–200 g (6–7 oz) plain flour**

Cream the butter with the sugar until light and fluffy. Beat in the sherry, then the oil and the egg yolk. Gradually work in enough flour to give a soft dough. Cover and chill for half an hour.

Roll out the dough to a thickness of about 5 mm (¼ inch) on a lightly floured board. Stamp out 5 cm (2 inch) circles and lay them on a baking sheet. Whisk the reserved egg white briefly with a fork to loosen. Brush the shortbread with the egg white, and then sprinkle evenly with sugar.

Bake in a moderate oven (180°C, 350°F, Gas Mark 4) for 15–20 minutes, until golden brown. Cool on a wire rack.

# OIL PASTRY

*Vary the oils in this excellent savoury pastry to vary the flavour: use all olive oil or all tasteless oil, for instance, or try half nut or sesame oil and half tasteless oil.*

**Makes 1 × 20–25 cm (8–10 inch) tart case**

**225 g (8 oz) plain flour**
**½ teaspoon salt**
**50 g (2 oz) butter**
**2 tablespoons oil**
**1 egg, beaten**

Sift the flour with the salt. Rub in the butter until the mixture resembles fine breadcrumbs. Make a well in the centre and pour in the oil, and the egg. Mix, adding enough water (about 1 tablespoon) to form a firm dough. Chill before using.

Use for savoury tarts, pies and quiches. Or, to make little biscuits, canapés or croûtons for soups, roll out as thinly as you reasonably can, stamp out 2.5 cm (1 inch) circles, or cut into smaller diamonds or other shapes and lay on a baking sheet. Chill for 20 minutes. Brush with beaten egg and, if you like, sprinkle with sesame, caraway, fennel, or poppy seeds, with finely chopped nuts, or with grated gruyère, or coarse sesame. Bake for 10 minutes in a moderately hot oven (200°C, 400°F, Gas Mark 6) or until golden brown.

OPPOSITE, TOP: SPANISH OLIVE OIL CAKE; BOTTOM: OLIVE OIL SHERRY SHORTBREADS

# VINEGARS, BOTTLED SAUCES & FLAVOURINGS

"Ten green bottles hanging on the wall…" A gross under-estimate in my kitchen, but then not all of them are green. Nor are they hanging, or, at least, not literally. Some are in racks hanging on the wall and the rest are amassed higgledy piggledy on shelves. Organization was never my strong point. If one of them should accidentally fall, let alone ten of them, I would be upset. These bottles contain a wide variety of strongly flavoured sauces and flavourings, from vinegar to fish sauce, pomegranate syrup to orange flower water. Not only would cleaning up the shards of glass be a pain, but the smell would linger on. Delightful in the case of the flower waters, but less alluring in the case of, say, fish sauce. Replacing the bottle would be the least of the problems.

# VINEGARS

WHITE WINE VINEGAR

CHAMPAGNE VINEGAR

RED WINE VINEGAR

Every country develops its own range of bottled sauces. Vinegars will be based on the predominant local alcoholic tipple – wine in France and Italy, rice wine in the East. In Britain, we have drawn the short straw with malt vinegar based on beer, harsh and crude compared with the vinegars made by our Continental cousins. Soy sauce and fish sauce are essential in Oriental cookery, varying in type from one country to another. Pomegranate syrup is a Middle Eastern creation, and has a sour and fruity flavour.

The best way to learn how to employ the more unfamiliar of these flavourings is to search out recipes from their country of origin and use them as they are meant to be used. There is no need to limit their potential, however. Once you have stoked up your confidence, you will discover that they can benefit everyday cooking. Purists insist that you should not transpose products from one country into the cooking of another. Bunkum. Foodstuffs have been appropriated left, right and centre throughout history (e.g. chillies in the Far East, or tomatoes in Italy) and there is no reason to stop now. It is just a question of working out how to slot them into your own cooking.

## Storage

Acids and salt are natural preservatives. Vinegars and other bottled sauces and flavourings, with high acidity or salt levels, are designed to keep – not necessarily indefinitely, but for a reasonable length of time, at least six months, and usually much longer. Buy small sizes at first, moving on to bigger containers if you find the level drops faster than anticipated.

Ideally, you should store them in a cool, dark, cupboard away from the ravages of light and heat. I fail miserably on this score – not enough storage space is the excuse. In fact, the only serious casualties seem to be vinegars. After a year or so out in the open (if they last that long), they lose much of their subtler flavour, leaving behind a harsh, sharp liquid. Thicker vegetable-based pastes should be kept, covered with a thin layer of oil as well as a lid, in the refrigerator once opened.

## WINE VINEGARS

The quality of wine vinegars varies considerably, but even the cheaper ones are preferable to the aggressive harshness of malt vinegar. The best wine vinegars are made by the old Orleans method. Barrels are filled with wine and vinegar, a starter, or "mother of vinegar", is added to launch the transformation, and then the whole lot is left quietly to get on with it. Slowly, slowly vinegar-making micro-organisms set to work on the alcohol, turning it into acetic acid. Once the task is complete, part of the vinegar will be drawn off and replaced with new wine. Faster methods involve heat, which destroys the more volatile complex flavours of the original wine, producing a vinegar with little subtlety. Vinegars made by the Orleans method will inevitably cost more.

A good wine vinegar will bear the hallmarks of the wine it is made from. Champagne vinegar is a pale yellow, delicately flavoured vinegar. Red Rioja vinegar is more robust, with the full fruitiness of Rioja. Bordeaux vinegar is made from Apellation Contrôllée Bordeaux wines.

BALSAMIC VINEGAR

SHERRY VINEGAR

CIDER VINEGAR

## BALSAMIC VINEGAR
*(Aceto Balsamico)*

When balsamic vinegar first started to attract attention outside its home patch, it was snob-value enough to possess even the tiniest of bottles. A year or so later, the masters of one-up-manship had moved on to balsamic vinegars matured for twelve years or more – the more prosaic four-year-old balsamic sneered at as common and passé, or even "not the real thing".

I loathe that kind of food snobbery which has nothing to do with the enjoyment of food. Balsamic vinegars, even the cheaper commercial ones (never that cheap, mind you), have a wonderful, sweet, spicy, nutty richness. Sure, the quality varies, and the bottom grade is the least interesting, but it is still a pleasure to use, and not to be sneered at.

Balsamic vinegar is made from the juice of, in the main, Trebbiano grapes, cooked down and thickened before starting a lengthy journey of fermentation. First, it sits in huge oak or chestnut barrels. Every year, as it evaporates and concentrates down, it is moved to new, smaller barrels of a different wood. It should have a minimum of four to five years in the barrel, but can

be matured for ten, fifteen, twenty, forty or more years until reduced down to a thick ambrosial liquid as precious as molten gold, if not more so.

Buy the most expensive balsamic vinegar you can afford. Not out of snobbery, but for your own pleasure. The older, more concentrated ones are powerfully flavoured and it will take only a few drops in a dressing, or on hot cooked vegetables to release the flavour. You may have to be a little more generous with younger versions, but it still will not take a great deal to do the trick.

Balsamic vinegar should be regarded as a condiment or seasoning, rather than a standard vinegar. Sprinkle lightly over grilled foods, or use to enhance sauces (particularly tomato sauces) and meat gravies. Add it towards the end of cooking, and never let it boil. Overheating decimates the flavour, leaving just a sharp mundane liquid. Balsamic vinegar is delicious on strawberries – sprinkle lightly over hulled, halved fruit and set aside for 30 minutes. A few drops added to fruit salads is no bad notion, either.

## SHERRY VINEGAR

This is a thrillingly rich, aromatic sweet vinegar from Jerez in Spain, made with the must used in sherry-making. Think of it as a seasoning, rather than an acidifier. It is often used in Spanish dishes, on salads, to deglaze pans, to enrich sauces, and, like balsamic vinegar, it is mellow enough to sprinkle straight on to hot cooked vegetables.

## CIDER VINEGAR

Cider vinegar has a relatively low acidity and, when it is good, has a gentle but distinguishable taste of apples. Its mildness makes it a good choice for pickling, for flavouring with herbs, or for use on salads when you do not want a dressing that will distract from the flavour of the main ingredients. Cider vinegar is popular in America, and has a growing band of devotees elsewhere. Like raspberry vinegar (see page 54), it can be used as a drink, lightly sweetened, and topped up with mineral water.

PERRY VINEGAR

WHITE RICE VINEGAR

BLACK RICE VINEGAR

SUMMER FRUITS VINEGAR

MANGO VINEGAR

## PERRY VINEGAR

Perry vinegar is made from perry, the pear-based "cider", and, like cider vinegar, is mild. If it is conscientiously made, a trace of fresh pear is detectable. Use this vinegar like cider vinegar.

## RICE VINEGAR

The Japanese vinegar *par excellence* and, as you would expect from the Japanese, a subtle vinegar with a clean, elegant flavour. Rice vinegar, made from rice wine, is sweetish, with a pale yellow colour. It is used in all kinds of ways, but perhaps most appealingly to season the rice for sushi.

I use it regularly whenever I want a mild, delicate flavour, in dressings, for pickling, to perk up a mayonnaise or a hot creamy sauce, or as a base for fruit vinegars. There is always a bottle in my kitchen, and I count it as an essential. Brown rice vinegar, made from brown rice, has a darker colour and a more pronounced flavour. Chinese white rice vinegars are usually sharper than Japanese ones.

## BLACK RICE VINEGAR

An inky black rice vinegar from China. It is thicker than most vinegars, with a rich spicy fragrance, sharper but reminiscent of balsamic vinegar. It is used for braising, enriching sauces, and as a dipping sauce. Chinkiang vinegar, from the province of the same name, is highly rated amongst black rice vinegars.

## FRUIT-FLAVOURED VINEGARS

Recently, raspberry vinegar was rediscovered, and thrown with abandon into all manner of fashionable culinary creations. It is really nothing new. Victorians were partial to a slurp of raspberry vinegar, and, no doubt, many of their ancestors before them. Our great-grandmothers sipped at glasses of slightly sweetened raspberry vinegar topped up with iced water, a blessedly refreshing drink on a hot summer day.

The cheaper commercial fruit vinegars often prove a profound disappointment, all too often made with over-sharp vinegar, and judging by the taste, precious little fruit. A good fruit vinegar will have a tremendous burst of fresh fruitiness and there is no mistaking it. There is nothing mysterious or complicated about making raspberry or other fruit vinegars. It is simply a case of macerating the fruit in vinegar over a period of days and then straining it. Try your hand at making your own when the soft fruit season is in full swing (the full method is given on page 62). Besides raspberries, currants, blackberries and blueberries all make excellent fruit vinegars with minimal effort.

Besides those long summer drinks, fruit vinegars are obvious candidates for fine vinaigrettes, balanced with either a light olive oil or, nicer still, hazelnut oil. Thin cream makes a good partner, too, for fruit vinegar dressings. Otherwise, use them for deglazing pans, adding a note of fresh fruit to simple sauces.

## HERB-FLAVOURED VINEGARS

You can flavour a vinegar with practically anything that takes your fancy. Tarragon vinegar is the only herb-scented vinegar I ever buy ready-made, and only because I like it so much that I get through it at a gallop. The bottle will insist on being empty

# SAUCES AND FLAVOURINGS

CHILLI VINEGAR

THYME VINEGAR

UMEBOSHI PLUM SEASONING

FISH SAUCE

at a time when my garden tarragon is as dead as a dodo and there is none to be had in the shops.

To make your own herb-scented vinegars, just push a few large sprigs of herbs, either one single type, or a mixture, right down into a bottle of vinegar. Do not expect poor vinegar to be transformed. Use a good quality white wine vinegar, rice vinegar, or cider vinegar, and never one that is aggressively harsh. Then leave the bottle on a warm, sunny windowsill for a week or longer. If the once-perky green sprig begins to look tired and bedraggled, strain the vinegar and rebottle it.

Chilli vinegar can be as strong as you care to make it. One or two chillies supplies a muted tingle, a generous handful builds up an explosive blast. Bruised spices, garlic, shallots, citrus zest – they all make fine vinegars. For a more refined, scented vinegar, loosely fill a jar with elderflowers or rose petals and cover with a good wine vinegar or, better still, rice vinegar.

## UMEBOSHI PLUM SEASONING

This is the liquid left over from pickling Japanese Umeboshi plums. Red in colour, clear and thin, with a sharp fruitiness, it should be used just like good wine vinegar. It makes a delicious salad dressing, is fine used to deglaze pans, or in a marinade. A dash added to a tomato sauce highlights the flavour of the tomatoes, particularly handy if they were dull greenhouse tomatoes to begin with.

## FISH SAUCE
(Nam pla, Nuoc cham)

Fish sauce is the liquid drained off from decomposing salted fish. I realize that this may not sound too appealing but do not let that put you off. The result is a salty, strongly flavoured, anchovyish thin sauce which can become quite addictive. It is used throughout South-East Asia as an essential seasoning, in much the same way as soy sauce. Quantities are small, not enough to give an overtly fishy taste. It goes into every conceivable sort of savoury dish – in dressings for salads, meat dishes, fish dishes, hot vegetable dishes, you name it.

I love fish sauce, and find myself throwing a spoonful into all kinds of foods, never mind their country of origin.

## SOUR POMEGRANATE SYRUP
(Grenadine molasses)

I bought a bottle of pomegranate syrup out of curiosity but I am sorry to say it sat on a shelf for several months before I actually opened it. How I regretted my neglect. Pomegranate syrup is extraordinarily good. It is made by boiling down the juice of sour pomegranates to a thick, dark brown-red sauce. The flavour of pomegranates is concentrated and gloriously vivid.

Pomegranate syrup (or grenadine molasses, not to be mistaken for grenadine, which is sweetened pomegranate syrup) is predominantly used in Iranian cooking, but it surfaces occasionally in other Middle Eastern cuisines, including Turkish. It is used in dressings for salads, but also in casseroles, the most famous of these being the Iranian faisinjan with a sauce thickened with walnuts. Heat does nothing to dispel the fresh fruity flavour – the syrup has already been boiled down hard to thicken, so that is hardly surprising. It is delicious with both lamb and beef, as well as game, and duck.

## SOY SAUCE
(Shoyu, Kecap)

There is soy sauce and soy sauce and they are by no means all the same. I once conducted an in-house personal soy sauce tasting, and was stunned by the divergence. My favourite at that sitting proved to be a Japanese soy sauce, with much more than mere saltiness to promote it.

All soy sauces are made along the same lines, but small variations in method give rise to the differences between the sauces of one country and another, or even between brand names emanating from the same country. Cooked soya beans are crushed with wheat, fermented, then mixed with copious amounts of salt. The mash is left to mature for a year or more and the liquid drained off.

As a rough and ready rule, soy sauces can be divided into "light" (or thin) and "dark" (or thick). The lighter ones are, of course, lighter in colour and consistency, but are saltier. Dark soy sauces are thicker, heavier, sweeter and have a more rounded flavour. Some Oriental countries also produce a middleweight soy sauce. Indonesian sweet soy sauce (*kecap manis*) is sweeter and darker than other soy sauces, and rarely available outside shops not specializing in Indonesian provisions.

## MUSHROOM and WALNUT KETCHUPS

The word "ketchup" comes from the East and originally described thin salty sauces. In Indonesia *kecap* means soy sauce, a far cry from thick sweet and sour tomato ketchup. Our own walnut and mushroom ketchups are much closer to their Oriental namesakes. Mushroom ketchup is made by

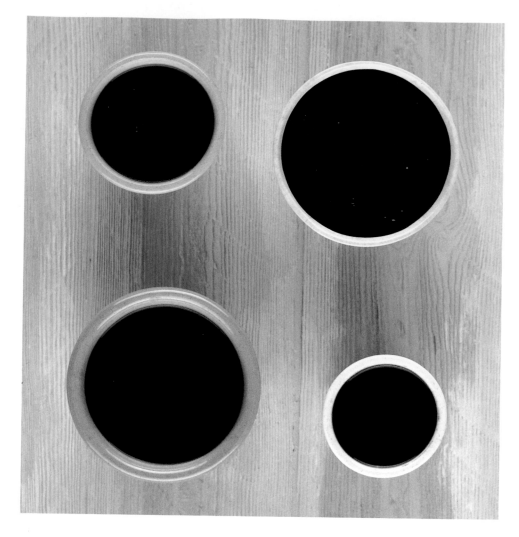

CLOCKWISE, FROM TOP LEFT: MUSHROOM KETCHUP,
SOUR POMEGRANATE SYRUP, SOY SAUCE, WALNUT KETCHUP

layering field mushrooms with salt, and leaving for several days to decompose, in much the same way as fish sauce. The copious liquid produced is strained off, then simmered with spices, and optional additions of vinegar and/or brandy, until it thickens to about the consistency of dark soy sauce.

Walnut ketchup is made in a similar fashion, using green walnuts, picked before their shells have hardened. Both sauces are used as seasonings, a splash added to gravies, sauces and stews. You can taste the mushrooms or walnuts in these

ketchups, but I suspect that in a blind tasting, most of us would assume that they were interesting variations on soy sauce.

## ANGOSTURA BITTERS

The "pink" in a pink gin is Angostura Aromatic Bitters, first made by Dr J. G. B. Siegert in 1824 in the town of Angostura, Venezuela. Angostura is now Ciudad Bolivar, and Angostura Bitters are now made in Trinidad. Dr Siegert's bitters were intended as a medicine but, as it turned out, people actually liked the taste, and what medicinal value they may have had soon ceased to be of relevance. The bitters themselves, however, are still made to the original recipe.

If you have a bottle of Angostura Bitters

in the house, it is likely to be lodged in the drinks cabinet, which is indeed a fine place for it to live. There is ample justification, however, for an occasional change of venue. A few drops can add a welcome twist of spicy bitterness to both savoury and sweet foods. Use it in fruit salads and jellies, ice creams and sorbets, dried fruit compotes, apple or mince pies. On the savoury range, it is good in gravies, marinades for meat or fish, casseroles, or even dressings for crisp green salads. Add it drop by drop until you get the balance just right.

HOT PEPPER SAUCES – TOP: TABASCO, JAMAICA; CENTRE: SWEET CHILLI, WEST INDIES; BOTTOM: SELIN, PILI PILI

## TABASCO and HOT PEPPER SAUCES

I once took part in a hot pepper sauce tasting. We worked our way through thirteen of them, ranging from hot to searingly hot. The prospect proved to be more terrifying than the event itself. By the time I had made it through to the end and back again, my mouth was tingling but by no means dysfunctional. Hot pepper sauces, like chilli peppers themselves, kick-start your taste-buds into full throttle.

The sauces had been collected from all over the world. There were sauces from the West Indies, from Thailand and China, from the Americas, and even one from south London. Colours ranged from green, through pillar-box red to murky browns. Some were thick, others thin, some contained a multitude of ingredients, others pared down to the absolute minimum.

Tasting over and done with, the names, origins and types were revealed. The overall favourite (and one of the hottest) had been that classic amongst pepper sauces, Tabasco from Louisiana.

Tabasco Pepper Sauce was created by Edmund McIlhenny, on Avery Island surrounded by the Bayou Petit Anse. The first bottles were sent out to wholesalers in 1868. Today, the McIlhenny family still make Tabasco on the island, and the method has not changed one iota. The only major difference is that most of the Tabasco chilli peppers (classified and named in 1888, twenty years after the creation of the sauce) are now grown off the island in Latin America.

The ripe, red Tabasco chillies are ground down to a pulp and mixed with salt from the mine on Avery Island, which is itself a great salt dome. The mash is left to ferment in barrels for three years. At the end of this period, a member of the McIlhenny family inspects each barrel, checking both colour and smell. If the mash passes muster, it is moved on to one of the huge vats, mixed with distilled white vinegar, and churned on and off for the next 30 days. A final filtering, and it is ready to be bottled.

Hot pepper sauces, wherever they come from, however they are made, have a dual purpose. The first is to add a shake of chilli heat, more controllable if you know your sauce than fresh chillies. The second, and every bit as important, is to add flavour. It pays to dabble and discover a hot pepper sauce with a fine flavour that you appreciate. One or two I have come across have a far from pleasant taste which spreads and upsets whatever it is they are added to. Chilli sauce devotees may well need several varying types, to suit their moods and whims.

FROM THE LEFT: HARISSA, CREMA PICCANTE, CHILLI PURÉE

### HARISSA

Harissa is a violently hot chilli paste, at its simplest a blend of red chillies, garlic and salt, with the more aromatic versions adding cumin, caraway, coriander leaf and/or seed and mint. Some recipes also include tomatoes, which softens the blow marginally. You can buy it in tubes or cans from Middle Eastern shops, but it is simple enough to make at home. It is added to soups and stews, gives a wonderful zip to a tomato sauce, and is served with couscous, or simply smeared on bread (for the brave only). I have also added it to mayonnaise, to serve with shellfish. However you use it, go cautiously, and warn friends of its strength if you serve it neat as a relish!

Harissa can be made with dried or fresh red chillies (the seeds are optional, but increase the fieriness). Dried chillies should be soaked in warm water for an hour. Use a pestle and mortar or a processor to grind ingredients to a paste. For every 25 g (1 oz) of chillies, add two cloves of peeled garlic, a generous pinch of salt, and all or some of the following: 1/2 teaspoon each of coriander seeds, caraway seeds, cumin seeds, dried mint, and 2 teaspoons chopped fresh coriander. Add enough oil to give a thick paste. Store in a screw-top jar in the refrigerator, the surface completely covered with a thin layer of olive oil. It will last for several months, as long as you make sure the layer of oil is renewed every time you dip in.

### ITALIAN CHILLI PASTES

The southern Italian answers to harissa. Several types of chilli paste are now being potted up and sold abroad. They are pungent, but nowhere near as aggressive as harissa. Besides red chillies, they may include red peppers, tomatoes (dried or fresh), garlic and herbs, blended together to give a full rich flavour. The name changes from brand to brand – two favourites of mine are Amati's "Red Pesto", and Taylor & Lake's "Crema Piccante". Simply mixed with olive oil or cream and heated gently, they can be tossed straight into hot pasta. Add a spoonful (or more but go slowly and keep tasting) to tomato sauces, soups, and casseroles.

### OLIVE PASTE
(Olive purée or pâté)

A paste made of black olives, ground finely with added olive oil, and occasionally a few extra spices, usually from Italy. As long as it is made with high quality black olives, it is delicious. Making your own olive paste demands no great skill, and once you have pitted all the olives, it is a matter of seconds to whizz them to a paste in a processor, adding just enough olive oil to get a relatively smooth consistency. Pot it up in small jars, and cover with a thin layer of olive oil.

Bought or home-made, olive paste is a great boon to have on hand. It makes a good instant sauce for pasta, as long as you are neither mean nor heavy-handed. With more time on your hands, use it to flavour the pasta dough itself. Smear on to pieces of bread, brushed with olive oil and baked in the oven until crisp, and eat as a first course or with drinks – even better topped with a slice of sweet tomato, or a strip of grilled red pepper. To make olive butter to serve with grilled vegetables, fish or meats, blend with unsalted butter and a generous squirt of lemon juice and chill.

### ARTICHOKE PASTE

Another Italian paste, this time a purée of artichokes and olive oil with a pale greenish tan colour. Again, this is delicious with pasta, and can be introduced into any dish where you think a touch of artichoke might be appreciated. Be aware, however, that this is a subtler substance than either olive or chilli paste, so there is little point in hopefully throwing a tablespoonful into a powerfully flavoured sauce, since it will be totally lost. One company who markets artichoke paste suggests using it to make a type of *bagna cauda*, the warm, pungent garlic and anchovy sauce from the Piedmont, served with raw vegetables, or over grilled red peppers.

CLOCKWISE FROM TOP LEFT: GREEN OLIVE PASTE, ARTICHOKE PASTE, BLACK OLIVE PASTE

TAHINA

## TAHINA
(Tahini)

Tahina is a thick, oily paste of crushed toasted sesame seeds. There are two types of tahina: the more usual is a beige colour, the other a darker muddy brown, made from unhusked sesame seeds. I do not much care for the latter, which has a bitter undertaste, although the fibrous husks no doubt make it the healthier of the two. Light or dark, tahina is inclined to separate in the jar, so flex your wrist muscles and beat the oil back into the paste before measuring out the required amount.

Tahina is used in copious quantity throughout the Middle East. It is an essential ingredient in many of the small dishes that are put together to form a meze. *Hummus bi tahina*, to give it its full name, is a purée of chickpeas and tahina. Moutabel (or *baba ganoush*) is a wonderful cream of roast aubergine with tahina. Simpler still is tahinasalat, tahina beaten with lemon juice and water until it emulsifies to a smooth light cream, flavoured with lots of garlic, olive oil, salt, cayenne and cumin. The curious thing about making tahinasalat is that as you gradually beat in the lemon juice and then the water, the paste first gums up to a heavy, crumbly gunge, and then thins down again to perfect smoothness. Alarming if you are not forewarned. All three of these are eaten with warm pitta bread.

Tahina is also used to thicken sauces, or as a sauce itself (beaten, as for tahinasalat with lemon, water or stock) in hot dishes, particularly for fish, and in soups – a delicious, filling soupy version of hummus is made by liquidizing cooked chickpeas, fried onion and garlic, tahina, and spices with good stock.

## MISO

I am a recent miso convert. I was put off the stuff as a result of its enthusiastic adoption by vegetarians of the brick-heavy lentil bake and open-toed-sandal tendency. It was only when I began to pay more attention to the recommendations of Japanese foodwriters than to my own prejudice that it dawned on me that miso must have something going for it.

Miso is more than just a single substance. There is a whole spectrum of types of miso, from the pale *shiro-miso* to dark brown *hatcho-miso*. In between these two extremes there is an extraordinary variety to choose from. All miso is made by mixing cooked soya beans with rice, wheat or barley, or a mixture, introducing a yeastlike mould, then leaving it to mature under pressure, adding a greater or lesser amount of salt, for anything from a matter of months to several years.

*Shiro-miso*, or "white miso", and most yellow misos are sweet and lightly flavoured, almost caramelish. *Ake miso*, red miso, is made with barley, and has a richer, more savoury flavour of yeast extract and olives. The darkest of all, *hatcho-miso*, is a pure bean miso, very thick, very rich, and very strongly flavoured.

Trying to decide which is which is not always easy. Assistants in both health food and Japanese shops are not always forthcoming, and can rarely pinpoint the precise virtues of the various misos they stock. As a rough guide, the lighter the colour, the sweeter the taste, but this does not always follow. In the end, it comes

down to trial and error. Be comforted by the fact that miso keeps for months and months in the refrigerator or a cool cupboard. Once you have opened the packet, decant the contents into a glass jar, tasting en route, and label with name and characteristics.

Miso, both sweet and salty, is the most versatile creation. The darker ones are marvellous for flavouring soups and casseroles, etc., more like concentrated stock and infinitely preferable to stock cubes. Add towards the end of the cooking period. Thinned down, practically any miso, or a mixture of two types, can be used as a dressing, or a sauce for vegetables or seafood, cold or lightly warmed through. A blend of mostly white miso and a spoonful of dark can be used to thicken sauces. In Japan, miso is used in pickling, and spread over grilled foods as a grand seasoning.

Japanese cookery books tell you never to boil miso. Why not? I tried boiling a couple of types, waiting for disaster to strike. It did not. I have since learnt that over-heating destroys some of the nutrients and the digestion-promoting enzymes, but it will not ruin the whole dish.

Once you begin using miso, you will find a hundred and one uses for it. As I have now discovered, you do not have to be vegetarian, or Japanese to appreciate it.

VARIETIES OF MISO

BITTER ALMOND ESSENCE    ROSEWATER    ORANGE BLOSSOM WATER    KEWRA WATER

## BITTER ALMOND ESSENCE

What makes bitter almonds bitter is a substance called amygdalin, also present in the stones of prunes and peaches. An enzyme in the almond works on the amygdalin when mixed with water to form benzaldehyde and prussic acid. Prussic acid is, of course, a deadly poison, and best avoided. Luckily, prussic acid is destroyed by heat, which means that there is no danger in eating a whole plateful of macaroons flavoured with ground bitter almonds, other than mild indigestion, the wages of gluttony.

Benzaldehyde is the essential oil of bitter almond, the element that supplies the characteristic flavour, and is harmless in small quantity. Bitter almonds themselves are hard to find in this country (though they are occasionally sold in Oriental supermarkets). Bitter almond essence, largely composed of benzaldehyde, can be found, however, and provides just the same flavour. Use it drop by drop as it is highly concentrated. The flavour of bitter almonds is delicious in any cake or biscuit which includes ground almonds. Where a recipe suggests using whole bitter almonds, substitute the same quantity of sweet almonds and a drop or two of essence. Note that plain almond essence is not the same thing, and almond-flavoured essence, or almond flavouring, is a synthetic and coarse substitute.

## ROSEWATER

Rosewater is made by macerating and distilling scented rose petals to produce a clear, perfumed liquid. Many delicatessens and food stores now sell it, but if you live in an apparently barren area, ask for triple or triple-strength rosewater at the chemist.

Rosewater was once a popular flavouring in Britain, but is now considered strange and exotic. In the Middle East it has never fallen out of favour, and many of the most exquisite sweet dishes are delicately perfumed with rosewater. It always surprises me that the scent of rosewater is not impaired by heat. But it is not, and so can be used in both cakes and biscuits, and baked creams. A thick sugar syrup can be laced with rosewater, and is delicious poured over a fresh fruit salad, with strawberries, or to moisten cake for lining a charlotte mould. Add to sorbets and ice creams, to whipped cream, *crème patissière*, jellies and jams, gelatine-set mousses and bavarois. Cream cheese, beaten with cream until soft and light, sweetened to taste, then spiked with rosewater makes a rich and wicked two-minute pudding. Serve with crisp almond biscuits and fresh raspberries.

Use rosewater cautiously, adding just enough to suit your taste. I like a well-defined waft of rose, but some might find that too much and will consider a gentle intimation quite adequate.

## ORANGE BLOSSOM WATER
(Orange flower water)

My paradise will be perfumed, not continually, but intermittently by a breeze carrying the scent of orange blossom on a balmy Mediterranean summer's night. The interval will be just long enough to recover from the sudden sheer pleasure each breeze brings, so that I can experience it all over again.

In the meantime, I will settle for an occasional sniff at a bottle of orange blossom water. Distilled from orange blossoms, this clear water is delightfully perfumed. It is used in similar ways to rosewater, often interchangeably (but reduce the quantity as it is stronger), to scent all manner of sweet delights. Orange blossom water is particularly good with its own fruit, the orange. Orange jellies (set with gelatine) and sorbets are that much more exotic with a dash of orange blossom water. Several Moroccan salads (served as savouries, rather than puddings) of orange slices alone, or with lettuce, carrot or radish, are dressed with orange blossom water, lemon juice, sugar, cinnamon and salt. Sounds unlikely, but they are cool, fragrant and refreshing.

## KEWRA WATER

This is derived from one of the pandanus plants (see page 16).

# VINAIGRETTE

*These are the basic proportions of vinegar, oil and mustard for a standard French dressing, which should be made with wine vinegar and light olive oil, groundnut oil or sunflower oil. The variations, using different oils and vinegars or other sharp liquids, are endless, and may require slight adjustments to quantities. Taste is the final arbiter. For a lemon and oil dressing, increase the lemon juice to 1 ½ tablespoons, use olive oil, and omit the mustard. I would use the same proportions for an umeboshi plum seasoning dressing, substituting 3 ½ tablespoons sunflower or groundnut oil and ½ tablespoon sesame oil. If using balsamic or sherry vinegar, you may find that you need a little less oil, and, again, there is no need for mustard.*

**1 tablespoon wine vinegar**
**4 tablespoons oil**
**salt and pepper**
**½ teaspoon Dijon mustard (optional)**

Either put all the ingredients in a screw-top jar, cover and shake well to mix, or whisk the vinegar with the salt, pepper and mustard, then whisk in the oil, a tablespoon at a time. Taste and adjust the balance, adding more oil or seasonings, if needed.

# POUSSINS WITH VINEGAR & GARLIC

*As the casserole simmers away quietly in the oven, the sharpness of the vinegar mellows out, and mixes with the meat juices to give a small amount of rich sauce, and very tender, well flavoured little poussins.*

**Serves 4**

**4 poussins**
**3 tablespoons olive oil**
**1 onion, finely chopped**
**2 sprigs thyme**
**1 bay leaf**
**16 garlic cloves, unpeeled**
**salt and pepper**
**5 tablespoons sherry vinegar or black rice vinegar**
**5 tablespoons chicken stock**

Brown the poussins in 2 tablespoons of the olive oil. Nestle them snuggly in a heavy casserole and tuck the onion, thyme, bay leaf and garlic around them. Season with salt and pepper, then pour over the vinegar, stock and remaining olive oil. Cover tightly and cook in a cool oven (150°C, 300°F, Gas Mark 2) for 1½–2 hours until the poussins are meltingly tender.

# FAISINJAN

*To be honest, this does not look awfully enticing – the thick sauce is a bit murky – but the smell alone will be enough to compensate, and then the taste… well, who cares what it looks like? Faisinjan is a classic Iranian dish, and this version is a slightly tweaked variation on the recipe given by Claudia Roden in* A New Book of Middle Eastern Cooking. *She suggests using wild duck instead of pheasant, and it can also be made with a good free-range chicken.*

**Serves 4**

**1 plump pheasant, cut into 8 portions**
**2 tablespoons oil**
**1 onion, chopped**
**225 g (8 oz) shelled walnuts, coarsely ground or very finely chopped**
**1 cinnamon stick**
**3 tablespoons pomegranate syrup**
**450 ml (¾ pint) water**
**salt and pepper**
**sugar**
**1 tablespoon chopped parsley**

Brown the pheasant pieces in the oil. Set aside, and fry the onion in the same oil until browned, stirring to prevent burning. Turn down the heat, add the walnuts and cinnamon and cook gently for a few minutes, stirring. Mix in the pomegranate syrup, water and a little salt and pepper. Bring up to the boil, stirring occasionally, then add the pheasant pieces. Cover and simmer gently for 30 minutes. Uncover and continue simmering until the meat is very tender and the sauce is thick – another 15–30 minutes. Taste and add more salt or pepper, or a little sugar to give a sweet and sour sauce. Sprinkle with the chopped parsley before serving.

# RASPBERRY VINEGAR

*This makes a fairly powerfully flavoured raspberry vinegar, certainly more fruity than the cheaper raspberry vinegars sold commercially. For a seriously intense one, repeat the infusion process a third time with another 225 g (8 oz) raspberries. Either way, remember that there is a three-day gap between using one batch of raspberries and another, so do not buy the full quantity all in one go.*

**Makes approx. 1 pint (600 ml)**

**2 × 225 g (8 oz) raspberries (see above)**
**450 ml (¾ pint) white wine vinegar**

Put 225 g (8 oz) raspberries in a preserving jar, crushing gently to bruise and release juices. Pour over the vinegar. Cover and leave for 3 days on a warm, sunny windowsill. Strain through a muslin-lined sieve, leaving the mixture to drip for a couple of hours without pressing down on it.

   Place the second batch of raspberries in the rinsed out preserving jar, again crushing gently, and pour over the vinegar. Seal, return to the windowsill and leave for a further 3 days, or even a whole week, then strain in the same way through a muslin-lined sieve. Bottle and seal well, then store in a cool, dark cupboard.

# VERA'S ORANGEADE

*A reader, Mr Ladelle, sent me some photocopies of the cookery pages of* Our Home, *a women's magazine of 1902. Amongst the cool summer drinks was this recipe for orangeade.*

**2 large oranges**
**65 g (2½ oz) caster sugar**
**100 ml (3½ fl oz) raspberry vinegar**

Squeeze the juice from the oranges. Chop the squeezed oranges up roughly and place in a bowl with the sugar. Pour over enough boiling water to cover. Stir to dissolve the sugar, then cover tightly with clingfilm.

   When the orange peel infusion is cold, mix in the orange juice and raspberry vinegar. Strain through a jelly bag or sieve lined with muslin, letting it drip through without pressing down on it. Store in a stoppered bottle or jam jar in the refrigerator.

   To serve, dilute with iced water, still or fizzy, to taste.

# UMEBOSHI PLUM & SESAME DRESSING

*A thick, nutty and fruity dressing, not the kind of thing you would toss into a green salad, but excellent with more robust salads, maybe served on the side rather than mixed right in, or with crudités.*

**Serves 6**

**4 tablespoons dry-fried sesame seeds**
**1 teaspoon dried green peppercorns**
**1 teaspoon soy sauce**
**1 tablespoon umeboshi plum seasoning**
**2 teaspoons sesame oil**
**4 tablespoons sunflower oil**

Grind the sesame seeds and peppercorns to a soft paste in an electric coffee grinder or in a mortar. Gradually work in the soy sauce, plum seasoning and then the oils.

WHITE WINE VINEGAR

UMEBOSHI PLUM SEASONING

UMEBOSHI PLUM AND SESAME DRESSING (TOP RIGHT), SERVED WITH A PEPPER SALAD; VERA'S ORANGEADE (BOTTOM RIGHT)

# GRILLED VEGETABLES WITH MISO

*You will probably have to grill the vegetables in several batches, unless you have an exceptionally wide grill. Vegetarians might like to add well-drained cubes of tofu to the collection.*

**Serves 4 as a main course, 8 as a first course**

1 aubergine
4 courgettes
salt
2 red onions
8 open-cap mushrooms
oil

WHITE MISO TOPPING:

**4 tablespoons white miso**
**1½ tablespoons sugar**
**2 tablespoons sake or dry sherry**
**finely grated zest of ½ lime**

RED MISO TOPPING:

**1 × 2.5 cm (1 inch) piece fresh root ginger, finely grated**
**3 tablespoons red miso**
**1 tablespoon white miso**
**1½ tablespoons sugar**
**2 tablespoons sake or dry sherry**

Slice the aubergine into discs 1 cm (½ inch) thick. Spread them out on a plate and sprinkle lightly with salt. Set aside for 30 minutes, then rinse and dry on absorbent kitchen paper. Halve the courgettes lengthwise, arrange them cut side up on a plate and sprinkle lightly with salt. Set aside for 30 minutes, then rinse and dry on absorbent kitchen paper.

Peel the onions and cut them into 1 cm (½ inch) thick discs. Push a wooden cocktail stick through each disc from one edge through the centre, like a lollipop stick, to hold the rings together.

Grate the ginger for the red miso topping, then squeeze to extract the juice. Reserve the juice.

While the aubergine and courgettes are being salted, prepare the toppings. For the white miso topping, mix all the ingredients except the lime zest in a small pan. Stir over a very low heat, without letting it boil, until smooth and hot. Draw off the heat and mix in the lime zest.

Red miso topping is prepared in exactly the same way, adding enough of the ginger juice to flavour it (about 1 tablespoon), after the topping has come off the heat.

Brush the aubergine, courgette, onion rings and mushrooms with oil and grill on both sides until they are patched with brown and tender. Spread half the aubergine slices and onion rings on one side only with white miso topping, the other half with red. Spread the cut sides of half the courgettes with white topping, the other half with red. In the same way, spread the cups of half the mushrooms with white, half with red miso topping. Return to the grill, miso-side up, for a minute or so more to heat through. Eat immediately.

# SPICED NOODLES

*Both the noodles and spice paste can be prepared in advance, leaving just the final frying and tossing for the last minute. The result is a spicy, steaming mountain of noodles, good enough to eat all on their own. In fact, if you want to turn them into a full main course, sauté pieces of chicken or pork fillet, shrimps or prawns, bean sprouts, mushrooms, peas, tofu or whatever in a separate pan then toss them in with the noodles.*

**Serves 6–8**

**I quail's egg-sized piece of tamarind pulp, or 2 tablespoons lemon or lime juice**
**450 g (I lb) Chinese egg thread noodles**
**I onion, chopped**
**3 garlic cloves, chopped**
**2 red chillies, seeded and chopped**
**I × 2.5 cm (I inch) piece root ginger, peeled and chopped**
**lower 10 cm (4 inches) of I stalk lemon grass, bruised and chopped**
**4 tablespoons oil**
**2 tablespoons fish sauce**
**I tablespoon tomato purée**
**I½ tablespoons palm sugar or dark muscovado sugar**

Break up the tamarind pulp and cover with 3 tablespoons hot water. Set aside for 15 minutes, then strain and reserve the tamarind water. Cook the noodles in boiling, lightly salted water for 4 minutes until just tender, or according to the packet instructions. Drain well, rinse under cold water, separating out the strands, then drain and cool. Cover until needed.

In a processor, or a mortar, grind the onion with the garlic, chillies, ginger and lemon grass to a fine paste. Fry this paste in the oil in a wok or pan large enough to take the noodles as well,

TOP: SPICED NOODLES; BOTTOM: OYSTER PO'BOY

stirring constantly, for about 3 minutes. Add 2 tablespoons of the tamarind water or lemon juice, fish sauce, tomato purée, sugar and 2 tablespoons water. Stir in well, and simmer

for 2 minutes. Tip in the noodles, raise the heat, and toss the noodles until they are evenly coated and wonderfully hot. Serve immediately.

# OYSTER (OR CHICKEN) PO'BOY

*We ate warm oyster po'boys oozing mayonnaise and Tabasco on Avery Island on a chilly December day, before setting off for a boat trip through the bayous. We spotted otters and egrets and staved off the cold with a large bottle of brandy. Happy memories. Po'boys are the classic New Orleans sandwiches, made with great French bread and a hearty shake of hot pepper sauce.*

**Serves 1**

**1 half baguette or ½ stick of French bread**
**6 shucked oysters or ½ chicken breast, cut into bite-sized pieces**
**fine cornmeal, or seasoned flour**
**oil for frying**
**mayonnaise**
**2–3 leaves crisp lettuce, shredded**
**1 small tomato, sliced**
**salt**
**Tabasco pepper sauce**

Split the loaf in half lengthwise. Clamp the halves together, wrap in foil and heat through in a moderately hot oven (200°C, 400°F, Gas Mark 6) for 10–15 minutes. Toss the oysters or pieces of chicken in cornmeal or flour, coating them evenly. Fry the oysters quickly in hot oil until lightly browned. Cook the chicken pieces a little more slowly, until medium-brown. Keep hot if the bread is not yet heated through.

Spread each half of the hot loaf generously with mayonnaise. Top one half with lettuce, then the fried oysters or chicken and, finally, the tomato slices. Season with salt and a generous shake of Tabasco and clamp the top on quickly. Eat immediately, while still warm.

# OLIVE PASTA

*Flavoured pastas always taste better for having been freshly made. This one is best served simply dressed with olive oil and garlic, and perhaps a hint of chilli.*

**Serves 3**

**2 large eggs**
**1½ tablespoons olive paste**
**175 g (6 oz) plain flour, sifted**

Whisk the eggs with the olive paste until evenly blended. Make a well in the centre of the flour, and add enough of the egg mixture (you will need most of it but possibly not all) to give a soft dough. It should be moist, but not wet. Gather the dough up into a ball. Knead for ten minutes, lightly flouring the work surface, if necessary. By the end of this time the dough should be silky smooth. Wrap it in clingfilm and rest in the refrigerator for 30 minutes.

If you have a pasta machine, roll the pasta through it, according to the instructions, and cut into 1 cm (⅓ inch) wide tagliatelle. Otherwise, divide the dough in two, and wrap one piece again in clingfilm and set it aside. Roll the other piece out in a rectangular shape on a very lightly floured board until it is 1.5 mm (¹⁄₁₆ inch) thin, thinner if you can manage it. Let it dry out for a few minutes, then roll it up loosely and cut into 1 cm (⅓ inch) wide slices with a sharp knife. Unravel the slices and lay them out on clean tea towels. Taking four or five strands together, wind them loosely around your fingers, then leave to dry on the tea towel. Repeat the process with the remaining dough. If you are going to cook the pasta within the next few hours, leave them where they are. The pasta can also be frozen.

To cook the pasta from fresh, drop it into a pan of boiling water and simmer for a few minutes until it is *al dente*. Frozen pasta can be cooked straight from the freezer, but allow an extra 3 or 4 minutes' cooking time.

# MOUTABEL (BABA GANOUSH)

*If possible, grill the aubergine over a charcoal barbecue to give a really smoky flavour to this sesame and aubergine cream. Moutabel is served as a first course, usually part of a mixed meze, with warm pitta bread to dip into it.*

**Serves 4–6**

**1 large aubergine**
**1 garlic clove, chopped**
**4 tablespoons tahina**
**25 g (1 oz) walnuts, chopped**
**juice of ½ lemon**
**generous ½ teaspoon ground cumin**
**salt**
**8 mint leaves, shredded**
**seeds of ½ pomegranate**
**2 tablespoons olive oil**

Grill the aubergine close to the heat, turning frequently until the skin is blackened and charred, and the flesh is soft. Alternatively, bake it in the oven, preheated to its highest setting, until blackened and soft. Peel the aubergine, chop the flesh roughly and drain in a colander until cool enough to handle.

Squeeze the aubergine to get rid of the remaining bitter juices, and process or liquidize with the garlic, tahina, walnuts, lemon juice, cumin and a little salt, until smooth and creamy. Taste and add more salt or lemon juice, if needed. Stir in two-thirds of the mint. Spoon into a bowl, cover and chill until needed.

To serve, bring the moutabel back to room temperature. Make a well in the centre, and fill with the pomegranate seeds. Drizzle the olive oil over the purée, and sprinkle with the remaining mint. Serve with warm pitta bread.

# PICKLES, PRESERVES & CANDIES

I am a hoarder. I hate throwing things out. Well, you never know when that old pair of curtains that I never liked might come in handy, or perhaps in a couple of years' time those trousers might swing back into fashion. My kitchen cupboards, too, are filled to overflowing with jars of this and that collected in the course of travels or purchased in order to test a particular recipe, or merely out of curiosity. A host of pickles, preserves, and candies are a hoarder's joy. Not only will they last, if not indefinitely, then at least for the foreseeable future, but during their lifetime you know for sure that they will always be useful when the occasion arises.

I go through phases of mild addiction to certain types of food. In a week when nothing but the spicy, aromatic nature of South-East Asian food will satisfy, I can work my way through a fair quantity of blachan but there is no way that I can polish off a whole block. A recurrent passion for the salty fermented taste of Chinese black beans slowly lowers the level in the jar, but after a year it is still not empty. It does not matter. They will keep.

There are certain items that never get a chance to prove their longevity. Sun-dried tomatoes or artichokes in olive oil are lucky to last out the week. I cannot resist dipping into the jar as I pass by, and munching contentedly as I carry on doing whatever it is that has brought me into the kitchen. My dentist would shudder if he knew how powerless I am to resist the temptation of a cake of palm sugar.

I work on the assumption that most people are far more disciplined than I am. Every one of the collection of pickles, preserves and candies in this chapter has an intrinsically lengthy shelf-life. Some are rarer than others, and worth buying if and when you come across them, without waiting until you actually need them. If needs be, they will wait patiently for your attentions, and more likely than not, their presence will encourage you to try your hand at using them. Many of the more outlandish items can be employed not only in the cooking of their country of origin, but adapted to heighten the flavour of more familiar dishes. Try them out first as they are meant to be used so that you know how to handle them properly, and what it is they contribute. Then, you can begin experimenting with confidence.

# PICKLES AND PRESERVES

## MOSTARDA DI CREMONA

This strange preserve has a decidedly medieval air to it. Pieces of fruit, melon, pear, cherries and others, are candied in a sweet syrup spiked with mustard and spices. It sounds bizarre, but tastes delicious. It is traditionally served with boiled meats, but makes a good accompaniment to roast game or dark meaty stews.

In the market in Turin I found another mostarda, this time made only with pears, cooked down in mustardy syrup to a thick gold-brown mush. This, too, is served with boiled meats.

## SUN-DRIED TOMATOES
(Pomodori secchi)

In the south of Italy halved tomatoes spread out to dry on black polythene sheets in the fields are a common sight in the summer. The moisture is sucked out by the heat of the sun, leaving behind a leathery wrinkled oval of concentrated tomato, with a deep caramelized flavour. They may be sold loose, or packed into jars and covered in olive oil, perhaps with added herbs, garlic or chilli.

If you buy them dry and loose, they will need to be rehydrated before use since they are as tough as old boots. Cover them with hot water and set aside for 1–1½ hours. Nibble a corner – they should still be chewy, but comfortably so, and bursting with flavour. Drain well, then dry them on absorbent kitchen paper. If you are not using them instantly, sprinkle with a little salt, then pack into a jar and cover with olive oil, adding herbs and garlic if you wish. Make sure there are no trapped pockets of

air, and that the tomatoes are completely covered, then seal the jar and stash it away until needed.

Most Italian foodshops and delicatessens will sell sun-dried tomatoes ready-packed in oil, to be used straight from the jar. Toss strips of dried tomato into pasta with a little of their oil, fresh basil, and crushed garlic. Or use them in sandwiches, or diced in salads, especially grilled pepper salads. I often slip a couple of sun-dried tomato halves, chopped up small, into a tomato sauce as it cooks to give a marvellous depth of flavour, or use them in stuffings, or braise with slow-cooking vegetables or meaty stews. And I eat them neat, straight from the jar.

## PRESERVED ARTICHOKES IN OIL
(Carciofini sott'olio)

These are small globe artichokes, carciofini as opposed to carciofi, the familiar large artichokes, so tender that you can eat them whole, choke and all. They are cooked in acidulated water, giving them a gentle sharpness, and preserved under olive oil. Sometimes they are sold loose, scooped out from a large bowl, but more usually they are packed tightly into glass jars. Do not confuse them with canned artichoke bottoms which are nowhere near as good, and certainly no substitute. If you are lucky you may come across the extra special roasted carciofini, streaked with brown from the heat of a charcoal grill.

Carciofini sott'olio are usually served as part of an antipasto misto, with plates of salamis, hams and cheeses, and can be added to salads – try them in a garlicy potato salad, or a tuna and bean salad. In fact, they go very nicely with canned tuna – as a student in Perugia I always made a dash at lunch time for the "panini al tonno", bread rolls filled with tuna, chopped artichoke, capers and mayonnaise. And tuna and artichoke pizzas are a hard act to beat.

## OLIVES

When two food-loving friends of mine decided to set up house together there was only one major bone of contention. Olives. She had a passion for them. He hated them. With unparalleled devotion, he set about remedying the matter. He ate an olive a day, gradually increasing the number over a period of two years, until finally he was every bit as keen as she was. A story of true love.

A taste for olives is worth acquiring if it does not come naturally, with or without the love-interest. Unfortunately, it is not made any easier by the poor quality of many of the most widely available olives. Some brands of canned or vacuum-packed olives are excellent, but far too many are not. As a general rule, it is safer to buy olives from those shops that sell them loose from the barrel. At least that way you can try one before handing over the cash.

How anybody ever discovered that the horribly bitter raw fruit of the olive tree could be transformed into a delicacy is a mystery. The process involves numerous stages of washing and soaking before you even get to the pickling proper.

The difference between green and black olives is only the degree of ripeness. Green, unripe olives will have a firmer texture than black, with a skin pulled tight and smooth. Avoid wrinkled or squishy green olives, clear indications that there is something amiss. Once the fruit has ripened to black or purplish-brown, the flesh softens and the skin may wrinkle. The extent of wrinkling depends on the precise stage of ripeness and on the variety. The tiny ink-black Niçoise olives are as crumpled and wrinkly as they can get, whilst the elegant purple-brown Kalamata olives have a taut, smooth skin. Either way, black olives should always be glossy.

Disappointing olives are not an entirely lost cause. Drain them, then tip them into a clean jar, tucking a few flavourings amongst

CLOCKWISE FROM TOP RIGHT: MOSTARDA DI CREMONA, WILD ONIONS IN OIL, PRESERVED ARTICHOKES IN OIL, SUN-DRIED TOMATOES, SUN-DRIED TOMATOES IN OIL

## WILD ONIONS IN OIL
(Lampascioni sott'olio)

Not really onions at all, but the bulbs of the Tassel hyacinth, a type of grape hyacinth that grows wild in the south of Italy. They do resemble tiny purplish onions, and are sometimes called *cipollini*, the Italian for little onions. In their raw state they are so bitter as to be inedible, but most of their bitterness is soaked away before cooking, leaving just a pleasing edge. They are boiled until tender, and preserved in oil. A few enterprising Italian delicatessens stock them, but by no means all, not even in Italy. A shame, since they are quite unique and remarkable in flavour. Serve them as part of an antipasto misto, with salamis, hams and cheeses.

TOP: SALTED BLACK BEANS, OLIVES; BOTTOM: FERMENTED BLACK BEANS, PICKLED CAPER BUDS AND PODS, SALTED CAPERS

them – halved cloves of garlic, sprigs of herbs, chillies, crushed coriander seeds, lemon or orange zest. Cover with olive oil, or a mixture of half olive, half sunflower oil, making sure the contents are completely covered. Seal and leave in a cool, dark place. A week later they will be much improved. Higher quality olives will emerge from this treatment with flying colours.

## SALTED CAPERS

The caper plant grows wild on rocky outcrops all around the Mediterranean. It is low and bushy with oval leaves and flowers of great beauty – a waterfall of long purple stamens against four white or pink petals. The flowers open in the morning, and by late afternoon they have wilted, overcome by the heat of the midday sun. Their scent

is a perfect blend of honeysuckle, jasmine, and caper.

Capers, that is caper buds, must be picked from the bush when they have reached just the right degree of plumpness, but before they burst open – a day-by-day harvesting of each bush, back-breaking work even with cultivated capers, let alone the wild ones. Much of the crop, and nearly all the exported capers, are pickled in vinegar, often harsh and penetrating. The rest are preserved in salt, usually sold locally, or at least in markets around the Mediterranean. Here, they will be graded according to size and quality, the larger, choicest ones, commanding the highest prices. I make a point of bringing salted capers back from trips to caper countries. The flavour is always so much fresher and the salt rinses away easily.

## CAPER PODS

The buds are not the only part of the caper plant that merit the pickling treatment. In Cyprus, the stems and young prickly leaves are submerged in vinegar. They are, I think it is fair to say, an acquired taste. The little spines make for uncomfortable eating, and though I have tried, I doubt that I shall ever acquire a taste for them. The tear-drop-shaped seed-pods are quite another matter. I can eat these like lollipops, biting the pod off its stem, and munching on the soft, slightly crunchy seeds inside. They are preserved in vinegar, but being of a robuster nature than the buds they survive the treatment in fine form. They are extremely good with a piece of mature cheddar, or when served as a pickle with cold meats.

## CHINESE FERMENTED BLACK BEANS
(Salted black beans, Tauco)

Ever-versatile, multipurpose soy beans in one of their classiest guises. Black soy beans are cooked, heavily salted, and fermented. Buy them in jars or cans in Oriental supermarkets, checking that you have picked up whole beans, not black bean sauce. Nice as it may be, the sauce is not half so useful and, besides, you can make it yourself with the whole beans.

The beans are used whole, chopped, or mashed to a paste in many Chinese dishes and some South-East Asian ones too. There is no reason to be territorial with them, though. These salty little nuggets are good in all kinds of less exotic dishes. I use them in salad dressings, with vegetables, in tomato sauces and stuffings, and sprinkled over soups together with pieces of fried garlic. They go well with poultry, meat, fish, shellfish and vegetables.

They need to be cooked, usually fried gently in oil along with garlic, onion, ginger or whatever else forms the basic flavouring in the recipe. To make a black bean sauce, mash two tablespoons of black beans to a paste with four crushed garlic cloves. Fry gently in oil, with 2 teaspoons grated ginger, and add around 85 ml (3 fl oz) stock, or stock with soy sauce and rice wine or sherry or whatever liquid seems appropriate. Stir and simmer until thickened. This is strong stuff, so use as a flavouring rather than a sauce all on its own.

Chinese fermented yellow beans are similarly processed yellow soy beans, but have a milder flavour, and may be sweetened.

## SALTED ANCHOVIES and SARDINES

There is at least one pickles and salted goods stall in every Mediterranean market, and no doubt in many other markets around the world. A major portion of the stand will be taken up with a display of salted fish of several types and grades. Most important are the sardines and anchovies – tightly packed silvery fish, grains of salt catching in the sunlight, neatly fanned out like the spokes of a cartwheel in cans or wooden tubs.

Salted anchovies or little sardines are used like the more familiar canned anchovy fillets in oil, but have a superior flavour. Rinse off the salt before using, scale them if necessary, and fillet – tedious, but it doesn't take long. If they taste excessively salty, soak the fillets in milk for 30 minutes or so. I like their saltiness, so rarely bother.

All the Greek-Cypriot grocers in my corner of London sell pretty, round, blue cans of salted sardines. Unopened, they keep indefinitely. Once opened they survive for several weeks in the refrigerator. If you bring loose salted anchovies or sardines back from a holiday, or have an opened can which you are unlikely to work your way through within the immediate future, set aside a little time to fillet the unused fish, pack them into a jar with, if you wish, a couple of halved cloves of garlic and a sprig or two of thyme, and cover with olive oil, or a mixture of olive oil and vegetable oil. Tightly sealed, they will last for ages, and taste marvellous.

## BOTTARGA
(Buttariga, Poutargue)

This is dried, pressed and salted grey mullet or tuna roe, enjoyed as a great treat all around the Mediterranean. The Greek *tarama*, the stuff of which real taramasalata is made, is also salted grey mullet roe but not pressed to the hard compactness of bottarga. Bottarga is usually coated with a greyish wax to keep it free from the ravages of the open air.

My first taste of bottarga was in Sardinia, grated generously over spaghetti tossed in first class olive oil. Not too generously, mind you, which would have been a mistake, since it is pungent. There is no better way to use bottarga. As good, however, is thinly sliced bottarga, dressed with olive oil and lemon on first class bread, or with potatoes in a salad.

You might find it in Italian or Middle Eastern delicatessens in this country, but it is unlikely. Bring it back with you from holidays in France or Italy. Be warned, it is pricy, but a little goes a very long way and it keeps well.

SALTED SARDINES AND ANCHOVIES

INGREDIENTS

## KETA

(Salmon caviar, Red caviar, Ketovaia)

Heretical though it may sound, I prefer keta, salmon caviar, to the genuine article. The salmon-coloured eggs are larger than those of real caviar, translucent and shiny as a heap of precious jewels. I like the fact that they are big enough to burst with my tongue against the roof of my mouth and I love the flood of salty richness that follows.

Properly speaking, keta is made with the roe of the Siberian or dog salmon, a species of Pacific salmon, but salmon caviar can be made from the roe of any salmon. Like all caviars it is simply salted and potted up. Small pots of keta are sold by smarter fishmongers, and many delicatessens. Once the pots have been opened, the keta should be eaten within a day or two.

Keta is lovely served with Russian blinis (yeast-raised buckwheat pancakes) and soured cream, or with smatana pancakes (see Dairy Products). It is used as a garnish, particularly for salmon dishes, or added to sauces for fish just before serving (but never heated), on canapés, to top elegant little savoury vegetable tartlets, etc, etc. Less sophisticated, but every bit as good, if not better, is keta on baked potatoes with lashings of crème fraîche, soured cream or smatana and chopped chives, or finely chopped red onion.

CLOCKWISE FROM TOP LEFT: PICKLED JAPANESE GINGER, BLACHAN, KETA, UMEBOSHI PLUMS AND SHISO LEAVES

## UMEBOSHI PLUMS

Ume are not actually plums, but a type of apricot, always used before it ripens. Umeboshi are ume pickled in brine with red shiso leaves, which give them a mid-puce colour. They are about the size of a big walnut, soft and wrinkled, with a sharp, clean fruity taste. The Japanese eat them for breakfast, which is not a habit likely to find great favour in the West. Save them for using, chopped or puréed, in cold "dipping" sauces or hot sharp sauces, in dressings, stuffings, or to serve whole as a relish with fish or poultry. To purée, halve and pit them, then rub them through a sieve. Puréed umeboshi (*bainiku*) is sometimes available in jars. Umeboshi plums keep indefinitely, stored in the refrigerator in their jar. I forgot all about a half-used jar at the back of my refrigerator which sat there happily for two years, and they still tasted fine!

## BLACHAN
(Balachan, Trasi, Terasi, Kapi)

Blachan is made of fermented salted shrimps, dried and pounded to a paste. It is sold in jars, still moist, or in solid blocks. It is an essential ingredient in South-East Asian cooking, used in small quantity to give an unidentifiable depth of flavour. The best satay sauce I have ever eaten was seasoned with blachan. Blachan has a forceful smell, like an intensified anchovy paste, and should be kept tightly wrapped or closed in a jar.

It is always cooked, never used raw. It may be ground to a paste with other flavourings and fried, or grilled, fried or roasted in a piece. In this last case it is sensible to wrap it in foil and dry-fry or roast it in the oven. If you do not, the smell is devastating and lingers for ages. Go easy with the salt when you use blachan, as it is pretty salty to begin with. Once you have used it a few times in Asian dishes, try adding a small piece to more Western-

style dishes – stews, for instance.

The southern Indian balichow (or Burmese balachong) is not the same thing. It contains salted shrimp, but other ingredients too, including lots of chillies, which transforms it into a relish to be eaten with other dishes.

## PICKLED JAPANESE GINGER
(Amazu-shoga)

Paper-thin slices of ginger lightly pickled in vinegar, salt, and sugar. *Amazu-shoga* has a delicate light salmon-pink colour, more attractive, I think, than *beni-shoga* which is dyed bright pink or red. Pickled ginger is served as a relish with sushi and sashimi, but it is delightful with cooked fish, particularly grilled salmon. I serve it, too, with poultry, or add it, finely diced, to salads. It is sold in plastic sachets or jars in Japanese food shops.

## STEM GINGER IN SYRUP

The Chinese were the first to preserve ginger in syrup. By the thirteenth century it was already being exported around the world. Much is still produced there today, though other countries now contribute their share, too. Very young ginger is chosen before it becomes tough and fibrous and too pungent. Although it is the tender shoots of the root that are used, it is known as "stem ginger". Once it has been trimmed it is simmered in syrup until tender and impregnated with sugar.

Every time I use these little spheres of ginger my mind wanders back to childhood, and the happy gatherings at the round dining table in my parents' house. My mother would cover the revolving dumb waiter set in the centre of the table with bowls of sweetmeats: pears and quinces poached in vanilla syrup, little biscuits, toasted nuts, clotted cream or ice cream, and, somewhere amongst them, a bowl of sweet stem ginger ladled out of the blue and white china ginger jar in the

STEM GINGER IN SYRUP

larder. A mixed hors d'oeuvre of a pudding, every guest turning the dumb waiter to help themselves to a little of this or that.

Stem ginger and cream or a scoop of home-made vanilla ice cream is still for me the epitome of luxurious desserts, but, like my mother, I use the ginger in other ways, too. Diced small, it goes into cakes, creams, soufflés, mousses, and sauces. A favourite cake filling, or soft icing for ginger biscuits, is made with cream cheese, sweetened with icing sugar and a little of the syrup from the ginger jar, studded with nuggets of ginger. The syrup is a marvellous ingredient in its own right, adding sweetness, gingeriness and moisture. The delicious shock of sweet ginger has its place in savoury dishes too. George Perry-Smith's creation of salmon with stem ginger and raisins, wrapped in pastry, has become a classic. Besides salmon, it can be excellent with lamb, chicken, or duck, pushed down in slivers into the meat, or added to a stuffing or sauce. A spoonful or two of the syrup can be made part of a marinade.

If an enthusiasm for using the syrup leaves the ginger in the jar exposed, cover it again with a thick sugar syrup which will soon take on the gingeriness of the original.

# SYRUPS AND CANDIES

## GOLDEN SYRUP

Golden syrup is vastly underrated in the world of haute-cuisine. Wrong. It does not even have a place in the world of haute-cuisine, where, if it is considered at all, it is immediately dismissed as a rather common taste. Well, I am happy to be common in that case. I love the taste of golden syrup, spread stickily over hot buttered toast, oozing over a suet pudding, or on Yorkshire pudding (minus the meat juices.)

Golden syrup is a by-product of sugar-refining, made from the syrup left behind after sugar crystals have been formed. This is an inverted sugar, i.e. one where a large portion of the sucrose molecules have been broken down into fructose and glucose, inhibiting the formation of crystals. The aversion to crystallization is a most useful property. For a start, it keeps the syrup runny, but it is also why small amounts are often used in recipes for toffees and brittle candies, discouraging unwanted crystallization.

Golden syrup is often referred to as treacle. Confusing, as treacle can also mean molasses (black treacle) or a refined version of molasses with a subdued taste. Those comforting winter puddings, treacle tart and treacle pudding, are usually made with golden syrup, whereas treacle toffee takes its name from molasses-type treacles. Except in these specific names, try to avoid using the word treacle. Quite apart from the ambiguity, it always sets me off giggling. In J. P. Martin's *Uncle and the Treacle Trouble* the mysteriously named Treac Levat tower is the cause of a hundred and one problems for Uncle the Elephant (clad as ever in a purple dressing gown) and his minions, culminating in a glorious sticky flood of treacle. Nothing mysterious at all, as it turns out, just a huge forgotten Treacle Vat.

## MOLASSES
(Black treacle, Blackstrap molasses)

Like golden syrup, molasses is a by-product of sugar-refining, particularly cane sugar. Beet molasses, though it exists, is pretty nasty stuff not usually considered fit for human consumption. Molasses comes in a variety of grades; the lightest still contains a fair quantity of crystallizable sugar whilst the darkest of the dark, blackstrap molasses, is left with very little. It has a strong, deep, liquorice flavour and is not the kind of syrup you would want to eat straight from the container. However, it does give a unique, dark flavour to fruit cakes, toffees, gingerbreads and biscuits, or steamed puddings, marvellous if not overdone. It can be used, too, with discretion, in savoury dishes, dark meaty stews, for instance, and classic Boston Baked Beans and Boston Brown Bread.

## MAPLE SYRUP

In *Little House in the Big Woods*, the first volume of her autobiography, Laura Ingalls Wilder describes how her grandfather collected the watery sap from his maple trees in the Wisconsin woods, and boiled it down to a syrup in a big iron kettle strung on a chain between two trees over a bonfire. That year (somewhere around 1875), there was a sugar snow. The sap begins to rise as winter draws to a close, around February or March. A late snowfall, a sugar snow, holds back the leafing of the trees and gives a longer run of sap.

Her grandparents threw a "sugaring-off" party to celebrate the long run. Family and friends danced into the night, and gorged themselves on maple candy. The syrup was boiled down to the thread stage and "Grandma stood by the brass kettle and with the big wooden spoon she poured hot syrup on each plate of snow. It cooled into soft candy, and as fast as it cooled they ate it . . . there was plenty of syrup in the kettle and plenty of snow outdoors."

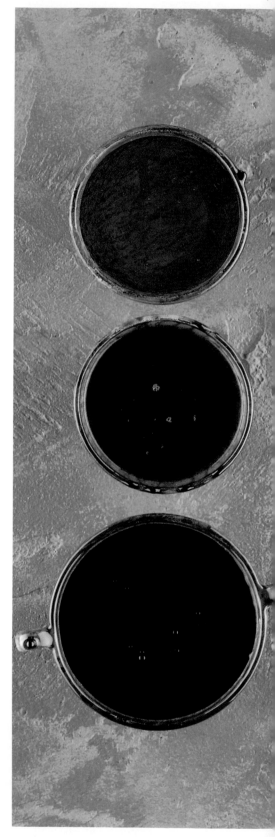

FROM THE TOP: GOLDEN SYRUP, MAPLE SYRUP, MOLASSES

Indians taught the first white colonists how to collect the sap of the maple and boil it down to use as a sweetener, and even today the basic method remains the same. Canadian maple syrup is carefully graded. Canada #1, Extra Light, Light and Medium are all thin, lightly flavoured syrups, best for pouring over pancakes, waffles and ice cream as a sauce. Canada #2 Amber is thicker and has a more concentrated taste. This is the best grade to use for cooking. Whilst you may be offered no choice over the grade, you should always check carefully when buying maple syrup. If the word "flavoured" appears on the label, often in small letters between the prominently printed words "maple" and "syrup", then it is a synthetic fake and not worth buying. It tastes foul and will ruin anything you use it in or pour it over.

Real maple syrup is another matter altogether. It is a delicious sweetener in all kinds of dishes, from cakes and candies, biscuits, fruity puddings and pumpkin pie to glazed hams and spareribs, or vegetables such as carrots and onions. The Ontario Maple Syrup Producers' Association gives this advice on substituting maple syrup for ordinary sugar: 1½ cups of maple syrup is the equivalent of 1 cup of ordinary sugar, i.e. 1½ times the volume provides the same degree of sweetness. When used in baking, you should also add ¼ teaspoon of bicarbonate of soda for every 250 ml (8 fl oz) syrup. When using all maple syrup instead of sugar, reduce other liquids in the recipe by one half. When substituting maple sugar for half the sugar, reduce other liquids by one quarter. A final word of advice from me, do not get reckless – too much maple syrup can be cloying and is no longer a good thing.

## MAPLE SUGAR

This is maple syrup taken a few stages further on, boiled down until it crystallizes and sets solid in sugar cakes. It is usually pulverized into sugar crystals, with a light tan colour, and, not surprisingly, a concentrated maple flavour. It should be used in the same way as vanilla sugar, as a flavouring rather than a direct substitute for ordinary sugar. To make your own maple sugar, boil maple syrup to a temperature of 116°C/240°F (soft ball stage), then draw off the heat and stir vigorously until it turns thick, opaque and creamy. Pour into a buttered dish and leave to set.

## UNREFINED BROWN SUGARS

To describe any sugar as "unrefined" is misleading. All sugar must be refined to some degree, to remove the other bits and bobs of plant matter and impurities. What is known as "unrefined" sugar is really "less refined", i.e. it has not been completely stripped down to a pure white crystal that is all sweetness and no flavour.

Real brown sugars come from sugar cane, although some so-called brown sugars are actually fully refined white sugar (made from either sugar beet or cane), coloured up with molasses or caramel. They have a shallow flavour compared with the equivalent unrefined brown sugars.

The newly harvested cane is crushed and squeezed through rollers to extract the sugar juice, which is then clarified to remove impurities. The juice is boiled to drive off water and thicken. Tiny sugar crystals are introduced to start off the crystallization process. As soon as the crystals have grown to the right size, they are separated out from the syrup by centrifugal force. The sugar from this first crystallization is *demerara*, with large mid-brown grains, and a slightly sticky texture. *Golden granulated sugar* is also from the first crystallization, but of a more thoroughly clarified sugar syrup. Unlike demerara, the crystals are steam-washed and dried to produce a free-flowing light golden sugar with a light flavour.

UNREFINED BROWN SUGARS

The syrup left over from the initial crystallization is put through the process twice more, and the fine sandy sugar crystals from the third crystallization become *light* or *dark muscovado*, or *molasses sugar*. Originally, these crystals were scooped into mesh-bottomed sugar bins, so that the remaining syrup – molasses – now dark and strongly flavoured, could drain slowly down and out of the bins.

The driest lightest brown sugar at the top of the bin, with the lowest residue of molasses was *light muscovado sugar*. In the middle, the sugar was stickier, more fully flavoured, and darker in colour, hence *dark muscovado*. Right at the bottom came the seriously sticky mass of crystals still mixed with a high proportion of molasses: this was *molasses sugar*, with its powerful liquorice taste.

PALM SUGAR, COCONUT PALM SUGAR

Molasses sugar carries the taste of molasses but is much sweeter. It must be used judiciously if it is not to dominate, but it does give the most superb richness when well employed. Like molasses, it is marvellous in Christmas cakes and puddings (and other steamed puddings too), toffee, savoury stews, brown breads, sweet and sour barbecue sauces, etc. Try it, too, in chutneys, pickles and jams, particularly marmalade (use half molasses sugar, half granulated).

## JAGGERY and PALM SUGARS
(Goodh, Gula jawa)

Jaggery is an umbrella word for the various "raw" or "crude" sugars used in India and South-East Asia. Most jaggery is made from cane sugar, and may be soft and sticky or solidified into hard cakes. The taste is similar to the purer muscovado sugars. Palm sugar jaggeries are, I think, the most delicious of all sugars. The flavour varies according to the type of palm, but they are all aromatic and richly flavoured. Their consistency ranges from moist and fudge-like, to dry and hard. The hardened lumps can be grated or pounded to a powder to use in cooking, but I can hardly bring myself to do it. I prefer to eat them neat with coffee as an end-of-meal sweetmeat.

Coconut sugar is made from the sap extracted from the flower of the coconut palm, and has a distinctive winy sharpness underlying its intense sweetness. Like other jaggeries, it may be sold in solid form, or moist and pasty, packed in large plastic sachets. Of all the palm sugars I have tasted, this is the one I like best.

## ROCK CRYSTAL SUGAR
(Rock sugar, Yellow lump)

Rock crystal sugar comes as clear, huge crystals, like uncut semi-precious gems. I am not talking about the comparatively small, brown or rainbow-coloured sugar crystals for coffee. Those ones look mean in comparison. Pieces of rock crystal sugar, from Indian and Chinese food shops, are big, an inch or more across, clear, maybe tinged with yellow. I can think of no particular culinary purpose for them, other than purely decorative. They just look beautiful. I serve them with coffee, to be admired, and crunched as they are, not dissolved away into the hot liquid.

## CHOCOLATE

Chocolate, or at least the definitive element of chocolate, comes from the cocoa bean. Different varieties of cocoa tree (*Theobroma cacao*) grown in different locations, yield beans with distinct flavours. Some of the finest cocoa is grown in Honduras, the Caribbean, Sri Lanka, Sumatra, Madagascar and the New Hebrides. Latin American cocoa swings in with a multitude of uses (notably cosmetic), and in inferior chocolate is often replaced by cheaper vegetable fats which inevitably distract from the flavour, and ruin the texture. When buying chocolate, scrutinize the packet. Somewhere it will tell you the percentage of cocoa solids used. The higher the percentage the more intense the flavour, and the less room there is for other unwanted additions. A quick scan of the contents list, if there is one, will indicate whether cocoa butter or less agreeable fats make up the bulk of the balance, and the position of sugar in the list gives a vague idea of the sweetness (if it comes first the chocolate is likely to be very sweet).

Whenever you are cooking with chocolate insist on the very best quality, with a relatively low sugar content – you can, after all, add more sugar if needs be. The flavour will be tempered by other ingredients, so for it to come through true and clear it must be forthright in the first place. At the very least, there should be a minimum 50 per cent cocoa solid content, but you can do a great deal better than that these days without going too far out of your way. 60–70 per cent should be what you aim for.

**Bitter Chocolate** Ideally, nothing but chocolate liquor and cocoa butter, so bitter that you could not possibly eat it straight, but the ultimate cooking chocolate. In most recipes (unless they specifically call for bitter chocolate) you will need to increase the quantity of sugar or other sweeteners. Some bitter cooking chocolates will be made of the chocolate liquor alone, less rich but more concentrated.

**Plain Chocolate** The best plain chocolate contains only chocolate liquor, cocoa butter, sugar and perhaps vanilla or cinnamon. The less sugar the better for cooking, and to my taste, also for eating. The flavour should be dark, slightly sharp, and verging on fruity, and the bar should snap satisfyingly when broken.

TOP: BROWN CRYSTAL SUGAR, SUGARLOAF SUGAR; BOTTOM: ROCK CRYSTAL SUGAR, COMPRESSED UNREFINED SUGAR

with second best, and the most intensive cocoa production, for the mass-market, from the high-yielding Forastero variety, is in Africa.

In its raw state the cocoa bean is bitter, astringent and far from enticing. Like coffee beans, they must be fermented and roasted to make them palatable and release their aroma. The next stage is to shell and grind them. The heat generated melts the natural cocoa butter (which makes up a good half of the weight of the beans), producing a thick liquid, known as chocolate liquor or mass. Some or all of the cocoa butter may be pressed out, leaving dry cocoa cakes which can be ground down to plain cocoa.

Extra cocoa butter (or other vegetable fats) is added to the chocolate liquor, along with sugar, flavourings and milk solids according to the precise product being made. The whole shebang is refined further by "conching" – rolling, turning and grinding down the mixture to make it smoother and smoother, and eliminate any remaining raw odours. The best chocolate is conched over a period of days, coarser chocolate gets a day or two if it is lucky. The mixture is "tempered" by careful controlled cooling, set in moulds – *et voilà* you have slab chocolate.

Cocoa butter is a precious commodity

**Bittersweet Chocolate**  Plain chocolate with very little sugar added, so that it really is bitter-sweet. Children will not like it. Grown-up chocolate connoisseurs will settle for nothing less. The perfect cooking chocolate.

**Milk Chocolate**  Plain chocolate blended with milk solids, which softens the bite of the chocolate liquor, and dilutes its flavour. Except perhaps for coating, there is little point in using milk chocolate in cooking.

**White Chocolate**  Not really chocolate at all, since it contains no chocolate liquor. This is, or should be, a blend of cocoa butter, milk solids and sugar. The light, milky flavour of white chocolate becomes cloying unless it is balanced by other more determined elements – orange and lemon, ginger, or very dark plain chocolate. Cheaper "white chocolate-flavoured bars" are unlikely to contain more than a trace of cocoa butter, possibly none at all. Instead, they are based on other solidified vegetable fats. Do not use these for cooking – when melted they inevitably separate into pools of fat and floating globs of white gunge.

**Xocolata a la Pedra**  Using chocolate in savoury recipes is not as outré as it sounds. Dishes of game, poultry and seafood with "chocolate" sauces are eaten on occasion in Spain, Italy and South America, but in Catalonia, in eastern Spain, they are more commonplace than perhaps anywhere else. These are not chocolate sauces in the sense of the thick dense chocolate sauce that you might pour over ice cream. A minimal amount of chocolate is added to enrich the sauce, giving a barely recognizable, subtle depth.

In Barcelona, I ate a dish of rice with seafood – langoustines, monkfish, hake, clams, mussels – bathed in a thin sauce made with an intense fish stock, saffron and something else that I did not at first recognize. Half way through, it finally

WHITE CHOCOLATE, PLAIN CHOCOLATE

clicked – chocolate. It was so good that I ate the whole lot, and felt uncomfortably full for the rest of the day.

The chocolate used here is not your standard plain chocolate. Xocolata a la pedra (chocolate "on the stone", a reference to the way it was once "conched" in stone troughs) is flavoured with cinnamon, rather than the more usual vanilla, and contains cornflour or rice flour. The cheaper types are fairly sweet, with more sugar than cocoa solids in the

ingredients, while the better quality bars, though still sweet enough, are higher in cocoa solids than sugar. If you are ever in the area, buy a few bars to bring home. Quite apart from the traditional Catalan recipes, a square or two of xocolata a la pedra gives an ordinary stew or sauce a velvety smoothness, and a subtle rich flavour.

# CHOCOLATE & GINGER MOUNTAIN

*Sheer indulgence. A mound of whipped cream, dotted with rum-soaked raisins, preserved ginger, white chocolate and nuts, coated in the darkest chocolate you can find.*

**Serves 6–8**

**40 g (1½ oz) raisins**
**2 tablespoons rum or brandy**
**300 ml (½ pint) double cream**
**1 tablespoon syrup from the ginger jar**
**40 g (1½ oz) toasted almonds, chopped**
**4 spheres preserved stem ginger, chopped**
**75 g (3 oz) white chocolate, chopped**
COATING:
**75 g (3 oz) plain chocolate, broken into squares**
**40 g (1½ oz) unsalted butter, diced**
**1 tablespoon syrup from the ginger jar**

Soak the raisins in the rum or brandy for 30 minutes. Whip the cream with the ginger syrup until it holds its shape, then fold in the raisins and rum, almonds, ginger and white chocolate. Pile up in a cone on a serving dish. Chill for an hour.

To make the coating, melt the plain chocolate, butter and ginger syrup in a bowl set over a pan of simmering water (make sure that the base of the bowl does not touch the water), stirring occasionally. As soon as the chocolate has melted, remove from the heat, stir to make sure it is evenly mixed, then leave until barely tepid and thickened. Spoon over the mound of chilled cream, covering it completely. Leave to set, preferably at room temperature, but if the kitchen is warm, in the refrigerator which will dull the gloss, but prevent collapse.

# RABBIT WITH CHOCOLATE & TOMATO

*Rabbit cooked in the Catalan style, in a tomato sauce thickened with a "picada" of parsley, nuts, saffron and chocolate.*

**Serves 4**

**40 g (1½ oz) raisins**
**1 rabbit, cut into 8 pieces**
**seasoned flour**
**2–3 tablespoons olive oil**
**1 onion, chopped**
**1 × 400-g (14-oz) can chopped tomatoes, or 450 g (1 lb) fresh tomatoes, skinned, liquidized and sieved**
**300 ml (½ pint) chicken, rabbit or game stock**
**2 sprigs rosemary**
**1 bay leaf**
**2 tablespoons finely chopped parsley**
**salt and pepper**
**2 garlic cloves, chopped**
**12 blanched almonds**
**12 hazelnuts**
**pinch saffron strands**
**15 g (½ oz) xocolata a la pedra or plain chocolate, chopped**

Cover the raisins with water and soak for 20 minutes. Coat the rabbit in the seasoned flour and brown in 2 tablespoons of oil, in a wide frying pan. Set aside. In the same oil, sauté the onion until tender and golden. Add the tomatoes, stock, rosemary, bay leaf, 1 tablespoon of the parsley, salt and pepper. Simmer gently for 5 minutes. Return the rabbit to the pan, cover and simmer for a further 20 minutes. Turn the rabbit pieces occasionally, and add a little more stock or water, if necessary.

While it simmers, mix the remaining parsley with the garlic, almonds, hazelnuts, saffron and chocolate. Process until smooth. If you do not have a processor, chop everything together finely, then pound in a mortar. Gradually work

in 6 tablespoons of sauce from the rabbit. Spoon this mixture over the rabbit, add the raisins, drained, and stir as best you can to mix. Cover again, and continue simmering for a further 10 minutes. Taste and adjust the seasonings. Serve with rice.

# BOTTARGA, POTATO & TOMATO SALAD

**Serves 8**

**1 kg (2 lb) new potatoes**
**6 tablespoons olive oil**
**1½ tablespoons red wine vinegar**
**salt and pepper**
**450 g (1 lb) cherry tomatoes, halved**
**10 large basil leaves, torn up**
**small bunch rocket, torn up**
**1 red onion, chopped**
**2 garlic cloves, crushed**
**50 g (2 oz) bottarga, sliced paper thin**

Scrub the potatoes and halve or quarter them, if large. Boil in lightly salted water and drain.

While the potatoes are cooking make the dressing: whisk the olive oil into the vinegar, a tablespoon at a time, and season with salt and pepper. Toss the hot potatoes in half the dressing and leave to cool.

When the potatoes are cool, mix in all the remaining ingredients except the bottarga, adding enough of the remaining dressing to coat. Cover and store in the refrigerator for 4 hours. Stir, then taste and adjust the seasoning, going easy on the salt. Just before serving, scatter over the bottarga.

RECIPES

# BROCCOLI & SUN-DRIED TOMATOES

*Cooked slowly, gently and at length, broccoli emerges with a heavenly melting texture and a sweet, mellow flavour. It is too good to serve as a side-dish, except with plainly cooked meats, roast chicken, maybe, or grilled lamb chops. Better, I think, to eat it as a course on its on.*

**Serves 4–6 as a first course or side dish**

**750 g (1½ lbs) broccoli**
**2 dried red chillies**
**6 whole, peeled garlic cloves**
**either 4 pieces sun-dried tomato, cut into thin strips, or 8 black olives, halved and pitted**
**5 tablespoons olive oil**
**250 ml (8 fl oz) dry white wine**
**15 g (1½ oz) fresh Parmesan, sliced into paper-thin shavings**
**salt and pepper**

Cut off the tough, woody ends of the broccoli stems. Leave thinner stems (5 mm/¼ inch thick) whole, but cut thicker ones in half or quarters along their length. Break the chillies into pieces and shake out the seeds. Cover the base of a wide, deep, heavy frying pan or saucepan with a thin layer of olive oil. Cover with half the broccoli, scatter over half the garlic, sun-dried tomato or olives, chilli, salt and pepper, and half the remaining olive oil. Repeat the layers. Pour over the wine. Cover and cook over a very gentle heat for 40–60 minutes until the liquid has almost all evaporated, removing the lid towards the end of cooking, if necessary. Spoon into a serving dish, and scatter with shavings of Parmesan. Serve immediately.

CLOCKWISE FROM TOP LEFT: BROCCOLI AND SUN-DRIED TOMATOES, ANCHOVY BREAD FRITTERS, CINNAMON AND MAPLE SUGAR TOASTS, ORANGES IN PALM SUGAR SYRUP

# ANCHOVY BREAD FRITTERS

## (CRISPEDDI DI ACCIUGHE)

*These small bread fritters, filled with salty anchovies, sweet tomato and fennel seeds, come from the south of Italy.*

**Makes 16**

**450 g (1 lb) strong white flour**
**pinch salt**
**1 sachet easy blend or easy bake yeast**
**warm water**
**2 tablespoons olive oil**
**50 g (2 oz) salted anchovies, rinsed,**
  **scaled and filleted**
**½ tablespoon fennel seeds**
**100 g (4 oz) tomatoes, skinned, seeded,**
  **and cut into strips**
**cayenne pepper**

Sift the flour with the salt, and mix with the yeast. Add enough warm water to form a firm bread dough. Knead for a good ten minutes until smooth and elastic. Place the dough in an oiled bowl, turning to coat it evenly with oil. Cover loosely and leave in a warm place for an hour until doubled in bulk. Punch down and knead for another 5 minutes.

Cut the anchovy into strips. Break off golf ball-sized pieces of dough. Roll each one out to form an oval about 7.5 cm (3 inches) long. Lay a strip of anchovy and a strip or two of tomato down the length of the oval. Sprinkle with a few fennel seeds and a little cayenne pepper. Brush the edges of the oval with water and pinch together very firmly to enclose the filling, then pat into a small elongated breadroll shape. Sit on an oiled baking sheet. Cover and leave in a warm place for 30 minutes until doubled in size.

Deep-fry in oil heated to 170°C/330°F, until golden brown. Drain briefly on absorbent kitchen paper, and eat while warm.

To bake, brush with olive oil and give them 15 minutes in a moderately hot oven (200°C, 400°F, Gas Mark 6).

# CINNAMON & MAPLE SUGAR TOASTS

*Cinnamon toast is a great tea-time treat, even more so when made with maple sugar.*

**Serves 1**

**1 slice good quality white bread, or**
  **brioche**
**butter**
**½ tablespoon maple sugar**
**½ teaspoon ground cinnamon**

Butter the bread generously on one side. Mix the sugar and cinnamon. Toast the bread on the buttered side until golden brown. Let it rest for a few seconds while the butter soaks in. Turn over and butter the other side. Cover with cinnamon sugar. Toast gently, not too close to the heat, until the sugar is melting and bubbling. Cool for a minute or two (if you don't you will burn your mouth something rotten), then cut into fingers and eat.

# ORANGES IN PALM SUGAR SYRUP

*Made with dark coconut sugar, this looks dramatic – orange fruit and translucent peel against an almost black syrup. It tastes every bit as good as it looks. Cane sugar jaggery, or dark muscovado sugar can also be used.*

**Serves 6**

**6 oranges**
**225 g (8 oz) moist coconut sugar, or**
  **other palm sugar**
**1 cinnamon stick**
**3 cloves**
**150 ml (¼ pint) water**

Pare the zest off 3 of the oranges, and cut into fine shreds. Blanch for 1 minutes in boiling water, drain and cool. Reserve.

Peel all the oranges with a sharp knife, cutting down to the flesh so that there is no white pith left clinging. Slice each orange, then reassemble and push a wooden cocktail stick through the centre to hold the slices together. Arrange in a snugly fitting serving dish, along with any juice.

Place the palm sugar, cinnamon and cloves in a pan with the water. Stir over a moderate heat, without boiling, until the sugar is completely dissolved. Add the orange zest. Bring up to the boil and simmer for 5 minutes. Lift out the orange zest with a slotted spoon, and leave to cool. Continue simmering the syrup for another 5 minutes. Draw off the heat, let the bubbles subside, then pour over the oranges. Leave to cool, basting the oranges occasionally with the syrup. Scatter over the zest. Cover and store in the refrigerator for up to 24 hours.

# SATAY SAUCE

*Satay sauce should not be peanut butter embellished with a bit of chilli, although far too often it is little more than that. The satay sauce here is undoubtedly the best I have ever eaten, based on a recipe given me by a friend many years ago. Blachan gives a particular depth of flavour, whilst the lemon grass and coconut milk provide more obvious attractions. Serve it with thin slivers of grilled beef, or chicken (marinate first with oil, lime, chilli, garlic and perhaps lemon grass), grilled prawns or vegetables.*

**Serves 6–8**

**75 g (3 oz) raw, shelled peanuts**
**4 tablespoons sunflower or peanut oil**
**2 stems lemon grass**
**2 red chillies, seeded and chopped or ½**
**    tablespoon chilli powder**
**3 shallots, chopped**
**2 garlic cloves, chopped**
**1 × 2.5 cm (1 inch) cube blachan**
**300 ml (½ pint) coconut milk**
**2 teaspoons dark muscovado sugar**
**juice of ½ lime**
**salt**

Fry the peanuts in 1 tablespoon of the oil over a high heat, stirring constantly, for 2 minutes. Drain on absorbent kitchen paper and cool. Grind finely to a dry paste. Take the lower 10–12.5 cm (4–5 inches) of the lemon grass, peel off the papery outer layers, then slice. Mix with the chillies, shallots, garlic, and blachan, and either process or pound to a smooth paste.

Heat the remaining oil over a moderate heat and add the spice paste. Fry, stirring constantly, for 2 minutes. Add half the coconut milk, the ground peanuts and sugar and bring up to the boil, stirring. Add the remaining coconut milk, lime juice and a pinch of salt. Simmer, still stirring, for 5–10 minutes until the sauce thickens. Serve warm, or cold.

SALMON WITH JAPANESE ASIDES

# SALMON WITH JAPANESE ASIDES

*This is no more than a variation on the Scandinavian gravad lax: cured salmon, thinly sliced, served not with a dill sauce, but a sharp fruity plum sauce, and slices of pickled ginger.*

**Serves 8 as first, 4 as main course**

**1 tablespoon granulated sugar**
**1 tablespoon coarse salt**
**2 teaspoons coarsely crushed black**
**    peppercorns**
**450 g (1 lb) salmon tail fillet in two**
**    pieces, skinned**
UMEBOSHI PLUM SAUCE:
**4 umeboshi plums**
**2 teaspoons rice vinegar**
**1 teaspoon dark soy sauce**
**1 tablespoon caster sugar**
**5 tablespoons light olive oil**
**pepper**

TO SERVE:
**16 pieces of pickled ginger**
**roughly chopped chives**

Mix the granulated sugar, coarse salt and coarsely crushed pepper together. Spread half on the base of a dish just large enough to take the salmon snugly. Lay the salmon fillets on top, and cover with the remaining seasoning mixture. Cover with foil, and weigh down with a heavy weight (cans of something or other will do fine) and leave in the refrigerator for at least 8 hours, preferably 24, turning the fish over occasionally. Shortly before serving, take the fish out of the bowl, shake off any debris and wipe dry. Slice thinly.

To make the plum sauce, chop the plum flesh and sieve. Beat in the rice vinegar, soy sauce, sugar and pepper. Gradually beat in the oil, a tablespoon at a time. Taste and adjust the seasoning.

Arrange the salmon slices on individual plates. Spoon a little of the sauce beside them, and make a small heap of pickled ginger nearby. Scatter with chopped chives. Serve the remaining sauce separately.

# PORK WITH BLACK BEAN TAPENADE

*The black bean tapenade is wonderful with pork, but it can also be tossed into pasta, or smeared thinly on toast, or bread brushed with olive oil and baked in the oven until crisp.*

**Serves 4**

TAPENADE
**1 medium tomato**
**3 large garlic cloves, unpeeled**
**1 small onion, chopped**
**4 tablespoons olive oil**
**1 teaspoon grated fresh root ginger**
**1 tablespoon salted black beans**
**50 g (2 oz) pitted black olives**
**1 tablespoon capers, salted for preference, rinsed**
**1 tablespoon chopped parsley**
**pepper**

**olive oil**
**4 pork chops**

To make the tapenade, grill the tomato whole, turning, until soft and patched with brown. Cool slightly and halve. Scoop out the pulp. Thread the garlic on to a skewer and grill until blackened and softened. Peel and add the pulp to the tomato. Cook the onion with the ginger in 1 tablespoon of the olive oil until softened.

Meanwhile, rinse the black beans, dry on absorbent kitchen paper, then add to the pan. Cook, stirring, for a further minute. Process or pound the beans to a paste with the tomato and garlic, and the remaining tapenade ingredients, gradually working in the last 3 tablespoons of olive oil.

Oil a shallow heat-proof dish, large enough to take the chops in a single layer. Spread each chop generously with the tapenade. Arrange in the dish, tapenade up. Drizzle over 1 more tablespoon of olive oil. Bake in a cool oven (150°C, 300°F, Gas Mark 2) for 25 minutes.

# STEAMED MOLASSES PUDDING

*A real winter comfort pudding, just the thing to dispel the gloom of short, cold days. The apple and walnuts soften the strong liquorice taste of the molasses. Serve with single cream, or home-made custard.*

**Serves 6–8**

**350 g (12 oz) cooking apples, peeled, cored and diced small**
**175 g (6 oz) self-raising flour**
**1 teaspoon ground ginger**
**¼ teaspoon ground allspice**
**¼ teaspoon ground cloves**
**¼ teaspoon freshly grated nutmeg**
**100 g (4 oz) butter**
**100 g (4 oz) light muscovado sugar**
**2 eggs**
**120 ml (4 fl oz) blackstrap molasses**
**75 g (3 oz) walnut pieces, roughly chopped**
**7 tablespoons milk**
**butter for greasing**

Toss the apples in 1½ tablespoons of the flour. Sift the remaining flour with the spices. Beat the butter with the sugar until soft and fluffy. Beat in the eggs and molasses. Mix in the flour in three batches, alternating with the milk, to give a batter of dropping consistency. Fold in the walnuts and apples.

Butter a 2 litre (3½ pint) pudding basin and fill with the mixture. Take a large sheet of silver foil, make a deep pleat down the centre, and lay over the pudding, pleat across the diagonal, pressing the edges down round the sides. Secure tightly with string, making a loop across the bowl with the trailing ends so that you can lift the bowl out of the pan. Set the bowl on a trivet, in a deep pan. Fill with enough water to come half way up the pudding basin. Bring up to the boil, cover the pan with a lid or a dome of silver foil, and simmer for 1½–2 hours, topping

up the water level with boiling water as necessary. Lift the pudding out of the water, uncover and let it stand for 3 minutes before unmoulding.

Those of you with a microwave can opt for the quicker method of cooking a steamed pudding (though the result is never quite so moist). Pour into a greased 2 litre (3½ pint) pudding basin and cover tightly with clingfilm. Microwave on full power for 10 minutes (650–700W oven). Stand for 5 minutes.

# BUTTERED MAPLE RUM TODDY

*A steaming hot toddy for cold weather celebrations. Try it as an alternative to mulled wine at Christmas.*

**Serves 6**

**1.2 litres (2 pints) medium sweet cider**
**120 ml (4 fl oz) maple syrup**
**2 tablespoons butter**
**1 cinnamon stick**
**4 cloves**
**1 teaspoon freshly grated nutmeg**
**150 ml (¼ pint) rum**

Place all the ingredients except the rum in a large pan, and slowly bring up to just below boiling point. Draw off the heat, stir in the rum, and serve.

# MUSHROOMS

Mushroom-hunting expeditions were an integral part of my family's autumnal sojourns in France. A warm but rainy day or evening would prompt us to set off the morning after, armed with a couple of plastic bags stuffed in our pockets. Overnight, the damp and the warmth would tease a new crop of mushrooms up through the leafmould of the nearby woods, prime targets for the Grigson threesome. Like many children, I had a good eye for mushrooming, and relished the pleasure of finding the first cluster of mushrooms amongst the shadowy trees.

We would bear home the spoils of our outing, amongst them, if we had been lucky, a few choice ceps, and some chanterelles. The evening ritual was then set. My father would spend an hour or so poring over the mushroom handbook, double- and treble-checking every detail to make sure that the mushrooms we had were edible. Then my mother would clean them, and cook them, usually in butter, with maybe a hint of garlic, a splash of white wine, and fresh parsley. For supper we sat down to a feast of fresh wild mushrooms on toast.

The mushroom-hunting instinct has remained strong. Whenever I walk through wooded areas, I find my eyes irresistibly scanning the ground. But I now live in London, and although the copses of Hampstead Heath and Highgate occasionally yield up the odd edible mushroom, they are few and far between. I have learnt instead to scan the smarter foodshops and market stalls, where the pickings can be more abundant.

There are dozens of kinds of wild mushroom that are good to eat, but only a handful make it to the point of sale. The advantage, of course, of buying wild mushrooms is that the identifying process has all been taken care of, and you do not have to worry about safety. The disadvantage is the price, high enough to bring tears to the eyes, especially when you consider that had you been in the right place at the right time, you might have picked them for free. Too bad. Dismiss this parsimonious thought from your mind, and focus instead on the marvellous meal you will shortly be enjoying.

If you are buying wild mushrooms it is usually a case of take what you can get. August may see an early crop, but September, October and November are the prime months for wild mushrooms. Ceps, chanterelles, and horns of plenty are the ones you are most likely to come across. Morels are a rare spring and early summer treat.

Cultivated mushrooms used to mean nothing but the familiar "champignons de Paris", sold at various stages of maturity from the neat white button to the wide, brown-gilled flat cap (which, incidentally, has by far the best flavour of this clan, excellent for soups and sauces). Matters are hotting up on the cultivation front, however, and thank heavens for that. Oyster mushrooms and the richly flavoured shiitake have now broken the erstwhile monopoly of the champignon de Paris.

There are two fundamental rules which apply to the preparation of all mushrooms, wild or cultivated. The first is do not keep them hanging around. If you have too many to eat immediately, make a duxelle (see page 93) or dry the excess, either by threading them on to string and hanging them in a dry, airy place, or by spreading them out on racks in a low oven, sliced if the mushrooms are large.

The second rule is do not wash them or peel them unless you really have to. Trim off really mucky stem ends and any damaged patches, then wipe the mushrooms clean with a damp cloth, or a soft-bristled brush. If you must wash them, then keep it brief. Swirl them quickly in water to dislodge stubborn grit, but do not let them soak. The one exception are morels with the honeycomb caps that are bound to harbour grit.

Most mushrooms exude some liquid when cooked, in many cases quite copious amounts. In many recipes this is a bonus and the juices will be absorbed into the other ingredients, permeating them with the flavour of the mushrooms. It only becomes a problem when you are simply frying the mushrooms. Start cooking them in a little butter or oil alone. If necessary, pour off the liquid (save for flavouring stocks and sauces), then add more butter or oil and other seasonings.

# FRESH MUSHROOMS

## MOREL

There was great excitement one spring morning when my father discovered half a dozen morels poking up through the grass right beside the gate of our small house in France. For a few weeks we rushed out early every morning to check for new arrivals before our canny French neighbours spotted them. Morels are unpredictable mushrooms – that was the one and only year we ever had doorstep delivery.

Now, like everyone else, I have to resort to handing over horrifying sums of money on the rare occasions when I find them for sale and feel justified in being extravagant. Lucky, then, that they have a powerful, sweet, full flavour that spreads itself generously over other ingredients.

In restaurants they are often stuffed with delicate forcemeats or mousselines, but

MORELS

this is far too fiddly to bother with at home. Your first priority with a treasure trove of morels is to clean them thoroughly. The strange honeycombed caps are bound to trap all kinds of grit and dirt – immerse them for three or four minutes in salted water, which will simultaneously flush out any unwanted insect life. Rinse under the cold tap, then spread out to dry briefly on absorbent kitchen paper or a clean tea towel, and you are ready to proceed.

Faced with a tiny haul, you will have to make choices – to eat them all yourself, or possibly shared with a loved one, simply cooked in butter and cream (they have a natural affinity with cream), or to be generous and spread them more thinly around a larger gathering. The simplest way of doing this is perhaps to slice and stew the mushrooms in butter, then stir into lightly scrambled eggs as a first course. Morels are wonderful with chicken, too, so try adding them to a simple creamy ragout of chicken, or a cream sauce to go with roast chicken.

## TRUFFLE

For years I wondered what all the fuss was about. I dutifully tried to convince myself that pâtés studded with flecks of black truffle were imbued with outstanding flavour, but to no avail. Maybe my palate was not fine-tuned enough to appreciate the subtlety of the truffle? Or maybe the mystique of the truffle lay purely in its rarity value and high price tag, and everyone was busy conning themselves and each other when it actually came down to the taste.

As it turns out, my palate is perfectly all right, but the second supposition is not without a grain of truth. By and large, preservation does the truffle no favours at all. Canned truffles are not worth shelling out on, unless you think snob-value worth paying for. But fresh truffles, now that is a totally different kettle of fish.

The black or Perigord truffle from France is the darling of *haute cuisine*. It is usually cooked, and is best with more delicately flavoured foods – fish, chicken, veal or eggs – where its flavour can shine through. If you are blessed with a gift of a fresh black truffle, try slipping thin slices under the skin of a good free-range chicken and roasting it.

It was the Italian white truffle, however, that finally dispelled all my doubts. White truffles have a unique, heady, pungent scent and the very thought of them makes me feel quite weak at the knees. Sadly, their price is exorbitant, but on a couple of occasions I have been lucky enough to have been given one of these gems.

Should you find yourself in the same happy position, you will want to make the most of them. Store them in an air-tight container in the refrigerator, loosely wrapped in absorbent kitchen paper, which should be changed morning and night. It is worth holding your guns for a couple of days (no longer or they might go off). Slip a few eggs into the same container. Within 24 hours they will have absorbed a good measure of truffliness, and you can treat yourself to the most wonderful scrambled eggs or omelette, as a preamble to the real thing. Never cook a white truffle as heat destroys the scent. Brush and/or wipe the grit off the outside, then grate or shave it over hot buttery pasta, a plain risotto, or any egg dish.

## CEP
(Porcini, Boletus)

We found ourselves stranded one night in a one-horse town in the wooded hills of Calabria. The only place to eat was the shabby hotel run by a mountainous glowering Italian – not a pleasing prospect. How wrong can you be. Food was his great joy and from the moment he laid in front of us a plate of his home-cured salamis and hams he was all smiles. With the antipasti came a bowl of *porcini sott'olio*, ceps preserved in oil, and there followed a plate of pasta tossed with more ceps, picked that morning in the woods. A real southern Italian feast.

Ceps, morels and truffles are the indisputable stars of the fungi world. The delightful thing about ceps is that they are relatively abundant. In the open market in Turin in October, for instance, there are a dozen or more stalls piled high with these bulbous fleshy mushrooms, and it would be a poor sort of a restaurant which did not feature at least three or four cep dishes on its menu.

Not that this makes them cheap to buy by any means – they are not that abundant – but since there is a distinct possibility that you might find one or two yourself on a meander through the woods, it makes sense to learn how to identify them beyond any doubt (but always treble-check with the help of a clear mushroom handbook).

Choose ceps that are firm, with few if any blemishes, and preferably no tell-tale holes which might conceal worms. Do not cut off the spongey part unless it is damaged or slimey. Wipe the ceps clean, and trim off the earthy base of the stem.

My favourite way of cooking them is to grill them in thick slices, brushed generously with olive oil and lightly seasoned. Alternatively, fry them in butter with parsley and a hint of garlic, or bake them whole in the oven. Fried ceps are excellent tossed with pasta, or with scrambled eggs. They go well with practically any type of meat you care to mention.

## CHANTERELLE
(Girolle)

One rung down on the gastronomic ladder from the cep, and some people might well dispute even that. Chanterelles have a more delicate, elegant flavour than gutsy ceps. They are one of the most charming of mushrooms to look at, too, varying in hue from primrose through egg-yolk to an orangey yellow, sveltley funnel-shaped and firm. Smaller specimens of the yellow oyster mushroom can look rather similar – do not be fooled. Oyster mushrooms, even young ones, whilst they may at first glance seem funnel-shaped, will in reality be more like a leaf, the lower edges curled round and close together in an attempt to form a cone. Nice but not a patch on a chanterelle.

Chanterelles are porous little things, so do not wash them. Brush off as much grit as you can with a soft brush and wipe clean with a damp cloth. Like many mushrooms, chanterelles have a tendency to exude a fair amount of liquid as they cook. Unfortunately, they have a tendency to toughen up if you raise the heat too high in an attempt to evaporate the liquid as it seeps out. When cooking chanterelles in butter, either pour off the juices to use as a stock to flavour a sauce, and return the cooked chanterelles to the pan with a fresh knob of butter to finish, or keep the chanterelles warm and reduce the stock, finishing with a generous slurp of double cream, and seasoning.

They can be baked, too, or simmered gently, whole or sliced in sauces. I have a particular penchant for chicken (as long as it is a good free-range bird) or guinea fowl with chanterelle.

## HORN OF PLENTY
(Trompette de mort)

"Horns of plenty" is a pretty but dewy-eyed name for these mushrooms. I prefer by far the sombre drama of the French name, *trompettes des morts*, trumpets of the dead. Ever since I was a child, my picture of the Day of Judgement has been one of angels blowing slender, matt black trumpets to summon up the dead from their graves. And that is exactly what horns of plenty look like.

Not that they are remotely deadly. Far from it. They are a delicious mushroom, with a fine earthy flavour. I remember picking them by the bagful in one particular wood in France. We ate as many as a family of three reasonably could and dried the rest for safe-keeping.

They appear fairly frequently in autumnal markets in France, and on rare occasions in up-market greengrocers and delicatessens in this country. They can simply be stewed in butter with a little parsley, and maybe, a few minutes before they are done, a splash of white wine or brandy, and/or a generous slug of cream. The contrast of their blackness against a creamy white sauce, or the pale tan of a soup made from cultivated mushrooms is eye-catching. Cook them gently in butter before adding, and they will do wonders for the flavour of the dish as well as the look of it.

## OYSTER MUSHROOM

Most of the cultivated oyster mushrooms you will come across will be of the characteristic pale oyster-grey colour, though now and again one finds the pretty pale yellow sort. They taste the same, and very good they are too; mildly flavoured in comparison to shiitake, with a softer, more melting texture. Oyster mushrooms give up vast quantities of liquid when cooked and, as a consequence, shrink to not much more than half their original size.

## SHIITAKE

Enterprising souls have started cultivating these Oriental mushrooms on a fairly wide scale in Europe and America, and it is a real blessing. They have by far the best flavour of any of the easily available cultivated mushrooms. Their texture is firm and substantial, so they take well to all kinds of treatment, and are a real bonus for vegetarians. They can be eaten raw, but they are far better cooked. Try stewing them simply in butter or olive oil with a hint of parsley and garlic, or grilling or baking them. Their rich flavour means that they are superb in meaty stews (add them only half an hour or so before the stew is done, since they can toughen with prolonged cooking) or with game.

SHIITAKE

OYSTER MUSHROOMS

## ENOKITAKE
(Enoki)

These Japanese mushrooms are the cutest little things, clusters of spindly stems tipped with a round ball of a head. They have a mildly lemony flavour and a crisp texture. Unfortunately, they seem to be a rare commodity outside Japan. Occasionally, very occasionally, a Japanese supermarket near me gets them flown in, neatly vacuum-packed. Buy a packet if you happen across them, but do not set your heart on using enoki mushrooms before you set off shopping. Unopened, they will last for up to a week in the refrigerator, assuming they have not been hanging around for days in transit.

Use them raw in salads, making the most of their decorative appearance, or serve them lightly steamed or stir-fried.

You may find canned enokitake, labelled Golden Mushrooms, in Chinese supermarkets, but they are hardly worth buying – floppy, overcooked and with a less than appealing flavour. Not recommended.

## STRAW MUSHROOM

Unlike enoki mushrooms, straw mushrooms are easy enough to lay your hands on. Every Oriental food shop sells them canned, though it is unlikely that you will ever see fresh ones. Do not expect any wild taste experience from them – it is the texture that counts, smooth, firm but tender, and cool. Use them straight from the can, drained and rinsed free of brine, in salads with a perky dressing, or add them to spicey casseroles towards the end of the cooking time. They are good, too, in stir-fried dishes, again added towards the end of the cooking period so that they just have time to heat through and absorb some of the flavourings.

# FUNGHETTO

*A delicious melting "stew" of aubergines, courgettes and mushrooms, that can be served as a side dish, a first course, or tossed into pasta (in which case this quantity will stretch around 8 people with no problems). It can be made in advance and reheated – add a little water to prevent it catching.*

**Serves 4-6**

I aubergine
225 g (8 oz) courgettes
225 g (8 oz) shiitake, oyster mushrooms, or ceps
85 ml (3 fl oz) olive oil
2 garlic gloves, finely chopped
3 tablespoons finely chopped parsley
3 sprigs fresh oregano
salt and pepper

Cut the aubergine into I cm (½ inch) dice. Spread out in a colander and sprinkle with salt. Slice the courgettes thinly, spread out in a separate colander and sprinkle these too with salt. Leave both for half an hour, then rinse and dry on absorbent kitchen paper or a clean tea towel. Cut the mushrooms into 5 mm (¼ inch) thick slices.

Heat the oil in a deep, heavy frying pan, large enough to take all the ingredients. Add the garlic and parsley, and fry for a minute. Add the aubergine, courgettes, mushrooms, and oregano and mix well. Turn the heat down low, cover and cook for 25–30 minutes, stirring occasionally, until the vegetables are meltingly tender, and all the liquid has evaporated. If necessary, add a tablespoon or two of water as they cook, to prevent their catching. Season with salt and pepper.

# ORIENTAL MUSHROOM SALAD

**Serves 4**

75–100 g (3–4 oz) enokitake mushrooms
225 g (8 oz) cherry tomatoes, halved
225 g (8 oz) thin asparagus, cut into
    2.5 cm (1 inch) lengths, *or* 225 g (8 oz)
    fine green beans, trimmed and cut
    into 2.5 cm (1 inch) lengths
I × 425g (15 oz) tin straw mushrooms,
    drained and rinsed
DRESSING:
I tablespoon Chinese salted black beans
2 teaspoons finely grated fresh root
    ginger
4 tablespoons olive oil
I tablespoon rice wine vinegar
½ teaspoon sugar
salt and pepper

To make the dressing, rinse the black beans thoroughly, dry on absorbent kitchen paper, and chop roughly. Heat 2 tablespoons of the oil in a small pan and add the black beans and ginger. Fry gently for about I minute. Draw off the heat and cool until tepid. Put into a screwtop jar with the remaining dressing ingredients, except the salt, and shake to mix. Taste and adjust the seasonings.

Drop the asparagus stem pieces into a pan of lightly salted boiling water. Simmer for a minute, then add the tips. Simmer for a minute or two longer until barely *al dente*. If using green beans, simmer them in lightly salted water for one minute. Drain either vegetable well, run under the cold tap then drain again and leave to cool.

Trim the bases off the enokitake, rinse well, and spread out to dry on absorbent kitchen paper. Just before serving, mix the mushrooms, tomatoes and asparagus or green beans in a shallow serving dish. Give the dressing a quick shake to mix again, and spoon about half of it over the salad. Save the remainder: it will keep in its jar, in the refrigerator for at least a week.

# MUSHROOMS WITH MASCARPONE

*This makes a wonderfully simple and luxurious first course, with the clash of hot, tender mushrooms and chilled mascarpone or cream, and crisp bread to soak up the juices.*

**Serves 4**

4 tablespoons mascarpone, crème
    fraîche, or soured cream
I tablespoon chopped chives
4 thick slices of bread, crusts removed
50–75 g (2–3 oz) butter, melted
4 small ceps or large flat cap
    mushrooms, or 8 shiitake
salt and cayenne pepper

Beat the mascarpone, crème fraîche or soured cream with the chives and salt and cayenne pepper to taste. Cover loosely and chill.

Cut a circle out of each slice of bread, just a little larger than the mushrooms. Pull a little of the crumb out of the centre so that the mushrooms will sit firmly on the bread. Brush the bread generously on both sides with melted butter, and place on a baking sheet.

Cut the stalks off the mushrooms (save for making stock, or flavouring a soup) and sit on top of the bread. Brush with butter and season with salt and pepper.

Bake in a moderately hot oven (190°C, 375°F, Gas Mark 5) for 20–30 minutes until the mushrooms are tender; the exact timing will depend on the thickness and type of mushroom. Quickly transfer the mushrooms and bread to warm serving plates, and top with a tablespoon of the chilled mascarpone, crème fraîche or soured cream. Serve immediately.

OPPOSITE, TOP: ORIENTAL MUSHROOM SALAD; BOTTOM: FUNGHETTO, MUSHROOMS WITH MASCARPONE

# FUNGHI
# SOTT'OLIO

*"Sott'olio", under oil, is the ubiquitous southern Italian way of preserving not only mushrooms, but peppers, aubergines and other vegetables too. The spicing is a very personal matter, but this is a combination I like with mushrooms.*

**Makes enough to fill 1 × 600 ml (1 pint) jar**

**450 g (1 lb) mushrooms (ceps, shiitake, button)**
**450 ml (¾ pint) white wine vinegar**
**250 ml (8 fl oz) water**
**grated zest of 1 lemon**
**2 bay leaves**
**1 teaspoon coriander seeds**
**1 teaspoon black peppercorns**
**1 teaspoon cumin seeds**
**5 cloves**
**4 garlic cloves, halved**
**approx 300 ml (½ pint) olive oil**

Wipe the mushrooms clean, and trim off the earthy parts of the stems. If using large whole ceps, quarter or slice them quickly. Place the vinegar, water, lemon zest, bay leaves, and spices in a pan large enough to take all the mushrooms. Bring up to the boil. Add the mushrooms and simmer for 7–10 minutes until just tender.

Drain and spread out on a triple layer of absorbent kitchen paper to dry. Reserve the spices and bay leaves.

Sterilize a large preserving jar, or several smaller jars. Pour 5 mm (¼ inch) of oil into each jar. Add a layer of mushrooms, ½ a garlic clove and some of the reserved spices. Cover with oil. Repeat the layers until the mushrooms are all used up. Make sure they are completely covered with oil. Let the jars stand, loosely covered, for half an hour, to settle, then top up with oil if necessary. Seal tightly, and store in a cool, dark place for at least one week before eating. They will keep for several months.

# GRILLED CEPS WITH CHILLI & CORIANDER

*How big is a large cep? The answer depends on what is available rather than any precise definition. You will have to rely on your own instincts here. Choose fine, firm specimens, large enough to slice thickly. If you suspect that they are too small to give anything but a mean little portion even as a first course, it would be expedient to add in a third one for good measure.*

**Serves 4-6, depending on the size of the mushrooms and your generosity**

**2 large ceps**
MARINADE:
**zest and juice of ½ lemon**
**6 tablespoons olive oil**
**2 fresh red or green chillies, seeded and finely sliced**
**2 tablespoons roughly chopped coriander**
**½ teaspoon salt**

Trim off the earthy ends of the stalks of the ceps. Wipe clean, and cut into 2 cm (¾ inch) thick slices. Mix all the marinade ingredients and pour over the ceps. Turn so that they are evenly coated, cover loosely and leave to marinate, turning occasionally, for half an hour. Take the ceps out of the marinade, brushing off any odds and ends of herbs, and so on. Strain the marinade. Grill the ceps close to a thoroughly preheated grill, brushing frequently with the marinade, until patched with brown and tender.

OPPOSITE: FUNGHI SOTT'OLIO

# ENHANCED MUSHROOM DUXELLE

*Making a duxelle is the classic French way of capturing and concentrating the flavour of mushrooms, wild or cultivated, on those happy occasions when you have far too many to eat immediately. The addition of dried mushrooms to a duxelle made from common or garden cultivated mushrooms gives it an added depth. The mixture will keep, covered, in the refrigerator for several days, or can be frozen for longer salvation. A tablespoonful or so stirred into sauces, soups, stuffings or pâtés, or spread underneath baked eggs (see the recipe right) will bring back the savour of the original mushrooms.*

**25 g (1 oz) dried mushrooms**
**85 ml (3 fl oz) oloroso sherry or Marsala (optional)**
**2 tablespoons finely chopped onion**
**25 g (1 oz) butter**
**450 g (1 lb) cultivated mushrooms (oyster, flat cap, button), finely chopped**
**salt and pepper**

Soak the dried mushrooms in the sherry or Marsala, or in 6 tablespoons water, for 30–40 minutes. Pick out the mushrooms and chop finely. Strain the soaking liquid through a sieve lined with absorbent kitchen paper or a double layer of muslin. Reserve.

Fry the onion gently in the butter until it is tender without browning. Add both dried and fresh mushrooms, a little salt, and pepper. Cook over a generous heat, stirring occasionally to prevent burning. When most of the liquid exuded by the mushrooms has disappeared, add the soaking liquid. Continue cooking until there is no trace of liquid left.

To preserve the duxelle, pack into small freezer containers and freeze.

# BAKED EGGS WITH DUXELLE

*Getting baked eggs cooked just perfectly, so that the white is set and the yolk still runny, is not as easy as you might imagine. Heating the ramekins through first means that the white begins to cook instantly, before the yolk is touched by any heat. Err a little on the side of undercooking, as the eggs will continue to cook in their own heat after they have been removed from the oven.*

**Per person:**

**1 egg**
**1 tablespoon mushroom duxelle (see left)**
**1 tablespoon single cream**
**salt and cayenne paper**
**butter for greasing ramekins**

Preheat the oven to hot (200°C, 400°F, Gas Mark 6). Get all the ingredients ready and to hand by the stove. Put the empty ramekins in the oven for 5–10 minutes until they are excessively hot. Meanwhile, bring a kettle of water to the boil and fill a roasting tin to a depth of about 2 cm (¾ inch) with hot water.

Whip the ramekins out of the oven and, working as fast as you can, butter each one. Spread the mushroom duxelle on the base and carefully break in the eggs, on top of the duxelle. Spoon over the cream, and season with cayenne pepper only. Cover the ramekins loosely with foil. Stand them in the roasting tin and rush back into the oven. Bake for 10–15 minutes until the whites are barely set. Season with a little salt and serve.

# DRIED MUSHROOMS

The big advantage of dried mushrooms over fresh, is that they keep, and once you have got your supply stored safely, they are always ready to hand. When an uncharacteristically housewifely urge to clean out my kitchen cupboards came over me recently, I discovered to my joy a hoard of dried mushrooms hidden behind the rest of the clutter, and all of them still in perfect condition. The bulk of the collection were dried porcini – Italian ceps – but there were a fair number of more unusual specimens, too, brought back from shopping sprees and holidays abroad. I ate exceedingly well for the next few weeks.

Porcini – most of the dried ceps sold here come from Italy, so I tend to use their Italian name – are the only dried wild mushroom you can be sure of finding and most delicatessens will stock them. Other European wild mushrooms are a rarer find, and I can never bear to pass them by when I see them. They tend to be cheaper on the Continent, and since they weigh next to nothing, and take up little room, they make worthy culinary souvenirs. Dried morels, horns of plenty and mousserons all make remarkably good substitutes for their fresh counterparts. The texture will be chewier, it is true, but the concentrated flavour is intense and true.

Oriental foodstores are sources of a wide range of dried mushrooms. Shiitake are ubiquitous, but there are many stranger, unfamiliar dried fungi worth experimenting with. Wood ears and cloud ears, relatives of European Jew's ear mushrooms are good buys, but strangest of them all is the white fungus ball.

Dried mushrooms need a good half hour's soaking before use, and longer will do no harm at all. Hot water speeds up the process, but it is not necessary. The liquid you use does not have to be water, either.

Stock or wine will add extra flavour when the soaking liquid is to be incorporated into the dish you are making. Whatever you use, do not waste it. Pick the mushrooms out of the soaking liquid, leaving behind any grit. Then strain the liquid through a sieve lined with absorbent kitchen paper or a double layer of muslin. If you do not need it straightaway, save it to use as a mushroom stock – it can be frozen like other stocks.

Pick over the soaked mushrooms before you go any further, and remove any earth-clad stems. If they are to be fried, spread out on kitchen paper to absorb some of the excess moisture. Most dried mushrooms can then be cooked like fresh ones, but keep the heat gentle and allow for the fact that they may need a few minutes longer in the pan.

Because the concentrated flavour of dried mushrooms is so powerful (with the exception of a couple of the Oriental ones), a few go a long way. A mere 15 g (½ oz) of dried mushrooms, reconstituted and cooked with a panful of cultivated mushrooms adds an incomparable flavour. Similar quantities are enough to scent a creamy sauce, or to enliven a soup. Try them in stews, in stuffings, with scrambled eggs, or omelettes – in fact, in practically any savoury dish where the rich flavour of wild mushrooms would be welcome.

Apart from the Ragout of dried mushrooms (see page 93) which demands an assortment of mushrooms, the dried mushroom recipes that follow can be made with any fully flavoured dried mushroom. Porcini and shiitake are probably the best bets, but merely because they are the most widely available.

## PORCINI
(Cep, Boletus)

Never be without a packet of dried ceps in your kitchen cupboard. Perhaps that is overstating the case a touch, but they are the most useful, approachable, available and most successful of dried mushrooms. They are sold in every Italian delicatessen and any other delicatessen worth its salt.

Reconstituted ceps cannot replace the fresh mushroom – they just will not regain that substantial solidity – so do not begin to think of them as a substitute. Employ them more as a seasoning than a main-line ingredient; they impart an earthy, meaty flavour to almost any dish they are added to. Used, for instance, in tandem with pale button mushrooms, sautéed, in soups, sauces, stuffings, etc, they instantly buck up the whole affair. Never waste the soaking liquid – it picks up the mushroominess to make the best mushroom stock around. If you are not going to use it immediately, freeze it until needed.

A hint of sweetness emphasizes the flavour of dried ceps. Not too much, mind you, we are not talking pudding. I often soak them in sweet sherry, Marsala, or for a mushroom risotto, a muscatel wine, adding the soaking liquid to the rest of the liquid used in the dish.

## CHANTERELLE

I would not go out of my way to hunt out dried chanterelles, but if I do come across a packet when I am rootling round an interesting food shop, I add them to the day's haul. Soaked and plumped up, they are good used in sauces, soups or casseroles, although they inevitably lack the fresh, light woodland aroma of newly-picked chanterelles.

## HORN OF PLENTY
(Trompette de mort)

These bounce back into shape in an exemplary manner when soaked, so you can use them in much the same way as you would fresh horns of plenty, bearing in mind that drying makes all mushrooms chewier in texture. They are often used as fake truffles as it is hard to distinguish between a black fleck of horn of plenty and a black fleck of truffle until you get down to eating. Given that nine times out of ten the truffle used in pâtés and the like has been preserved and is therefore pretty tasteless, it probably does not matter one jot which it is even then. I reckon it is a waste of a good mushroom unless you are out to impress. Far better to use them for their own sake.

CLOCKWISE, FROM TOP LEFT: DRIED HORNS OF PLENTY, DRIED MORELS, DRIED PORCINI

## MOREL

Reconstituted dried morels are a surprisingly good substitute for fresh morels, a little chewier but retaining much of the original flavour. Just as well, really, since fresh ones are a rare and unpredictable commodity. Your enthusiasm for dried morels may well be tempered by the heart-stoppingly high price, but console yourself with the thought that a 15 g (½ oz) handful will go a long way. Use them sparingly, in dishes with plenty of other ingredients, but where they will still be seen, admired and appreciated. Personally, I would be loathe to chop them up, or hide them in a pie. Do not waste any of the precious soaking liquid. Rinse morels under the cold tap after soaking to flush out any lingering grit.

## MOUSSERON
(Fairy ring mushroom)

Mousserons have a surprisingly full flavour for something so weedy and small. They cannot compare with the grandeur of ceps or morels, but they have their own clear-cut character. I feel that they are too insubstantial to make a meal of, so keep mousserons to use as a garnish – not the totally pointless radish rose kind of garnish, but as a final small fillip, adding not only to the visual appeal, but, more importantly, to the overall taste of a dish. Soaked, drained and fried briskly in butter until they begin to brown and crisp at the edges, or more slowly with a splash of white wine so that they remain tender, they make good last-minute additions to softly scrambled eggs on toast, soups, creamy mashed potatoes, or celeriac and potato purée, and a hundred and one other dishes.

TOP: DRIED SPANISH ST GEORGE MUSHROOMS; BOTTOM: MOUSSERONS

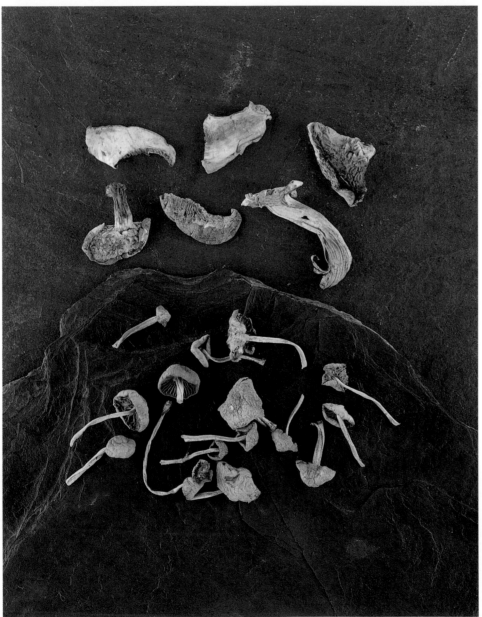

## WHITE FUNGUS BALL
(Jelly fungus, Silver wood ear)

A most extraordinary dried mushroom, but before you get too excited, let me make it clear that in terms of taste it has precious little going for it. No, the white fungus ball's charm lies in its appearance and its crunchy texture. In its dry state it looks like a natural sponge, honey-coloured and tightly furled. When soaked it turns snowy white and swells up to three of four times its original size.

Use them for their decorative appearance. I have usually braised them gently for 15–30 minutes along with other dried mushrooms, or poached them in stock, and they do absorb some of the flavours around them. Cooked for long enough (an hour or more), they lose their crunchiness and become soft and gelatinous. However, I have found that by the time they get to this stage, they look so bedraggled that it hardly seems worth it.

In China they are often used in sweet dishes; Yong Yap Cotterell gives several sweet recipes in his book *The Chinese Kitchen* (Weidenfeld & Nicholson Ltd, 1986), but I cannot honestly say that I find the idea appealing. I may well be wrong about this, but for the time being I cannot summon up enough curiosity to find out. Sorry.

## CLOUD EAR and WOOD EAR
(White back fungus, Black fungus)

Dried cloud ears and wood ears look similar in the bag, like crumpled scraps of black-brown suede. The main visual difference is size – cloud ears are smaller. The suede-like "white back" is actually a dusty grey in the cloud ear, browner in the wood ear. And if you are still not sure which is which, look at the price tag – cloud ears are two or three times more expensive than wood ears.

They both have a pleasing middle-of-the-range flavour, though that of the cloud ear is a mite more subdued. This is more than made up for by its delicious texture when braised, retaining a slight crunch, but at the same time smoothly gelatinous. Wood ears are a tougher number altogether, and remain crunchy and rather chewy, though not unpleasantly so.

Either kind can be used in stir-fried dishes, or braised in stews or soups. Do not keep them just for Oriental cooking either – they are delicious with poultry, meat or fish, served with or without a creamy sauce.

## SHIITAKE

(Forest mushrooms, Chinese dried mushrooms, Winter mushrooms, Flower or Floral mushrooms, etc)

Conversation in a Chinese supermarket:
Grigson, holding out an unlabelled packet of dried mushrooms: What kind of mushrooms are these?
Assistant: Chinese dried mushrooms.
Grigson: Yes, but what is their name?
Assistant, smiling wearily: Chinese dried mushrooms.
Grigson, trying new tack: Are they black mushrooms? Winter mushrooms? What about floral mushrooms?
Bemused assistant sticks to his guns: They are just Chinese dried mushrooms.
No joy there. The problem was that practically every Chinese cookery book I own used different names for what I suspected were exactly the same kind of mushroom. Just to complicate matters, several authors implied that ordinary Chinese dried mushrooms, and floral or flower mushrooms were completely separate entities, yet in one single packet I found specimens which matched the identifying pictures of both.

Further rootling around in books with a more scientific bent finally confirmed my suspicions. The whole damn lot are all

TOP: DRIED CLOUD EARS; BOTTOM: DRIED SHIITAKE

shiitake mushrooms (sold as forest mushrooms in Japanese foodshops). Floral mushrooms, with their cracked surface, are considered the best quality.

Floral or no, dried shiitake are almost on a par with dried porcini, when it comes to taste. Like porcini, their savour is full enough to allow them to be used almost as a seasoning; a few reconstituted shiitake cooked with plain button mushrooms improves the flavour no end. They are good on their own, too, but the stems are inedibly tough. Use them to flavour stocks, or throw straight out.

# RAGOUT OF DRIED MUSHROOMS

*A delicious way to show off a collection of different types of dried mushrooms, both Oriental and European. Serve in small portions as a rich first course with fingers of toasted brioche or as a main course with rice or noodles.*

**Serves 4 as a main course, 8 as a first course**

**450 g (1 lb) pearl onions**
**50 g (2 oz) assorted dried mushrooms (use at least three kinds, perhaps morels, horns of plenty, shiitake, cloud ears)**
**50 g (1 oz) butter**
**1 tablespoon oil**
**150 ml (¼ pint) soured cream**
**salt and pepper**

Top and tail the pearl onions. Cover with boiling water and stand for 1 minute. Drain and slip off the skins. Cook them in boiling salted water for 5 minutes. Drain well, and spread out to dry on absorbent kitchen paper or a clean tea towel.

Cover the mushrooms generously with hot water and leave to soak for 30 minutes. Pick out the mushrooms. Strain the water through a sieve lined with absorbent kitchen paper or a double layer of muslin. Make up to 600 ml (1 pint) with water.

Fry the mushrooms gently in the butter for 2 minutes. Add the onions, salt and pepper and the soaking liquid from the mushrooms. Simmer until virtually all the liquid has evaporated. Stir in the soured cream and simmer for a couple of minutes longer until slightly reduced. Taste and adjust the seasonings and serve.

OPPOSITE, TOP: RAGOUT OF DRIED MUSHROOMS; BOTTOM: SALSA AI FUNGHI

# SALSA AI FUNGHI

*This is a mushroomy version of pesto and can be used in the same way, tossed into hot cooked pasta (there is enough to breathe life into pasta for eight people here), rice or potatoes. Or try smearing it on to crostini – thickly cut pieces of good bread brushed with olive oil and baked in the oven until crisp and golden brown. Once you get going, you are bound to find plenty of other ways to use it up.*

*It keeps happily in the refrigerator for up to a week. Spoon what you are not using immediately into a screwtop jar, bang the jar down on the work surface a few times to expel any air bubbles, then cover the surface with a thin layer of olive oil. Cover and keep chilled.*

**Serves 8 on hot pasta**

**15 g (½ oz) dried mushrooms**
**135 ml (4½ fl oz) olive oil**
**100 g (4 oz) firm tomatoes**
**50 g (2 oz) pine kernels**
**3 garlic cloves**
**1 small bunch parsley, roughly chopped**
**2 anchovy fillets, roughly chopped**
**salt and pepper**

Cover the mushrooms with water and set aside for half an hour. Scoop out the mushrooms, and chop roughly. Strain their soaking water through a sieve lined with absorbent kitchen paper or muslin to remove any grit, and reserve. Fry the mushrooms in 1 tablespoon of the olive oil in a small pan for about 2 minutes. Add the soaking water, and simmer until the pan is almost dry.

Grill the tomatoes until tender, then skin and seed them. Place them in a blender or liquidizer with the mushrooms, pine kernels, garlic, parsley and anchovy fillets. Process, gradually trickling in the remaining olive oil, to give a thick paste. Add pepper to taste and a small amount of salt, if necessary. Cool.

# CHICKEN WITH MUSHROOM & DILL BUTTER

*I cannot honestly tell you that the dark mushroomy butter under the skin of the roast chicken has instant visual appeal, but the smell should make up for that as it arrives at the table, and the first taste of the moist, mushroom-scented flesh will dispel any lingering doubts.*

**Serves 4**

**1 plump, oven-ready roasting chicken**
**salt and pepper**
FLAVOURED BUTTER:
**15 g (½ oz) dried mushrooms**
**50 g (2 oz) butter, softened**
**finely grated zest and juice of ½ lemon**
**1 tablespoon chopped dill**
**black pepper**

To make the flavoured butter, cover the mushrooms with warm water and soak for 30 minutes. Pick out the mushrooms and chop roughly. Strain and save the soaking liquid to add to a stock, soup or sauce on some other occasion.

Process the butter with the mushrooms, lemon zest, dill, pepper and a generous squeeze of lemon juice. Taste and adjust the seasonings, which should be fairly generous. If you do not have a food processor, chop the mushrooms and dill very finely, then mash them into the butter with the other ingredients.

Starting from the neck end of the chicken, ease your fingers between the skin and flesh of the chicken, gradually loosening the skin without pulling it right off. Now push the flavoured butter up under the skin, smearing it over the flesh with your fingers, making sure that the breast, in particular, is nicely coated. Season the skin with salt and pepper.

Roast the chicken in a hot oven (220°C, 450°F, Gas Mark 7) for 15 minutes per pound, plus an extra 10–15 minutes. Serve with its buttery pan juices.

# VEGETABLES

I am not amongst those who pine for the old days of seasonality and are offended by the sight of a strawberry or courgette in February. Misconceived nostalgia. If you withdrew every vegetable or fruit that could not be grown outdoors in a northerly climate in winter, we would be left for three or four months with a monotonously limited selection. I love carrots and cabbage and potatoes and the handful of other true winter vegetables, but to be stuck with them and nothing else for that long is not a scenario to be relished.

Besides, there are still seasons. Summertime sees a proliferation of soft fruits, tomatoes, courgettes and the like, with better flavour than their winter counterparts, and so much cheaper too. Chestnuts and new season apples in the autumn, Jerusalem artichokes and Brussels sprouts as Christmas approaches. What a pleasure, then, that we can, nowadays, also find a fascinating and intriguing number of fruit and vegetables flown in from across the world, to supplement our own supplies.

My interest in the stranger foreign vegetables began when I was a student in Manchester, living in an area with a large Indian community, and later in one with a Caribbean population. Manchester's Chinatown, in the heart of the city, added a third patch to explore. In those days it was as much the restraints of a student grant as plain curiosity that motivated me. Many of the vegetables I first encountered there are now a regular part of my cooking and are these days often available in supermarkets. Some got the thumbs down; I cannot, for instance, raise any enthusiasm for yams.

I still make regular visits to small ethnic grocers shops often discovering new treats. This year kantolas and tindoori have become firm favourites. Over the past few years wholefood and healthfood shops selling organically grown vegetables have turned up other surprises, above all a fine collection of squashes. Trips abroad, and not necessarily that far afield, have introduced me to cardoons and fiddlehead ferns, amongst others.

Britain, too, has its own store of quite unfairly neglected vegetables. Wild samphire, salsify and seakale have all been popular in the past, but for whatever reasons have fallen from favour until recently. The wheel has almost turned full circle, and all three are now creeping their way back into chic groceries and occasionally supermarkets. With luck it will not be long before they are as familiar as aubergines or fennel.

It is always worth trying something new. Good advice given me by my mother, and to her by her mother. When you see a pile of vegetables that you have never tasted before, buy a few and give them a try. Ask the shopkeeper how to cook them. This does not always produce results, but it is worth a go. Although you are unlikely to be handed an exact recipe, you may get some idea of how to proceed. If your booty is not amongst the selection that follows and no other reference book comes up trumps, use common sense.

Cook them along the lines of whatever commonplace vegetable they most resemble, check frequently as they simmer, steam, bake or fry, and keep your fingers crossed. There will be times when you will be disappointed, but more often than not you will be happily surprised – if somebody thinks that vegetable worth selling, then there is likely to be something going for it.

## ROCKET
(Arugula, Rokka, Rucola)

Rocket has become *très à la mode* and *le prix aussi*. This is by no means surprising. Rocket leaves have a delicious peppery taste, that makes you sit up and take notice when you happen across a leaf in a mixed green salad. Unless you grow it yourself (which does not require green fingers), the youngest, tenderest leaves are inevitably going to come in expensive small posies or packets, making a pure rocket salad for more than two an extravagant gesture.

However, once you are hooked on the taste and ready for a more robust version, keep a sharp look out for Cypriot rocket, labelled "rokka", in Greek and Greek-Cypriot greengroceries. It is sold in big bundles at rock-bottom prices. Once you have located a good supply, the culinary rocket field opens wide before you. I love it cooked, simply dropped into a pan of boiling water, brought back to the boil and instantly drained. Squeeze out excess water and serve like spinach with butter, and/or lemon juice. Leftovers, if there are any, are good cold. From Italy, where rocket is commonplace, come recipes for pasta with rocket (throw the roughly chopped leaves in with the pasta a few seconds before it is done), and potato and rocket soups, and rocket- and ricotta-filled ravioli.

Delicate or robust, raw rocket should not be confined to the salad bowl. One of my favourite sandwiches is composed of

ROCKET

rocket, Parma ham, thin slices of Parmesan and a generous dusting of freshly ground black pepper, clamped between slices of Italian or granary bread heavily laced with olive oil.

## RADICCHIO

*Radicchio* and *cicoria* are both Italian for chicory. *Radicchio* is, on the whole, reserved for the beautiful burgundy leaved-chicories of the Veneto – all of them, not just the cabbage-rose of a radicchio that has become familiar in Britain and America. That one is either *radicchio di Verona* or *di Chioggia*.

The leaves of *radicchio di Treviso* are also deep red, streaked with white, divided by a vertical white rib. It is shaped something like those crinkly-edged tulips, just at the point when they are on the verge of opening up in the heat of a warm room. It may also be forced, grown in the dark like our own forced rhubarb, to give a red and white copy of the better known Witloof or Belgian chicory. *Radicchio di Castelfranco* opens wider than the others, with pale green outer leaves and white inner leaves and heart, all splashed with garnet red.

All radicchios can be used raw in salads, imparting their characteristic edge of bitterness, married with a delicate sweetness, and all of them are delicious cooked, though the beautiful red turns a less inspiring brown. Forced radicchio should be used just as you would Belgian chicory. The more supple, thinner leaves of the other three mean that they flop out of shape when heated. Grilled radicchio salad is a favourite of mine – strips of radicchio leaves, tossed in vinaigrette, mixed with cubes of goat's cheese, then grilled briefly until the leaves begin to wilt and the cheese to melt. Sweated briefly in butter or oil, with a dash of lemon or balsamic vinegar, perhaps some garlic, or some diced bacon, radicchio becomes either a powerful vegetable side dish, or a dressing for hot pasta. Radicchio may also be used in ravioli stuffings, to wrap around little parcels of food as you might spinach or lettuce, and in risottos.

PURSLANE

GREEN AND WHITE PAK-CHOI

## PURSLANE
(Pigweed, Portulaca)

Ambling through a basil field in Italy, we were distracted for a few moments by the wild purslane, flourishing in the dry soil. We nibbled at the little fleshy leaves and red stems, sorry not to have time to pick enough to make a salad.

Wild purslane is unusual in Britain (though sea purslane, also edible, grows on saltmarshes on southern and eastern coasts), but so, too, is cultivated purslane (much the same as the wild), at least in shops. It is easy to grow at home, but be sure to sow seeds generously since it takes a fair number of purslane plants to make up a salad, even a mixed one.

So far, I have been talking about red-stemmed purslane. There is a second kind that you may come across in Arab shops,

which is much sturdier, with leaves a good 2½ cm (1 inch) across, green stems, and has a more pronounced flavour. The stems can be tough and stringy, so I discard them except for the top couple of inches. The oxalic acid, present in both sorts, is more noticeable in green-stemmed purslane, making it less suitable when raw for salads except in small quantity, chopped up. On the other hand, being larger and more robust, it cooks well, though needs only the briefest of dips in boiling water – add the purslane, bring back to the boil and drain instantly. Dress with melted butter or olive oil, or toss in vinaigrette and cool.

Purslane is eaten in France and Italy, throughout the Middle East, across much of Asia and parts of Africa. In Nice it is one of a quartet of wild herbs known as *refréscat*, simmered in soups, and it does give a wonderful smoothness and flavour to a soup. The fleshy leaves are perfect for pickling – submerge in a spiced and lightly sweetened vinegar.

## PAK-CHOI
(Bok-choy, Mustard greens, Chinese white cabbage)

Pak-choi is amongst the choicest of the Chinese brassicas, with its broad, juicy white stems and mildly mustardy green leaves. When young and tender, both can be used raw in salads. Like the more familiar Swiss chard, leaves and stems are best cooked separately. Pak-choi can be substituted for Swiss chard, bearing in mind that the more tender green leaves will require briefer cooking. Chinese "seaweed", that delicious mound of crisp, translucent green shreds, is often made with the leaves of pak-choi, briefly deep-fried.

Pak-choi takes equally well to Western and Eastern flavourings. The stems are good stir-fried, adding the sliced leaves for the last minute or so. Or you could save them to cook like spinach. Both parts can be boiled, or steamed or microwaved. Pak-choi, leaves and stems pre-cooked, makes a delicious gratin, mixed with Béchamel sauce, diced olives or anchovies, scattered with grated Parmesan and baked until patched with brown.

## ROMAN or ROMANESCA CAULIFLOWER

This is one of the most beautiful vegetables known to man, if not the most beautiful. The lime-green curd swirls up in geometric spiralling cones, as if sculpted patiently and lovingly. Since they taste much like ordinary cauliflowers, it seems pointless to break up the head into small pieces and lose the visual delight it offers. Cook them whole, in the microwave for the best colour, or on the hob with the base submerged surrounded by water, but with the top exposed (it will cook in the steam). Do not, whatever you do, overcook it. Remove it from the heat while it is still *al dente*, for both flavour's and look's sake. Serve as it is, or drizzle over a "sauce" of olive oil, heated with garlic and flakes of dried red chilli, or salted with chopped anchovies, cooked until they dissolve.

## MIZUNO

A Japanese salad leaf, now grown by at least one organic market gardener in Britain, and there may be others. If not, they should be encouraged. The spiky green leaves have a firm texture and mild flavour, but it is the stalks that I really like, crisp and juicy. In theory, it is a winter salad, though I have bought it in July. I would not go out of my way to track it down, but it does on occasion make a welcome change, particularly in mid-winter.

## FIDDLEHEAD FERN

Tightly-curled round like a bishop's crozier, fiddlehead ferns are quite charming to see, and have a pure green flavour with touches of asparagus and green bean. Do not, however, be tempted by just any old fern shoot poking its pretty head up in the woods. There are those that assure us that ordinary bracken is perfectly safe to eat at this young stage, but many botanists warn fiercely against. The ostrich fern, which

grows wild in northern America is the only one that everyone seems to agree is edible, but only at this immature fiddlehead stage. Once the head begins to unfurl, and the leaves open up, the toxins develop and it should be left to grow in peace.

Still if you are in America or Canada in the spring, you may just hit the brief season for fiddlehead ferns. I have eaten them in a London restaurant, flown over for the occasion, and I am told that frozen fiddlehead ferns can be found in very esoteric delicatessens, albeit rarely. I have yet to see the proof of this, although I did once find a jar of pickled fiddleheads, which are delicious and decorative, served with cheeses, or cold meats and charcuterie, or scattered over salads.

If you do happen to be blessed with a cache of fiddleheads, trim the stem down to a couple of centimetres (an inch) or so long, and, if necessary, rub off any downy brown scales. Rinse thoroughly and steam or boil until tender – 4–6 minutes should be ample. Serve like asparagus with melted butter or Hollandaise sauce.

## CHINESE ARTICHOKE
(Crosnes, Chorogi)

Chinese artichokes are still a rarity in Britain, though I have seen them for sale once or twice in chic greengroceries in the past couple of years. There is no good reason why they should not be sold on a wider scale and relatively cheaply. They have an exquisite flavour, somewhere between Jerusalem artichoke and salsify, and grow easily and abundantly, needing precious little encouragement. I am sure that soon their time will come. There is many a comparatively dull vegetable that has inched its way on to the supermarket shelves in recent times. All it needs is an enterprising duo of grower and retailer to launch it.

When you do lay your hands on a bag of Chinese artichokes, you will find that they need little preparation. If you have the

choice, pick ones that are firm and pearly white, indicating that they are absolutely fresh from the ground, or a yellowish beige, a few days older, but still perfectly good to eat. To cook, top and tail, and rinse thoroughly. Simmer in just enough salted water to cover, or steam them. A dash of lemon juice will heighten their flavour. Cook them until tender rather than *al dente*, though not mushy and collapsing. Serve them as they are, with a large knob of butter and a sprinkling of chopped parsley, chervil, chives, or tarragon, or finish them in a rich cream and butter sauce. If you opt for the latter, enjoy them as a first course, with triangles of fried or toasted bread or brioche. They make a delicious salad, too – toss the hot cooked artichokes in vinaigrette, cool, and add fresh herbs.

## SEAKALE

Though seakale grows wild on beaches, it can be cultivated well away from the sea. It is grown commercially, albeit on a very small scale, and is sometimes sold in greengroceries and supermarkets. The long, thin spears gain their ghostly translucence from blanching; the young shoots are deprived of light either by mounding earth or sand up around them, or covering them with opaque cloches. Thus, they develop only the most delicate and seductive of flavours; a joy of a vegetable.

To prepare seakale, trim off the root and stalk base, and rinse thoroughly. The tender young leaves can be trimmed off to use in salads, or left *in situ*. Simmer in lightly salted water or steam until just tender. Drain well, and serve as a first course, like asparagus, with melted butter sharpened with lemon juice, or even a restrained hint of horseradish. Seakale vinaigrette, i.e. seakale turned in vinaigrette when it is hot, and left to cool, then sprinkled with chopped fresh parsley, and/or a few capers, is extremely good.

## MARSH SAMPHIRE

(Glasswort, Saltwort, Poor man's asparagus)

Jointed like green coral polished smooth and shiny by the sea, marsh samphire is a wild, seashore plant that grows profusely on mud-flats below the high tide line. It has been particularly associated in England with East Anglia. One friend remembers hearing as a child the samphire seller singing his wares as he toured the streets with his horse and cart, and that was a mere thirty or so years ago.

Samphire is sold by fishmongers, or at least by some fishmongers, from spring through to early summer. It is at its prime in May, when the shoots are large enough to have some substance but before the central core begins to get woody. At this time it can be eaten raw in salads. However, it is more usual to steam or boil it (with no added salt). A few minutes are all that are needed; much longer and you destroy the fresh salty tang of the sea. To prepare the samphire, rinse thoroughly, and trim off any damaged parts and the woody base. Eat like asparagus with melted butter.

It has a natural affinity with fish, so take advantage of this by steaming the two together; make a bed of samphire on a heatproof plate, lay fillets or steaks of fish over it, season and steam together. It can also be pickled, briefly blanched, submerged in a spiced and lightly sweetened wine vinegar.

## ROCK SAMPHIRE

This is no relation whatsoever to marsh samphire, though it can be cooked or pickled in the same way. Rock samphire, as the name suggests, grows on seaside rocks, with fleshy flat leaves of a grey-green colour. It has a distinct taste of iodine, which some people dislike, but others find most attractive, me amongst them. Of the two samphires, I think this makes the

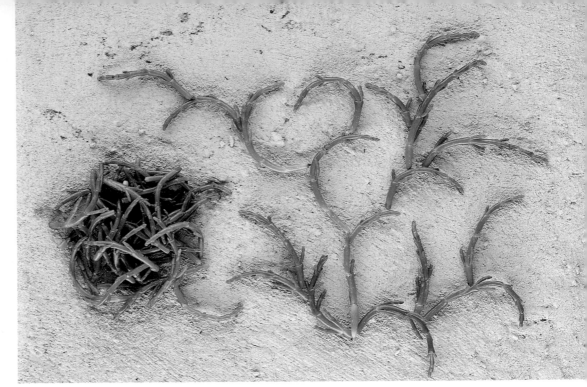

MARSH SAMPHIRE

better pickle. I have never seen it for sale, but have often picked it for myself. Nobody much seems to be interested in cropping rock samphire, which is a bonus for those who do appreciate it.

## NOPALE

(Cactus pad, paddle or leaf)

You can eat cactus fruit, so why not the swollen stems? Apart from the off-putting prickles, no reason at all. Strange, then , that the juicy pads of the prickly pear are eaten only in Central America, particularly Mexico, and not in other countries where the fruit is relished.

Only the younger leaves, still tender, are eaten. They have a gentle sharpness, a crisp but soft texture combined with a mucilaginous juice not unlike that of okra.

If you do get the chance to cook fresh nopales, this is how to set about it. Unless you are 100 per cent sure that they are of the prickleless cultivated variety, or that some kind soul has already shaved off the prickles, do not pick them up with your bare hands; wear gloves or grasp them with a piece of newspaper or you will regret it. With a sharp knife or vegetable

parer, slice off the "eyes", along with any prickles. Trim off the edge of the paddle all the way round. Get rid of the trimmings, rinse the knife and any other utensils used, and the cactus paddles themselves. Now you are safe. The paddles can be cooked whole, sliced or diced as you wish. They can be steamed or boiled, either briefly to preserve the crispness, or for a longer time to soften, in which case they will loose some of their slipperiness.

Rick Bayless, in his book *Authentic Mexican Cooking*, suggests grilling them whole. Score each side lengthwise three times. Brush with oil, sprinkle with salt and a little lime juice. Grill over a moderate-low charcoal fire or ordinary grill, for 15–20 minutes, turning occasionally, or roast in a moderate oven (180°C, 350°F, Gas Mark 4) for about 25 minutes. Finely diced or sliced thinly, they can also be stir-fried. Cooked nopales are good with egg dishes, in salads and salsas, and *au gratin* with tomatoes, cheese and breadcrumbs.

Canned or bottled nopales with additional spices and herbs are a tolerable substitute for fresh and should be used as cooked nopales, bearing in mind the extra seasoning, usually chilli-hot.

WATER CHESTNUTS

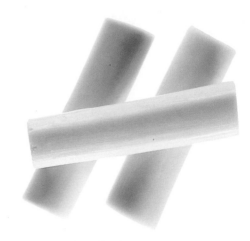

PALM HEARTS

## WATER CHESTNUTS

How confusing names can be. Chinese water chestnuts, the crisp, sweetish spheres that you can buy readily in cans, are not at all the same as the true water chestnut, which is indeed a nut with a most peculiar horned appearance. The latter is clad in a hard slate-black shell, which is a real pain to get off. The starchy interior is, in my opinion, not worth the bother.

Not so with the Chinese water chestnut. They can well, but they are even better fresh. They look much like gladioli corms, a dark skin, fringed with rings of papery brown scales. When you see them snap them up fast. They keep unpeeled, for up to a week (store in the vegetable drawer of the refrigerator), as long as they are firm and unbruised. They can be eaten raw, and a real pleasure they are. All you need do is peel them, discarding any that are discoloured. Once peeled they will survive in the refrigerator in a bowl of lightly salted water for a couple of days.

One of the big bonuses of water chestnuts is that they retain their texture and taste when cooked. This makes them a favourite ingredient in Chinese cooking, in stir-fries, casseroles, stuffings for dim sums, soups, and so on. They make a good addition to many a Western dish, too – in salads, in casseroles, with mixed vegetable dishes, in stuffings for poultry and whatever else you can dream up. Try them "on horseback" – wrapped in a thin strip of bacon, exposed bits brushed with oil (or marinade them first), and grilled until the bacon is cooked.

## ARROWHEAD

These starchy Chinese tubers have a smooth ivory surface often partially or wholly hidden by dry, wispy rings of papery brown skin. They do not look remotely like arrowheads, but more like flower bulbs. The name refers to the shape of the leaves. Some writers describe the flavour as bland, but I find their mild chestnut taste very appealing.

They are used in Cantonese, Szechuan and Yunnan dishes, often braised with other ingredients, but they are quite good enough to enjoy plainly cooked in place of potatoes. To prepare, slice off the top and bottom, and peel. Drop them into acidulated water as you work to prevent discoloration. Boil them in acidulated salted water, or steam, for about 10 minutes until tender. Serve them whole, or sliced with a generous knob of butter or splash of olive oil. They can also be diced and sautéed with garlic and chilli, or baked in the oven.

## PALM HEARTS
(Palmitos)

I have had a couple of brushes with fresh palm hearts, bought in the south of Spain, and have returned rather thankfully to canned palm hearts. The fresh ones taste fine, once you have stripped off the seemingly never-ending tough layers that surround the tender heart, but the returns seem niggardly compared with the amount of waste, and the price. Perhaps in Brazil, where they are a common vegetable, presumably cheaper, and probably fully stripped and prepared before you buy them, it makes more sense to go for the fresh ones. If you do decide to try your lot with fresh palm hearts, simply boil the inner cylinder in lightly acidulated, salted water, until tender.

From now on, however, I shall be sticking with the canned variety, which I love. The difference in flavour is not so very remarkable. In fact, it is really the texture that is so pleasing, firm, cool and smooth, whilst the taste is mild, slightly sharpened by the marinade they float in. They make an excellent addition to salads, dressed with vinaigrette, or mayonnaise, particularly good with shellfish, the sharp fragrance of lime, and sweet herbs. The saltiness of crisp little pieces of browned bacon is always a good addition.

OKRA

## OKRA

(Bamia, Bhindi, Gumbo, Ladies fingers)

Either you like the mucilaginous texture of okra, or you do not. If you do not, ignore those recipes that come with the promise to reduce the slipperiness of okra. That is how okra are meant to be, and there is no point wasting time and money if you do not appreciate their texture. If they are new to you, buy a handful, cook them simply and see what you think.

Okra are an important vegetable right across the globe, from India, through the Middle East and Africa, to the Caribbean and Louisiana. Their juices add a smoothness to stews and soups, and thicken them slightly, but okra are also a good vegetable in their own right.

Always pick out the smallest, liveliest-looking okra, with no brown patches, or at least very few. Larger ones can be stringy. To cook whole, trim off the conical cap, trying not to pierce through to the interior, though it is not the end of the world if you do. Steam, boil, sweat gently in butter or olive oil, or microwave until just tender, but still retaining shape and substance.

Although I like okra plainly cooked, they are even better married with tomatoes — for instance simmered in a tomato sauce, or in a tomato-y stew or soup. My other particular preference is for okra, sliced thickly, tossed in seasoned cornmeal, and fried in olive oil — serve with lemon

wedges. Cream and okra is an unhappy combination, best avoided.

## MELOUKHIA

Meloukhia is a type of mallow, related to the marsh mallow, hibiscus, and okra. Like okra, meloukhia gives soups and stews a pleasing velvety smoothness, thickening slightly in the process. Though it is used throughout the Middle East, Egypt is the country where it is most highly rated. Meloukhia soup is one of Egypt's national dishes. Since the flavour is muted, it can be incorporated into all manner of savoury dishes with a fair complement of liquid, and is well worth experimenting with.

Fresh meloukhia makes a rare appearance in this country, but you will probably have to settle for dried. The dried leaves should be crumbled and soaked in hot water for half an hour or so, before adding to the pot. Simmer for half an hour. Fresh leaves just need to be washed and finely chopped, and require a mere 5–10 minutes' simmering.

## CARDOON

Why don't we cultivate cardoons, or at least import them into this country? We have happily adopted that more famous

Mediterranean thistle, the artichoke, but not a trace of the majestic cardoon. We are missing out, but if you are curious and happen to be in the south of France or Spain, or in Italy (particularly the Piedmont), in the autumn and early winter, look out for them in markets, and ask for them in restaurants. The flower of the cardoon can be eaten when young, or may be dried and used as a vegetable rennet, but the thick stalks are the real delicacy.

It is hard to miss them on market stalls — huge, silvery white stems, like overgrown, prickly celery. They have a slightly milder flavour, but can be a little bitter, though this disappears on blanching. If you do have the luck to bring one home to your kitchen, the stalks can be eaten raw (for instance with a *bagna cauda*, the hot anchovy and garlic dip from the Piedmont). Pull off the tougher strings, and pare off the tougher white inner skin. Cut the trimmed cardoons into suitably-sized pieces and drop them into acidulated water as you work to stop discoloration. To cook them, save time and just chop the stalks up, simmering them in acidulated water until tender. Taste a corner after 5 minutes, and if it seems bitter, drain and rinse the cardoons, then simmer until tender in a fresh pan of water. Once they are cooked, they can simply be served with butter, lemon, salt and pepper, or napped with a cheese sauce, a cream sauce, or a punchier olive oil and anchovy sauce.

## SQUASHES

The squash family (Cucurbitaceae) includes many familiar vegetables – courgettes, cucumbers, pumpkins – and hundreds of others besides. Since I have no intention of writing a two-volume book, I have picked out four of the most worthwhile of this clan, commoners apart. This does not mean that the rest are of little interest, though a few of them can be dull. Incidentally, bitter gourds, tindoori and chayote, which all have individual entries here, are also types of squash.

Squashes are roughly subdivided into two groups, summer and winter, which is not absolutely determined by season. Summer squashes are varieties that are best picked young and tender, with seeds, skin and all quite edible. Because of their youth, the flesh is usually lightly coloured, with a relatively subtle flavour. Courgettes are a prime example. Winter squashes are picked more mature, with hard inedible skins, on the whole a more pronounced flavour, and with more intensely coloured flesh. Spaghetti squash confuses the issue – it is usually classed as a summer squash, although the skin is far from palatable.

**Patty pan squash (Custard marrow or squash, Scallop squash):** There is no doubt about the shape of a patty pan squash, round, slightly flattened like a flying saucer, and with scalloped edges. The colour is another matter. As far as I am concerned it is white, or pale green. The bright yellow version is what I think of as a custard marrow – well, it makes sense at least in terms of colour. Other writers insist on switching the names around the other way, and yet others treat all names as interchangeable. In the end, it makes scant difference to the cook, since they taste just the same and one's choice is likely to be limited to one or other anyway.

Pick the smallest, when their mild flavour is most concentrated, and steam or boil them whole as you would young courgettes. Larger specimens, 10 cm (4 inches) in diameter and upwards, are best briefly blanched, then stuffed and baked in the oven, so masking their tendency to wateriness.

**Butternut squash** is a winter squash with a bottle-gourd shape. Unlike, say a pumpkin, the flesh is densely packed, buttery and deliciously nutty and sweet. Unless you are making soup with it, which is not such a bad idea, keep it away from excessive water to preserve the full flavour. Baking, which really concentrates the flavour, steaming or microwaving whole (pierce the skin for the microwave), halved or in chunks, are better methods of cooking. Cut into cubes, the barely cooked flesh is wonderful sautéed in butter or oil, perhaps with slices of chorizo. Sliced, it is good for gratins with the contrasting savouriness of cheeses like Parmesan or Cheddar, or egged and crumbed fritters.

Though of more ample girth, **Red Kuri** is similar in texture to the butternut, but a little waxier and smoother. It has a distinct taste of chestnuts, and is to my mind the best of the bigger winter squashes. It can be cooked in the same manner as butternut, and makes a sensational purée that is just bliss with roast game.

**Vegetable spaghetti** (Spaghetti squash) is a most peculiar, and engaging vegetable. The derivation of the name is straightforward; when cooked the flesh separates quite naturally into long spaghetti-like strands. It is a dieter's dream (do not let that put you off if weight-watching is not relevant to your menu), a filling pasta-replacement with negligible calories. And, in fact, it is best treated in much the same way as pasta. Its crisp strands are happy to be bathed in any pasta sauce, whether as simple as butter or olive oil and Parmesan, or something a little more involved like a tomato-y seafood sauce, or a Bolognese.

To cook the squash, carve it in half lengthways – it is easier to do this à deux, one to hold it still, the other to cut. The halves can be boiled (cut into large chunks if it makes life easier and if you do not want to serve it in its shell), but I find that this makes them rather watery, however well I think I have drained them. Better, though slower, is to bake them in a moderate oven, cut side down, with a scant centimetre (half an inch) of water around them. If I am short on time I will microwave them, again cut side down with a little water, tightly covered with clingfilm. Whichever way, cook them until the skin can easily be pierced with a skewer. Once cooked, drain well. Nibble on a seed – if it is soft, the seeds can be left right where they are and eaten along with the rest. If not, scoop them out. Then all that is left to do is to fork up the flesh and add your chosen sauce.

## SQUASH FLOWERS

Summer markets in Provence, Italy and Spain are a glorious sight, a riotous celebration of colours under the hot sun. Bunches of courgette flowers splash egg-yolk yellow across the scene. Picked early that morning they will still be vigorous and bright, but by lunch-time, as the stall-holders pack up, the few left unsold will be beginning to droop. Squash flowers have a

SQUASH FLOWER (COURGETTE)

SQUASHES – TOP ROW, FROM LEFT: VEGETABLE SPAGHETTI, MARROW, YELLOW COURGETTE (SUMMER SQUASH), DOODHI; BOTTOM ROW, FROM LEFT: CHAYOTE, BUTTERNUT SQUASH, KOBOCHE SQUASH, PATTY PAN SQUASH

brief life-span off the vine, and though they can still be eaten when crumpled and floppy, they are at their best within a few hours of being picked. The flowers of all squashes from courgettes to pumpkins are edible, and if you grow your own, should not be wasted.

If you are lucky you will be able to buy or pick the flowers still attached to a junior vegetable, a finger-length courgette maybe, or a tiny patty pan squash, and the pair can be cooked together. This is the only time when I will go through the inevitably fiddly and lengthy process of stuffing individual flowers. On its own, a stuffed squash flower disappears in a brace of insubstantial

mouthfuls, and it takes a fair few per person to make anything but the meanest offering. At least with a delicate little courgette attached you can get away with stuffing a mere two or three each. If you do decide to take on the onerous task of stuffing squash flowers, they really do have to be fresh and perky. I have tried filling floppy ones and they tear and rip mercilessly. There is more room for stuffing if you remove the thick pistil. Whatever the stuffing, the flowers can then be steamed or baked in the oven, simply basted with olive oil or with a sauce. They can also be fried, but if the flowers are just the teensiest bit over-filled the stuffing has

an irritating habit of swelling up and bursting out.

Squash flower fritters are a much more straightforward proposition. Shake out any unwelcome insect life, then coat the flowers lightly in flour to help the batter stick, dip into a fritter batter and deep fry. They can also be deep-fried neat in hot oil for a few seconds, which gives them an elegant translucence. Mind you, cooked this way, they make a better garnish than a dish in their own right. One modern Italian recipe suggests tossing deep-fried courgette flowers with hot tagliatelle, chunks of tomato and basil to create a beautiful summer pasta dish.

TINDOORI

## TINDOORI
(Ivy gourd, Tindola)

You will find these little green gourds, some 4–5 cm (1 ½–2 inches) long, striped with pale green, in Indian and, more rarely, in West Indian shops. Piled up in a heap, they look pretty and inviting, with their tight shiny skins. I would not, to be honest, go far out of my way to find them, but if I see them *en passant*, I usually buy a bagful. The inside is tightly packed with tiny seeds, all edible (there would be precious little left if they were not), and pleasingly crunchy and juicy. They taste similar to cucumber, but guard their texture much better when heated.

The first time I cooked them, I simply steamed them whole, and ate them hot with salt, pepper, a dash of lemon juice (balsamic vinegar, or sherry vinegar would be even nicer) and a knob of butter, and very pleasant they were too. The wife of the man who runs my local Indian shop prefers to halve them, then sweat them in oil or butter for 10 minutes – never any water, she says firmly – and sprinkle with garam masala a few minutes before they are done. Now, I usually salt them, halved, to extract some of their water, concentrating the mild flavour that they have, before I do anything else.

They are extremely good tossed in flour, seasoned with salt and pepper, and a few spices or a touch of curry powder, then deep-fried briefly. They adapt well to Western styles of cooking – maybe just simmered in a tomato sauce, or baked with tomato slices in the oven, topped off with cheese and breadcrumbs. Infinitely adaptable, they can be slipped into curries, stir-fries, and a hundred and one other vegetable dishes.

## BITTER GOURD
(Bitter melon, Karela)

Bitter gourds are. Bitter, that is – very bitter. If you find the bitterness of endives or chicory hard to stomach, then do not even consider tangling with a bitter gourd. If, on the other hand, you like endives and chicory, then it is worth your while experimenting with bitter gourds, but in moderation.

They are intriguing-looking vegetables, with their warty skin. In practice I have found that middling-sized ones, about 10–13 cm (4–5 inches) long, less bitter than tiny ones, but they are still strong going. The Chinese often stuff the gourds then fry them, but I find the ratio of gourd to stuffing too much. Stir-frying them, amongst a mass of other ingredients, so that you get a more subtle hint of bitterness, is a way of using them much more to my taste.

Salting or blanching reduces the bitterness, and should never be omitted. First, halve each gourd lengthways, and scoop out the seeds. To salt them, cut them first into thin rings, or chop, and spread them out in a colander. Sprinkle lightly with salt, and leave for at least half an hour, preferably an hour. Rinse and pat dry. To blanch, drop the halves into a pan of boiling salted water, bring back to the boil, and simmer for 3 minutes. Drain and rinse under the cold tap.

BITTER GOURDS

## KANTOLA
(Spiny bitter gourd)

In my experience, kantolas, or spiny bitter gourds, have not been terribly bitter, and certainly not a patch on their larger cousins, karela, or bitter gourds. Balls of soft green "spines" 2.5 cm (1–1 ½ inches) long, they have a short season, six weeks or so, around June and July and are worth experimenting with. I was introduced to them by the salesman in my local Indian grocery, who has a passion for them, and I can understand why. They have a subtle, delicious bitterness. The feel of them in the mouth is quite unique too. First, there is the soft roughness of the skins against the tongue, followed by the slight crunchiness of the seeds inside.

Kantolas are at their best when still green, but, if possible, try to include a few that have matured to a yellowy colour when buying them. When you get home, halve the yellow ones to reveal the stunningly coral red seeds inside. Save them to sprinkle over the finished dish, adding a vibrant splash of colour.

Kantolas can be cooked like tindoori, though there is no need to halve them first (unless you intend to stir-fry them). They can be soaked in brine for a few hours, or blanched for 3 minutes if you are wary of the bitterness, but I never bother. Sweat them in butter or oil, deep-fry them, steam them, add to curries, or cook in a tomato sauce, Western-style. Plain boiling is not such a hot idea, as they become sadly water-logged.

## CHAYOTE
(Alligator pear, Cho-cho, Chow chow, Christophene)

Chayotes do not rate high on the flavour stakes, but they come in with a tremendous score on texture, smooth, firm and juicy. There is little point in trying to be subtle when cooking chayotes. They beg big gutsy flavourings – chillies, spices,

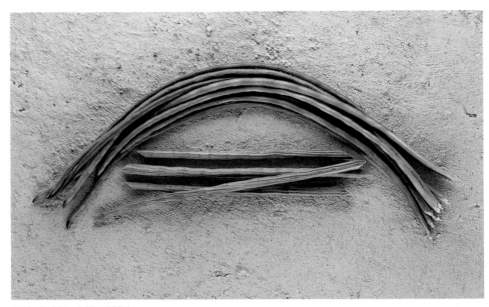

YARD LONG BEANS, DRUMSTICKS

garlic, tomatoes, cheese – and are perfect vehicles for stuffings. Simmer them whole in lightly salted water until just tender, halve, remove the "stone" (which is actually soft and edible), and some of the insides, then fill with whatever filling you fancy, top with breadcrumbs mixed with grated cheese, drizzle with a little olive oil and return to a hot oven until browned. They are also good *au gratin*, cooked, sliced and layered with a punchy tomato sauce, again topped with cheese and crumbs and baked. Alternatively, try simmering chunks of chayote in a spicy sauce, allowing them to absorb some of the flavour as they cook.

Their mild, almost non-existent taste means they can be, and often are, used in sweet dishes, maybe simmered in a scented syrup like pears, and served cold, or baked in slices with cinnamon, nutmeg, sugar or honey, lemon and butter. For more ideas look particularly in Caribbean and southern and Central American cookery books.

Use chayotes as quickly as possible. Though they appear to remain in fine fettle when stored in the refrigerator for a week or more, they soon develop an unpleasant mouldy flavour.

## YARD LONG BEANS

What fun these are – like an ordinary string bean crossed with a runner bean then stretched out to an extraordinary yard or more in length. They have the curious rough skin of a runner bean, and a firmness and taste that lies somewhere between the two. They should be cooked like other fresh beans, but it seems a terrible shame to cut them up – you might as well have stuck with straight string beans (although, incidentally, yard long beans from a small Indian shop can turn out to be cheaper).

I always cook them whole, curling them into a large pan of boiling water. To make the most of their peculiar length, I sometimes roll up and knot three or four cooked beans together to form a flattish nest. These can be reheated, covered, in the oven, or in a creamy sauce, or alternatively, dressed while still hot with a vinaigrette and served cold in a salad, adding other vegetables, too, if you wish. Even better is to brush the knots with olive oil, or marinade them, then grill them on the barbecue until patched with brown. Imagination is the key here, and once you have located a regular supply, you can really go to town.

## SUGAR SNAP PEAS

The best of both worlds. Like mangetouts, once topped and tailed, you can eat the whole thing, lock, stock and barrel. Like common peas, there are plump fully formed little peas lined up inside the pod. Sugar snaps are sweet, juicy and tender, as delightful eaten uncooked as cooked. Add them raw to salads, or a dish of crudités. Steaming keeps the truest flavour, boiling comes second best. Either way, do not overdo it – a couple of minutes will usually suffice. I think they need no more than seasoning with salt and pepper – butter or olive oil is gilding the lily, though a drop or two of balsamic vinegar does not go amiss.

## AKEE

When ripe, the red fruit of the *Blighia sapida* splits open to reveal three glossy black seeds, each wrapped in primrose yellow curd. This yellow curd, the aril, is the one part that is eaten, and only when the fruit is ripe enough to burst open without human encouragement. The seeds and the unripe aril are poisonous. Since you are unlikely to come across fresh akee outside the West Indies, there is no need to feel nervous about this. Canned akee is as safe as houses, all preparation and preliminary cooking taken care of. I cannot comment on the difference in taste or texture between fresh and canned as I have never had the opportunity to taste akee freshly cooked. One day perhaps…

Canned akee are as soft as scrambled eggs, with a delicate flavour quite unlike anything else. On their own and unadorned, they might be described as bland. Cook or rather reheat them with punchy flavourings, chillies and spices, herbs, tomato, onion, garlic, salty bacon or olives, and they are transformed.

Salt fish and akee is virtually Jamaica's national dish, a mixture of salt cod, salt pork, tomato, chilli and ackee, quite wonderful when properly put together. Taking this as my cue, I often sauté onion, garlic, chilli and diced bacon, add a few chopped, seeded tomatoes, and herbs, simmer down until they are all but dry then stir in the drained and rinsed akee, turning carefully until heated through. It makes a good side dish, or light main course with toast. Akee can also be puréed, and reheated with flavourings and a good knob of butter. The purée makes a good filling for small pasties – add finely diced onion and other vegetables, sweated in butter until tender, for extra interest.

## "EGG" AUBERGINE – White, Yellow or Purple

Aubergines are not necessarily big, purple and bulgy. They can be long and thin, streaked with white, or as tiny as the West Indian "pea" aubergine. I have a particular soft spot for the egg-shaped group, varying in girth from large chicken egg to duck or goose egg.

The beautiful sleek ivory egg aubergine is now grown in Holland and has made its way into many a supermarket. It has a decidedly creamy texture. Although it can

A SELECTION OF "EGG" AUBERGINES

have a hint of the bitterness so often found in aubergines, it is rarely pronounced, so these are the best of the egg aubergines for cooking whole.

African garden egg aubergines are bright yellow, and can often be found in West Indian food shops. Purple egg aubergines are much used in Middle Eastern and Indian cookery. Both of these varieties can be quite bitter. Given that the shape is part of their charm, slicing and salting in the normal way is not appropriate. Several alternatives, then, depending on intended use. Firstly, if the aubergines are to be kept

whole and uncut, pierce the skin in several places and soak in brine for 30 minutes– 1 hour. Squeeze gently to expel as much liquid as possible, then rinse. A more effective method is to simmer the pierced aubergines in salted water until tender. Drain, cool slightly, and squeeze gently. Rinse.

If you are stuffing or filling the aubergines in some way, either cut them in half, or cut them lengthwise into four slices, stopping 1–2 cm (½–1 inch) short of the stem so that they hold together. Rub salt into the cuts, and leave for 30 minutes–1 hour.

Rinse and dry. It is worth buying a few extra aubergines, so that you can quickly cook one to see if the salting has done its job, or whether it needs more time.

Egg aubergines can be steamed, boiled or microwaved whole, or stuffed with any of the fillings used for larger aubergines. Sliced as above and fanned out, they are good deep-fried. They are just the right size for pickling; at London's fine Lebanese restaurant, the Al Hamra in Shepherds Market, they serve a wonderful dish of pickled aubergines, slit down the centre to form a pocket holding a filling of chopped walnuts. Mediterranean pickled aubergine recipes can be adapted this way, filling the slit with finely chopped herbs and garlic, with or without walnuts, or with pine kernels, perhaps.

## LOTUS ROOT

A packet of exotic "crisps" contained amongst other bits and bobs what appeared to be potato crisps with holes punched out like a wagon-wheel. Not the latest designer crisp at all, but thin slices of deep-fried lotus root. The whole root resembles links of fat, yellow-brown sausages, that some unfortunate shopper has dropped in the mud. Long holes run down the length of each root, hence the lacy cross-section.

Lotus roots are starchy, with a crisp texture which they retain when cooked, and a hint of sweetness. To prepare, wash off the mud, separate the links and lop off the ends. Peel and slice, thickly or thinly according to your recipe, dropping the pieces quickly into acidulated water as you work to prevent discoloration. They can simply be boiled, again in acidulated water, or steamed (exact time will depend on the age of the root and thickness of the slices – taste a piece after 10 minutes) and served with a knob of butter, salt and pepper.

In the Far East they may be stuffed for special occasions, but that is a fiddly job,

to be undertaken only by those with generous reserves of patience and time. You can bake them, too, or add them to stews, where they will absorb other flavours willingly. Thin slices, 5 mm (¼ inch) or so, can be sautéed gently – irresistible, done like sautéed potatoes, in butter with fresh thyme, rosemary and a hint of garlic.

## BEETROOT

Beetroot is so regularly maltreated and mistreated, bullied and brutalized that it must be fast attaining vegetable sainthood. How can people massacre this king amongst vegetables with such odious frequency and conviction? Beetroot cooked plainly, the vinegar bottle banished from sight, has a sweet, nutty and unique flavour. Not so long ago, I dished up a salad of beetroot with fromage frais and chives to two surprisingly polite friends. I could almost see their noses wrinkling in distaste as they gingerly took a single slice each. Five minutes away in the kitchen, and I returned to an all but empty dish and two complete converts.

There are three ways to cook beetroot. Before you begin, clean them, trim the stalks close but not right down, cut the root off a short distance from the ball so that the juice does not leach out. They can then be simmered in lightly salted water, which will take 1–2 hours. The flavour is even better if they are baked, wrapped tightly in foil, for 3–4 hours in a low oven. By far the fastest way, and almost as good as baking them, is microwaving. Pierce the skin of each beetroot in three or four places, then wrap them individually in cling-film. Cook them on full power, for approximately 8 minutes for 225 g (8 oz). Beetroot are done when the skin scrapes easily away from the root. In all cases, the smaller the beetroot, the better the flavour. Smaller beetroot also cook more evenly in the microwave.

Once they are cooked, you can have a field day. They like the fruitiness of tart apples or oranges, the sharpness of lemon, soured cream or fromage frais, the freshness of herbs like parsley, chives or dill, the saltiness of anchovies, or cheese, the crispness of baked breadcrumbs or fried bread, the softness of potatoes and hard-boiled eggs. Eat them hot with butter, lemon juice and dill. Bake them alternated with slices of apple, dotted with butter, covered, just long enough to heat through. Turn them into a salad, by slicing and dressing with vinaigrette while hot. Eke out with other vegetables, like potatoes, celery, onion, or with apples or oranges when cold, arranging the ingredients elegantly in a large shallow dish so that the beetroot does not bleed messily over the rest. Similarly, if you are serving them hot or cold with soured cream, dollop the cream on top, rather than mixing it in.

If using beetroot for soups or to flavour and colour a stock, be sure to add a good squirt of lemon juice to prevent the rosy colour deteriorating to a dull brown.

Look out, too, for golden beetroot, which have a flesh of rich golden-ochre. I think they do taste a little different, sweeter, purer, a mite better, though this may be because I have only ever eaten them when tiny, no more than 4 cm (1½ inches) in diameter.

## SWEET POTATO

There were few culinary matters that my mother and I disagreed about, but sweet potatoes were one of them. She insisted that white-fleshed sweet potatoes were nicer than orange-fleshed. I would go for the orange-fleshed any day.

Orange-fleshed sweet potatoes, clad in pinkish purple skins, have a densely packed, buttery texture and a sweet chestnutty flavour. White-fleshed are mealier and milder. Both can be cooked like plain potatoes, with one exception. Much of their sweetness leaches out into the water when boiled, leaving them dull and water-sodden. Better to bake them, serving them in their jackets with salted butter, or mashing the flesh to a purée with butter, milk or cream. Mashed sweet potato mixed evenly with half its volume of unsweetened apple sauce is a welcome change. Though it sounds a little strange, mashed potatoes make a delicious topping for an otherwise traditional fish pie. Sweet potatoes make wonderful chips, deep-fried or better still, tossed in oil, seasoned and baked in the oven, turning occasionally to caramelize the outside evenly.

For more involved recipes turn to Caribbean and South American cookbooks, or to North America, especially Louisiana, where they are often known as yams, which they are not. Do not dismiss American recipes for sweet potato baked with extra sugar and spices, or "candied" in sugar syrup, to be served along with the main course. Yes, they are very sweet (the quantity of sugar can usually be reduced by a third to a half) but they work, and can taste marvellous.

There are many ways of serving sweet potatoes as a pudding, too. In America sweet potato pie may be dished up in tandem with pumpkin pie at Thanksgiving. Though sweet potato puddings have a tendency to be heavy and stodgy, they are a happily comforting indulgence on a cold winter's night.

## SALSIFY
(Oyster plant, Vegetable oyster)
## and SCORZONERA
(Black Salsify)

The long rods of salsify and scorzonera are so similar in taste that even experts would be hard-pushed to tell the difference. Though they are not varieties of the same plant, the only noticeable difference is the colour of their skin, salsify's being yellowy white, scorzonera's nigh on black. Just to confuse the issue, what is now sold as salsify is nearly always black-skinned scorzonera.

ROOT VEGETABLES – CLOCKWISE FROM TOP RIGHT: JICAMA, SALSIFY, SWEET POTATO, CELERIAC, BEETROOT

The health-conscious will reheat them for a minute or so in water, which is fine, but I would advise the rest of you to go for something rather richer as a special treat. Reheat them in butter, sizzling until just patched with brown, and sprinkle with fresh *fines herbes*, or nutmeg. They are heavenly finished in cream (add a generous slurp to the pan once browned), or partnered with Hollandaise sauce. Salsify fritters offer a pleasing contrast of crisp and waxy textures. Salsify vinaigrette (see Seakale, page 104) is a delight.

## JICAMA
(Yam bean)

The dull, tan exterior of the jicama looks far from promising. You would never guess that this covers crisp, juicy flesh, with the sweetness of freshly picked young peas. The fibrous skin peels off easily, and then all that you need do is slice the jicama thinly, dress it with a squeeze of lime or lemon juice, and maybe a sprinkling of chilli and cumin, and it is ready to eat. It can be cooked, but I think that on the whole this is a waste. The only time I would heat it through would be in a mixed Chinese stir-fry, giving it just enough time to hot up, but not enough to destroy its freshness. In fact, it is similar enough to water chestnuts to replace them in Chinese recipes, ideally in those where the cooking time is brief.

Jicamas are a favourite in South America, but the best place to find them in this country is in Chinese food shops, where they will be sold as "yam beans", a confusing name since they are neither yam nor bean. Choose the smallest ones – as they grow larger the flesh becomes more starchy and less interesting – and reject any that are soft, or bruised. Uncut, they will keep happily in the refrigerator for a couple of weeks. Once cut, they should be used up quickly, although, tightly wrapped in clingfilm, they will hold out in the refrigerator for a day or so.

Nomenclature aside, I suspect that many people are put off by the earthy appearance, or just plain mystified. They should not be – salsify and scorzonera are easy to prepare, and even easier to eat. They have a smooth, soft texture and a delicate flavour which hints at globe artichoke. Peeling them raw is a terrible waste of time and vegetable. Just scrub them well, slice off top and tail, and cut

them into manageable lengths – 5 cm (6 inches) or so – as the pan of lightly salted and acidulated water comes to the boil. If, for whatever reason, you divide them into shorter pieces, drop them into acidulated water as you work to prevent discoloration. Simmer the salsify until just tender. This can take as little as 5 minutes, or it may take up to 30. Drain, run under the cold tap and then strip off the skins.

# LOTUS ROOT CRISPS

*Designer crisps? Well, maybe, but none the worse for that. Lotus root crisps are more than just a decorative fancy, since they have a pleasing nutty taste into the bargain. They should be eaten, as should any type of crisp, fresh from the pan – do not leave them hanging around.*

**lotus root**
**oil for deep frying**
**salt, or salt and spice mixture such as the one used in the Jicama salad (page 121)**

Peel the lotus root and slice into cartwheels about 2 mm (1/16 inch) thick. Drop into lightly acidulated water as you work. Either deep-fry the slices in a proper deep fryer (best if you are cooking them in any quantity), electric for preference, or heat a 2 cm (3/4 inch) layer of oil in a frying pan. The temperature of the oil should be 190°C/375°F, i.e. when a cube of bread takes 40 seconds to brown.

Whilst the oil is heating, drain the lotus root well, and dry thoroughly on absorbent kitchen paper or a clean tea towel. Fry in small batches, turning as they brown, until golden brown on both sides. Drain briefly on absorbent kitchen paper, and sprinkle with salt, or salt and spices. The crisps crisp up as they cool, so serve them when they are warm, or cold, rather than really hot.

# STIR-FRIED BITTER GOURD WITH CHICKEN

*The thin slices of bitter gourd provide a welcome but not overwhelming contrast to the richness of wind-dried sausages. Or is it the other way round? Either way, this is a good introduction to the strange charm of the bitter gourd.*

**Serves 4**

MARINADE:
**1 tablespoon dark soy sauce**
**1 tablespoon rice wine or dry sherry**
**2 teaspoons rice vinegar, or cider vinegar**
**pepper**

**6 boned chicken thighs, skinned and thinly sliced**
**225 g (8 oz) courgettes, sliced 5 mm (1/4 inch) thick**
**1–2 bitter gourds 50–70 g (2–3 oz), halved, seeded and blanched**
**2 tablespoons oil**
**2 Chinese wind-dried sausages (liver or plain pork), sliced 5 mm (1/4 inch) thick**
**2 garlic cloves, thinly sliced**
**1 × 2.5 cm (1 inch) fresh root ginger, peeled and cut into matchsticks**
**1 green chilli, seeded, and thinly sliced**
**2 teaspoons sesame oil**
SAUCE:
**2 teaspoons cornflour**
**4 tablespoons stock or water**
**1 tablespoon light muscovado sugar**
**1/4 teaspoon five-spice powder**

Whisk together the marinade ingredients, and pour over the chicken. Stir to coat evenly then leave for 30 minutes.

Spread the courgette slices out in a colander and sprinkle lightly with salt. Leave for half an hour, then rinse and pat dry. Slice the blanched bitter gourd into very thin semi-circles.

Heat the oil in a large wok until smoking. While it heats, take the chicken out of its marinade and pat it dry. Reserve the remaining marinade. Add the garlic, ginger and chilli to the oil and stir-fry for 30 seconds. Add the chicken and courgettes and continue stir-frying for about 1 minute. Now add the gourd and the sausage. Stir-fry until all the ingredients are lightly browned.

Mix together the sauce ingredients and add the reserved marinade. Pour the sauce mixture into the wok. Keep stirring as the sauce sizzles and thickens. Draw off the heat when the ingredients are nicely glazed with sauce. Sprinkle with the sesame oil, and serve with rice or noodles.

OPPOSITE, TOP: LOTUS ROOT CRISPS; BOTTOM: STIR-FRIED BITTER GOURD WITH CHICKEN

concentrate on. A squeeze of lemon or, better still, lime juice brings out the full fresh flavour. I have tried recipes that involve puréeing papaya, but this process seems to destroy a good deal of the flavour and texture.

Like the mango, papaya is delicious partnered with salty, smoky cured meats, or in chilli-hot salsas. Or try alternate slices of papaya, with segments of grapefruit and/or avocado, dress with vinaigrette, or simply lemon juice, and a dust of cayenne, ground cumin and coriander. The flavour survives the rigours of cooking.

Papaya does have one very particular property. It contains an enzyme called *papain*, a natural meat tenderizer. Try wrapping thin pieces of meat (chicken breast is extremely good this way) in papaya skins, or sandwich between thinly sliced papaya (add grated fresh ginger and chopped garlic for extra flavour), and leave overnight, then brush with a little oil and grill. Serve well seasoned with fresh slices of papaya, or a salsa. *Papain* is, unfortunately, quite partial to a slurp of protein-packed gelatine. It is a dead loss trying to embed cubes of papaya in jelly, as the jelly will never set (the same goes for uncooked pineapple).

Green, unripe papaya can be used to make chutneys, or steamed and served as a vegetable, with plenty of salt and pepper.

## CARAMBOLA
(Starfruit)

This looks like a small, translucent yellow rugby ball with long wedges gouged out of it. Sliced, it falls into elegant star shapes, hence the name starfruit. Pick fruits that are firm and unblemished – a fine trace of brown along the ridges is acceptable, but more than that and it is moving past its prime.

The taste of the raw carambola is sharp, citrus-like, juicy and pleasing, if not exceptional. Many people who have only ever eaten it raw assume that its greatest attribute is its pretty shape. They are wrong. The full scented flavour develops when it has been sliced and lightly poached in a sugar syrup until just tender, but still whole. Add the cooked slices to a fruit salad, along with a little of their poaching syrup. Save the rest of the syrup and use it for making fruit sauces, sprinkling on sponge cakes or finger biscuits for fruit charlottes, trifles or other puddings. Or use it in cool drinks, diluted with sparkling mineral water, perhaps with a shot of gin, vodka or what-have-you for a stunning cocktail.

## KIWIFRUIT
(Chinese gooseberry)

The fortunes of kiwifruit are like those of many a pop star. A meteoric rise to fame, a few years at the top with endless appearances on any conceivable excuse, then boredom set in, and the kiwifruit was terribly *passé*.

All very unfair. The kiwi is not a star amongst fruit, but it is certainly no dud either. In the enthusiasm for this new, decoratively green fruit, it was madly over- and mis-used, and its true value got lost along the way.

If you have dismissed kiwifruit as dull and boring, then try again. Do not mess around with them, because they cannot take it. Enjoy them as they are. They should simply be halved and eaten with a teaspoon, cool and refreshing with a gentle fragrance.

There are only two other ways in which I use them. When they are very cheap, I make a sorbet, enlivened with a dash of Marsala. Instead of throwing away the skins, I use them like papaya skins, to tenderize meat. Do not try to incorporate raw kiwifruit into jellies set with gelatine. You end up with a pool of liquid. Note, too, that kiwi curdles milk and thin cream.

## PASSIONFRUIT

The passion of "passion fruit" is of the religious kind and has nothing to do with the fruit itself. Spanish priests in South America read the flowers as a representation of Christ's Passion on the cross. The nails were symbolized by the three styles, the crown of thorns by the filaments, Christ's wounds by the stamens, the apostles by the petals.

The hard, egg-sized wrinkled shell of the purple passionfruit looks distinctly unpromising, and the mass of yellowish grey pulp inside is no more attractive. But who cares about that, when they discover the intense sharp perfume of the juice. The translucent pulp clings tightly to small crunchy black seeds, and can be eaten neat, but that is rather a waste. Two mouthfuls and it has gone. Better to extend the flavour to the full by using it in jellies, mousses, fools, ices, and sauces.

To extract the maximum amount of juice, scoop the pulp into a small pan with a spoonful of sugar. Heat gently until warm, but not boiling then press through a sieve. Reserve the seeds to scatter over the pudding as a decoration. Passionfruit and orange juice are natural bedfellows, so mix the two together to make a scented drink, to use in desserts, or to make the best possible fruit curd (substitute for lemon juice in lemon curd recipes).

## GRENADILLO
(Granadillo)

The orange-brown grenadillo is a larger form of passionfruit. It has a smooth, hard round shell, and a stiff stalk, just like a *maraca*. The name means "little pomegranate". If you tend to enjoy your passionfruit flesh neat, this is the one to go for since each one carries a greater volume of flesh, with a slightly less concentrated flavour.

## KARUBA
(Banana passionfruit)

The Brazilian karuba, or banana passionfruit is a rare find. Pale green, with a downy covering, it is about 7.5 cm (3 inches) long and cylindrical. My one encounter with these was in Fauchon's in Paris. There they had sieved the flesh, and whizzed the juice with milk to make the most sophisticated of milk shakes.

## TAMARILLO
(Tree tomato)

With smooth plum-red skin, and tapering egg-shape, the tamarillo glows like a precious jewel. A strange fruit, barely sweet, with an unusual flavour, aromatic, tomato-ish, maybe with a hint of apricot or coconut.

Do not try eating a tamarillo until it gives slightly when pressed, and even then avoid the skin. The tannic acid in an underripe tamarillo dries the mouth faster than a high-speed hair dryer.

I usually halve the fruit lengthways and scoop out the juicy, soft, scarlet and yellow flesh with a spoon, but they can also be used in salads, savoury or sweet, and cooked. To peel them, advisable before incorporating them in most dishes, cover with boiling water and stand for 30–60 seconds to loosen the skin. At one fashionable London restaurant they dredge halved tamarillos (unpeeled) with sugar and grill them for pudding. Reduce the sugar to a scant sprinkling and they go just as well with meat.

# BLUEBERRY FRANGIPANE TART

*Any soft fruit that takes well to being cooked, such as blueberries, mulberries, or raspberries, can be used in this almondy tart, at its best served warm, but almost as delicious cold.*

**Serves 6-8**

**225 g (8 oz) shortcrust pastry**
**icing sugar**
FILLING:
**75 g (3 oz) butter**
**75 g (3 oz) vanilla sugar**
**1 egg**
**1 egg yolk**
**2 teaspoons lemon juice**
**25 g (1 oz) flour**
**90 g (3½ oz) ground almonds**
**450 g (1 lb) blueberries**

Line a 24–25 cm (9½–10 inch) pie tin with the pastry. Rest for half an hour in the refrigerator. Place a baking sheet in the oven and preheat the oven to hot (200°C, 400°F, Gas Mark 6). Prick the pastry base with a fork.

Make the filling. Cream the butter with the vanilla sugar until light and fluffy. Gradually beat in the egg and yolk, then the lemon juice. Stir in the flour and almonds. Spread just under half the filling on the pastry base. Cover with the blueberries, and then spoon the remaining filling over the blueberries. Do not worry if it does not cover too evenly, as it will spread out as it cooks.

Bake the tart on the hot baking sheet for 10 minutes. Reduce the heat to moderate (180°C, 350°F, Gas Mark 4) and cook for a further 15 minutes until the almond cream is just set. Dredge the surface with icing sugar and return to the oven for 10–15 minutes until the tart is nicely browned. Serve warm or cold, with cream or ice cream.

## Variation: *TAMARILLO FRANGIPANE TART*

Replace the blueberries with 5 ripe tamarillos. Pour boiling water over the tamarillos. Stand for 30–60 seconds then drain and peel. Halve the tamarillos lengthwise, then slice thinly across the width. Arrange each sliced half on the frangipane cream, like the petals of a flower. Press the halves down, fanning out the slices. Cover with the remaining frangipane cream and bake as above.

# MISSION FIG, WALNUT & RUM FOOL

*Ingredients for this rich and creamy fool cover the whole range of this chapter: dried fruit, nuts and the juice of fresh citrus fruit.*

**Serves 4-6**

**225 g (8 oz) mission figs**
**2 tablespoons rum**
**1 tablespoon lemon juice**
**300 ml (½ pint) double cream**
**100 g (4 oz) walnuts**

Snip the woody stem ends off the figs. Place in a bowl and pour over enough water to cover. Soak for 4 hours. Liquidize or process the figs until smooth with a generous 150 ml (¼ pint) of their soaking water, the rum and lemon juice.

Spread the walnuts out on a baking tray and bake in a hot oven (200°–230°C, 400°–450°F, Gas Mark 6–8) for 4–10 minutes until they turn a shade darker. Shake them in a metal sieve over a sheet of newspaper to get rid of any papery flakes of skin, then chop them roughly and leave to cool. Whip the cream until it holds its shape, and fold in the fig purée with the walnuts. Taste and add more rum or lemon juice, or a little sugar, if necessary.

OPPOSITE: THE FRANGIPANE TART MADE WITH HALVED AND SLICED TAMARILLOS

# DRIED FRUIT

Glancing along the shelves of the average supermarket, you might well assume that the only fruits it is possible to dry are grapes, plums, apricots and figs. You would be wrong; most fruits can be dried, and in many countries the choice is wide.

In New York I bought dried strawberries, kiwi, blueberries, cranberries and bing cherries. In the market in Tel Aviv, I found dried sour cherries and apricot and pineapple "leathers". A little bit of leg-work has unearthed sources of unusual dried fruit on home territory as well. Wholefood shops have by far the widest selection, and Middle Eastern delicatessens come a close second.

Some dried fruits are dried naturally out in the sun, whilst others are trundled through hot-air tunnels. "Evaporated" fruits retain a residual moisture of around 25 per cent, which leaves them soft and ready to eat straight from the package. "Dehydrated" fruits have precious little moisture left, and will need a good long soak before they are edible. Most "evaporated" fruits will have been treated before drying with sulphur dioxide to prevent browning and give longer shelf-life. Final dressings of vegetable oil or glucose syrup may be applied to give them an extra gloss and prevent any further loss of moisture.

## Storage

Store dried fruits in air-tight containers to prevent loss of residual moisture – i.e. so that they do not become as tough as old boots – and to keep them safely out of reach of fruit-flies and moths. If the worst comes to the worst and you discover unwelcome visitors having a high old time in your fruit, you will have to discard the whole lot, and rinse the container thoroughly with boiling water before using it again for storage.

However air-tight you think your container is, keep it in a dry, cool cupboard, well away from the steam of the kettle or stove. You do not want your fruit to dry out, but nor do you want them to turn mouldy.

## Using Dried Fruit

I eat more dried fruit straight from the packet than I do cooked, sprinkled over cereal, in fruit salads, or simply mixed with Greek yoghurt or fromage frais for pudding.

To soften up most dried fruit it is enough merely to soak them for a few hours in water, or some other appropriate liquid. As long as they are not leathery dry you can skip this stage and simply simmer them until tender. Use just enough water to cover, and a few spices or strips of orange zest, then sweeten to taste when they are tender. If there is a vast quantity of liquid left swilling round, scoop out the fruit and boil the liquid until syrupy. Pour over the fruit and leave to cool. Even better, simmer dark fruit in red wine, or lighter coloured fruit in a sweet dessert wine such as Muscadelle. Whatever cooking medium you use, keep an eye on the fruit as they cook, and whip them off the heat before they collapse to a mush.

Softened dried fruit, soaked or cooked, can be puréed to make sauces or a base for an ice cream or mousse. The concentrated fruity taste, often balanced by a pleasing acidity, means that dried fruits go terrifically well with all kinds of meat, too.

## HUNZA APRICOTS

Hunza apricots look fairly insignificant – mousey beige, the size of a peach stone – and taste anything but. They are grown in Kashmir, spread out to dry on the corrugated iron roofs of houses, then transported along the Korkoram highway on the first step of their journey to the wholefood shops of the West.

Hunza apricots are simplicity itself to deal with. Plump them up merely by soaking for 3 or 4 hours, or by simmering in just enough water to cover for 5 minutes or so, the method I prefer. There is no need to add sugar, but a dash of lemon juice brings out the flavour. Serve them hot or cold and wait for the round of applause.

If time allows, extract and crack the stones, and add the almondy kernels to the cooked apricots.

## UNSULPHURED DRIED APRICOTS

Unsulphured dried apricots have a deep toffee-ish taste, quite unlike that of sulphured apricots. The colour, too, is different, a dark chestnut-brown. Only buy them from wholefood shops with a fast turnover. Stored in bad conditions for too long, they develop an unpleasant fermented undertaste. Eat them raw, or use them as you would ordinary dried apricots, compensating for their lack of acidity with a squeeze of lemon juice.

## MUSCAT RAISINS

Just as Muscat grapes, with their deep musky sweetness, are the choicest of grapes, so plump, silky-skinned Muscat raisins are the choicest of raisins.

Spanish Muscat raisins are often dried on the stalk in their original bunches, arriving in Britain around Christmas time. I search them out in smart delicatessens, particularly Spanish ones, to savour with after-dinner coffee.

CLOCKWISE, FROM TOP LEFT: UNSULPHURED DRIED APRICOTS, MUSCAT RAISINS, FRUIT LEATHERS, HUNZA APRICOTS, DRIED PEARS

## FRUIT LEATHERS

Fruit "leathers" are thin pliable sheets of dried fruit purée. The commonest is apricot, but I have found wonderful pineapple and raspberry "leathers" as well. They have a minimal residual moisture content so keep extremely well. Tear off strips to chew as a snack, or cut into shapes with scissors or a sharp knife to decorate cakes and puddings. Roughly chopped, and simmered with a little water they quickly collapse to give a thick delicious purée.

## DRIED PEARS

Biting into a dried pear is like sinking your teeth into the most delicious slightly chewy fudge, sweet, but not too sweet, with a concentrated waft of pear taste. Dried pears, like no-soak apricots and prunes, are "evaporated" fruit, which means that they still hold some 25 per cent or so of their original moisture. Whether you eat them as they are, or use them in cooking, there is no need to soak them to make them palatable.

You can use them in cakes and puddings, or simmer in water and lemon juice, or white wine to make a compote. Cooked and puréed they make a delicious sauce, savoury or sweet. They go marvellously well with meat, too. I often use them in stuffings for poultry, or pork, or add to casseroles. Try simmering them in stock to serve alongside a pork roast.

## MISSION FIGS

Mission figs are small and black with an intense dark, almost burnt flavour, quite different from that of ordinary dried figs.

They are moist enough to be used straight from the packet in cakes and pastries (snip the woody stem off first). I find, as with most figs, that simmering in water or water and sugar draws much of their flavour out, leaving a fruit that is all crunchy seeds and no taste. So, if you do want to soften them up (to make a purée, perhaps as a base for a sauce, or ice cream) it is better just to soak them for four or five hours.

MISSION FIGS

MEDJOOL DATES

## MEDJOOL DATES

I have one gripe about medjool dates: they make all other dried dates pale into insignificance. Plump and succulent, they have a voluptuous buttery texture, and a dense brown sugar taste. You may come across them neatly boxed, or loose and rumpled, but none the worse for that.

The first arrivals in mid-November are terrifyingly expensive, and the price only eases marginally as Christmas approaches. Console yourself with the thought that they are so rich that you can get away with only two per person. In fact, if you offer them as part of a selection of *petits fours*, one each will not look too mean.

## DRIED CRANBERRIES

You could not eat fresh cranberries raw. Well, you could but it would not be much fun. It would be fair to assume, then, that in a dried cranberry the bitterness would be concentrated, making them good only for cooking with a heap of sugar. Not so. The dried cranberries I have eaten have been delicious just as they were, tart but not unpleasantly so, with an intense fruitiness that is most appealing. I made a sauce with them, which was good, and used them in stuffings which was better, but in the end, I preferred them raw, dry, and chewy.

DRIED CRANBERRIES

## DRIED WHITE MULBERRIES

A rare find, and one worth watching out for. Dried white mulberries are occasionally stocked by very superior wholefood shops. They look like large, off-white knobbly raisins, but have the musky sweetness of fresh mulberries. There is not a lot you can do with them apart from eat them raw. When cooked they collapse to an unpleasing tasteless mush. I usually mix them with pistachio nuts and pine kernels to make a sophisticated version of "nuts 'n raisins", to nibble at with drinks, or to give away as presents.

Before you do anything at all with them, they must be cleaned of grit and whatever else. Place them in a large bowl and cover generously with water. Let them sit for a few minutes, so that any grit has time to settle onto the bottom. Scoop out the mulberries, and dry them on kitchen paper. If you are not going to eat them immediately, dry them more thoroughly, by spreading out on a baking sheet, and leaving in a cool oven for 15 minutes or so.

## ELVAS PLUMS

Portuguese Elvas plums are candied and semi-dried greengages, so they do not truly belong in this section, but I could not bear to leave them out altogether.

They are made around the medieval towns of Elvas and Estremoz close by the Spanish border. The ripe greengages are picked in late July and August, and taken to one of the many farmhouse "factories". There they will be lightly cooked, ladled into wide earthenware bowls and left to steep in a sugary syrup for three months. Some are sold locally at this stage, and the rest are laid out to dry on wooden slats, before being packed away, often by hand, into charming little boxes and baskets.

With perfect timing, the year's crop of Elvas plums are ready for distribution in November.

## DRIED SOUR CHERRIES

I bought a big bagful of dried sour cherries in the market in Tel Aviv. Throughout the Middle East they are cheap and plentiful, but not so elsewhere. One Middle Eastern shop I know in London has them from time to time, but by no means regularly. Luckily, they last well in an airtight container. My Israeli horde kept me going for two years!

Shiny, black and wrinkled, like over-sized currants, they have a marvellous sour fruity flavour. I rather like them raw, but they will not be everyone's cup of tea. To enjoy them at their best, they need to be soaked for 24 hours, then simmered in their soaking water for 10 minutes until they are plump and tender. To serve as a pudding, add sugar to taste, and maybe a stick of cinnamon before simmering. Better still, use the powerfully flavoured cooking liquid as a sauce with lamb (see the recipe on page 145), pork and game. Try braising a joint of pork with the soaked cherries and their liquid (top it up with extra water if needed).

## DRIED SWEET CHERRIES
(e.g. dried Bing cherries)

Not quite as good as dried sour cherries, but not far off, and they may be easier to find. They can be substituted for sour cherries in savoury dishes, but cry out for a generous dash of lemon juice to balance the flavours.

For puddings and pie fillings, cook as for sour cherries, but go easy on the sugar. Cherries and almonds have a natural affinity. Try serving stewed dried cherries with a creamy cinnamon-scented slow-baked rice pudding, scattering toasted almonds over the top. Sounds homely, tastes divine.

## DRIED PAPAYA

Translucent pink cubes of dried papaya are so pretty that they are hard to resist. They are usually sugared, with a soft, slightly chewy texture – delicious sweets all on their own.

I use them, diced, like glacéed cherries or angelica, but only in dishes where both flavour and colour show to full effect. Try adding to simple cakes and muffins, or folding into a cream cheese mousse, or uncooked cheesecake.

DRIED PAPAYA

DRIED SWEET CHERRIES

## DRIED MANGO

Thin leathery strips of dried mango need at least three hours soaking before they become useable. Once they have plumped up the flavour is remarkably similar to that of fresh mango. Not quite as fragrant and subtle, of course, but there is no doubt whatsoever that they are the same fruit. Their big plus is that they retain much of this flavour when cooked, unlike fresh ripe mango. Reconstituted dried mango makes a much better chutney or jam, and as an added bonus is less messy to prepare, and less expensive too.

DRIED MANGO

CLOCKWISE, FROM TOP LEFT: COOKED WHOLE CHESTNUTS, UNSWEETENED CHESTNUT PURÉE, MARRONS GLACÉS, CHESTNUT FLOUR, SWEETENED CHESTNUT PURÉE

*Marrons Glacés* Luxurious, sweet and sensationally rich, the most perfect of all glacéed fruits. Treat them with due respect, serving just a few per person, with strong black coffee as a counter-balance. None but the truly gluttonous will consume more than three at the outside. There are plenty of recipes incorporating broken chips of *marrons glacés* but it does seem churlish to smash them up. However, if you do have just a few left over this may be a practical way to stretch them further.

*Whole Chestnuts in Syrup (canned)* Essentially a wet version of *marrons glacés*, and very nearly as expensive. Two or three of these per person, served in small bowls or glasses with a little of their syrup spooned over the top, a dash of kirsch, and a swirl of whipped cream, make a swish, quick pudding.

*Broken Marrons Glacés (in tubs)* Like off-cuts of smoked salmon, they cost about a third less than perfect whole *marrons*

*glacés*, and keep almost indefinitely, to be used in puddings and chocolates.

*Chestnut Flour* Dried chestnuts ground down to a fine powder. The flour is used in northern Italy and Tuscany to make thick porridges, fritters and sweet cakes called Castagnaccio, flavoured with rosemary, and olive oil. Chestnut pancakes, made by substituting chestnut flour for plain flour, are very good with a savoury filling.

## COCONUT

Emerging from a shady street into some heat-swollen piazza in Italy, one is occasionally charmed by the sight of a coconut "fountain". Tiered circular basins, rising one out of the other, carrying fragments of fresh coconut floating in a pond of water, glinting in the sun. Time for a break, relaxing on a bench chewing a piece of the crisp, cool white flesh.

Cracking open a whole coconut is not child's play. A workman's vice and tools make it a good deal easier. The coconut can be clamped firmly in place, with the three "eyes" upward. Drill holes through two of the eyes. Otherwise, get a friend to hold the coconut steady, and pierce the holes with a sturdy skewer. Drain out the coconut water to drink chilled. Now bash the coconut hard around its middle with a very heavy hammer and break it in two and then into pieces. Ease the white flesh away from the shell and peel off the thin brown skin with a vegetable peeler.

When buying coconuts, choose one that is heavy for its size. When shaken close to your ear, you should be able to hear the juice sloshing around inside. Nearly all coconuts that reach us are mature. I have never been lucky enough to try young green coconut, but I gather that it is a marvellous treat.

So for the time being I shall have to put up with the occasional fully ripened coconut, which is treat enough. Add slivers to fruit salads, or lightly spiced salads of shellfish, or chicken, and fruit. Grated, it can be used in any recipe which includes desiccated coconut, and will give a heightened coconut scent and moistness. And then there are recipes, like the American "Southern Ambrosia" where only fresh grated or shaved coconut will do – layer slices of peeled orange with grated fresh coconut and icing sugar in a glass bowl. Chill for a few hours before serving. I did once try it with desiccated coconut and it was like eating sawdust.

Coconuts are an everyday ingredient throughout the tropics, used predominantly in savoury dishes, often with chillies, a match made in heaven. Caribbean stews and soups are often laced with coconut, and many of the subtle aromatic curries of Thailand and Malaysia are simmered in coconut milk. I sometimes use coconut milk instead of milk in Western-style puddings. It makes a sensational custard, runny or baked, and marvellous *crème brulée*.

## COCONUT MILK

Coconut milk is not the liquid inside the coconut. It is extracted from the flesh of the coconut. You can buy it ready-made in cans or frozen but it is simple enough to make at home from fresh, desiccated or creamed coconut.

Grate the flesh of half a fresh coconut into a bowl. Cover with 300 ml (½ pint) of boiling water and let it cool. Tip into a fine sieve and squeeze to extract as much liquid as possible. The process can be repeated but the second extraction will be much thinner. To make the milk from desiccated coconut the method is exactly the same. Use 225 g (8 oz) desiccated coconut to

300 ml (½ pint) of water.

Creamed coconut is sold in hard blocks. Grate or chop 75 g (3 oz) creamed coconut and dilute with 300 ml (½ pint) of hot water. Alternatively, it can be added straight to the simmering liquid in the pan towards the end of cooking.

Coconut milk may separate if left to stand; just give it a quick stir and it will be as right as rain. It does not keep well.

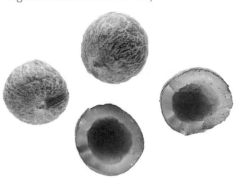

## MINIATURE COCONUTS

The pack of woody marbles had no label on it at all. Inveterately curious, I bought them anyway. They were tiny whole coconuts, shelled so that you could eat them straight from the box. They are a little too hard to make them useable in, say, a fruit salad, but they are fun to chew neat as a snack, or at the end of a meal.

# CABBAGE WITH COCONUT MILK AND SPICES

*This is a quick way of dressing up plain white cabbage. Use just one chilli for a mild hint of heat, two for something a mite more punchy.*

**Serves 6**

**half a head of white cabbage, shredded**
**300 ml (½ pint) coconut milk**
**4 allspice berries, bruised**
**1–2 green chillies, seeded and finely chopped**
**2 teaspoons caraway seeds**
**salt**

Place all the ingredients in a pan and bring up to the boil (the cabbage will produce more liquid, so do not worry that there seems very little). Cover and simmer gently for five minutes. Remove the lid, stir, and simmer for a further 10–15 minutes, stirring frequently until the cabbage is just tender, and most of the liquid has been absorbed.

# HORCHATA DE CHUFAS

*On a hot day, a glass of creamy* horchata de chufas *is a real reviver. I prefer it not too sweet, but add more sugar if you wish.*

**Makes 900 ml (1½ pints)**

**225 g (8 oz) tiger nuts**
**75 g (3 oz) sugar**
**finely grated zest of ½ lemon**

Wash the nuts well in several changes of water. Soak in water for at least 3 hours, or overnight. Drain. Liquidize or process with enough water to give a fine paste. Mix with the sugar, lemon zest and 1 litre (1¾ pints) of water. Leave to stand for 4 hours. Strain through a muslin-lined sieve, taste and add more sugar, if necessary. Chill until ice-cold.

# PECAN & FENNEL SEED BISCUITS

*These biscuits go well with cheese or pâtés, or can be used as canapé bases. Unused dough can be kept until needed in the freezer.*

**Makes approx. 18 biscuits**

**100 g (4 oz) 100% wholemeal flour**
**225 g (8 oz) plain flour**
**½ teaspoon baking powder**
**½ teaspoon salt**
**50 g (2 oz) butter**
**1 tablespoon fennel seeds**
**50 g (2 oz) shelled pecans, finely chopped**
**1 egg, beaten**

Mix the flours, baking powder and salt. Rub in the butter until the mixture resembles fine breadcrumbs. Stir in the fennel seeds and the nuts. Add just enough water to form a dough. Pat into a 7.5 cm (3 inch) thick sausage shape, wrap in clingfilm or foil and chill until firm (or freeze until needed).

Dip the blade of a sharp knife into very hot water, dry quickly and slice as many 5 mm (¼ inch) thick discs as you want biscuits. Warm the knife again in the water if necessary. Lay the biscuits on a baking sheet, prick with a fork and brush with beaten egg. Bake in a moderate oven (180°C, 350°F, Gas Mark 4) for 12 minutes.

MACADAMIA NUTS (ABOVE), PECANS

# BUTTERSCOTCH NUT TARTLETS

*Throw caution and calorie-counting to the wind. These tartlets are thoroughly irresistible, and furiously fattening. Vary the mixture of nuts as you wish, although the combination of macadamias, almonds and pecans is very good.*

**Serves 8**

**350 g (12 oz) shortcrust pastry**
FILLING:
**175 g (6 oz) light brown sugar**
**175 g (6 oz) unsalted butter**
**50 ml (2 fl oz) double cream**
**25 g (1 oz) plain flour, sifted**
**100 g (4 oz) macadamia nuts, coarsely chopped**
**50 g (2 oz) almonds, coarsely chopped**
**50 g (2 oz) pecans, coarsely chopped**
**50 g (2 oz) hazelnuts, coarsely chopped**

Roll the pastry out thinly, and line eight 9 cm (3½ inch) tartlet tins. Rest for half an hour, then prick the bases with a fork, line with greaseproof paper and weigh down with baking beans. Bake in a moderately hot oven (190°C, 375°F, Gas Mark 5) for 10 minutes. Remove the beans and paper and return the pastry cases to the oven for 5 minutes to dry out.

Heat the butter gently with the sugar in a pan large enough to take all the filling ingredients. Stir constantly, and bring up to the boil. Add the cream, and the sifted flour and beat well until evenly mixed. Stir in the nuts and bring back up to the boil. Spoon into the pastry cases. Return to the oven for 10 minutes. Leave to cool and serve with whipped cream, or vanilla ice cream.

BUTTERSCOTCH NUT TARTLETS

I am not complaining. It took me a while to get any further than rice and chickpeas. But slowly, I have worn down my foolish resistance to anything with a reputation for puritanical healthiness. It took some time for me to realize that wholesome healthiness does not exclude the possibility of enjoyment. Not entirely my fault – "whole grain" or "lentil bakes" of a certain type are not amongst the great dishes of the world, and boy, do they lie heavy on the stomach. Still, step by step, I have worked my way through the grains and pulses on offer at my local healthfood shop. I have brought back others from trips abroad, in Europe and further afield. What a choice there is. An inexhaustible supply, it seems.

Both pulses and grains range from the pleasant, warming and homely, to the downright delicious. I have picked out more grains than pulses for inclusion here, not because I think them superior, but because they have suffered greater neglect. Rice is about the only grain we turn to regularly as an accompaniment to our meals. Too often, it is white rice of abysmally poor quality, that merely serves to sop up juices and pad out the stomach, with no individuality or character of its own. Basmatti rice gets an occasional look in, and, when it does, stands head and shoulders above the common crowd. Thai fragrant rice has perhaps the purest, clearest rice flavour. Poor little millet seeds, good for nothing but the budgie, are undoubtedly superior to soggy dull rice. Buckwheat, whole barley, or wheat, none of them tricky to handle, are interesting, pleasing alternatives.

Flour is generally taken to mean wheat flour, but any grain or pulse can be ground to a fine powder. Wheat is unique in that it forms gluten, and lots of it, when combined with water. Without gluten, yeast breads will not rise. Fine, so you will not be making breads with low-gluten flours alone, but that does not make them redundant. Distinct flavours, smoky, leguminous,

whatever, mean that they can contribute more than just bulk.

Wheat flour is, however, the only flour that can be manipulated to make two of the most sophisticated pastries imaginable, paper-thin filo, and fine threads of kadaif or konafa pastry, proof, if any were needed, of the grandeur of Middle Eastern cookery. It requires enormous skill to make them well, but no more than imagination and a few minutes' patience to put them to good use in cooking.

## Storing grains and pulses

Buy grains and pulses from shops with a high turnover. Wholefood and healthfood shops usually have the greatest variety, but be suspicious if business is sluggish every time you visit. Dried grains and pulses are meant to keep, but they are not immortal, and after all, they ought to be keeping at your convenience, not the retailers! Grains should really be used up within four months of purchase before their natural oils turn rancid, pulses within, at the outside, two years. The older they are, the longer they will take to cook. Since you cannot possibly have the faintest idea how long it has taken them to get from the field via wholesaler and retailer to your kitchen, it is probably best to polish them off within the year.

Always decant grains and pulses into airtight containers, and do not mix new purchases with the dregs of the last lot. Keep the containers in a cool, dark cupboard, away from heat and light. If you work your way through them speedily, they will not suffer disastrous consequences if they sit on an open shelf, but do not let them linger.

I loathe weevils. I do not know quite why I find them so repulsive, but I do. Storing grains, flours and pulses in airtight jars should keep them safe from infestation, but I am afraid it is no guarantee. Weevils, the horrid little so-and-so's, lay their eggs in grain when it is still in the field. Sometimes the eggs survive

processing, and emerge as fully grown specimens in your kitchen. There is nothing to be done but throw the whole lot out (I put them down the waste-disposal unit, with callous satisfaction), wash the jar thoroughly with soapy water, rinsing it out with boiling water. Airtight containers will at least prevent them migrating to other grains nearby. Weevil eggs, by the way, are absolutely and totally harmless.

# GRAINS

Before I talk about my chosen grains, a few words about cooking them. There are two basic methods.

## Basic Pilaff Method

When you decide to serve a grain, any grain, as a partner to a main course you could opt for plain boiling. They will taste okay, not wonderful, but okay. You will get more out of them if you opt for the pilaff method, frying them first in a little oil, then adding a measured quantity of liquid which they absorb as they cook with no further disturbance. Minor refinements, adding a little onion and garlic, a few herbs, nuts or dried fruit, using stock instead of water, improve them further. Major additions – vegetables, meat, fish – can turn the pilaff into a meal on its own. The fundamental method stays the same:

For every 225 g (8 oz) whole grain:
2 tablespoons oil or butter
2-3 times its volume of liquid, water or stock
salt and pepper

1 medium onion, finely chopped (optional)
1 garlic clove, finely chopped (optional)

Slow-cooking grains, e.g. whole wheat or barley, or brown rice, can be soaked for a few hours or overnight, to speed up the cooking process.

If using onion and garlic, cook them gently in the oil or butter until tender without browning. Add the grain, and stir over a medium heat for 2–3 minutes to toast lightly, and coat evenly in fat. Add the liquid, salt and pepper. Bring up to the boil. Lower the heat right down, cover the pan tightly, and leave to simmer very gently, avoiding the temptation to stir. Check after 15 minutes (longer if it is a slow-cooking grain), taste and – if really necessary – add a little extra hot liquid – some grains will absorb more than twice their volume. Cover again and continue cooking until the grains are tender and all the liquid has been absorbed. When cooked, turn off the heat and let the pan stand, still covered, for 5 minutes, letting the steam plump up and separate the grains. Fluff up with a fork, check the seasoning, and serve, adding a large knob of butter unless you are worrying over your cholesterol intake.

### Absorbtion Method

This is the pilaff method minus the oil, and best reserved for cooking rice. Generally speaking, you use twice as much liquid as rice (in terms of volume, not weight), put them both into a pan with salt, bring up to the boil, cover tightly, and leave to simmer quietly over a low heat for 10–20 minutes until the rice is tender, and the liquid all absorbed. Add a little extra liquid if you have to. Turn off the heat, let it sit, still covered, for 5 minutes, then fluff up the grains with a fork (unless it is glutinous rice, in which case they are meant to stick together). Butter or yoghurt can be added to moisten.

## RICE

Classifying rice merely as long- or short-grained, brown or white, is over-simplifying the subject and just will not do. There are literally thousands of different varieties of rice. Admittedly, many of them are barely distinguishable in terms of culinary use, but a fair number stand out

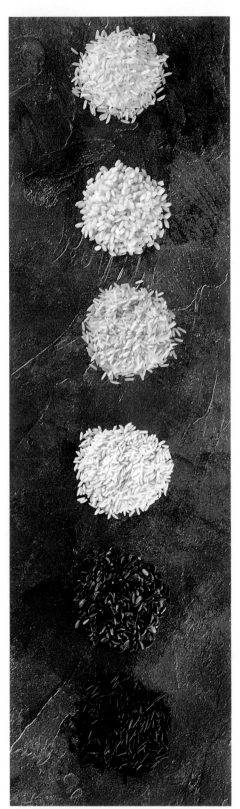

FROM THE TOP: VALENCIA RICE, ITALIAN RISOTTO RICE, BASMATI RICE, WHITE GLUTINOUS RICE, BLACK GLUTINOUS RICE, WILD RICE.

from the crowd with clear individual virtues.

Naturally, the rice dishes of any rice-growing country or area take advantage of the particular properties of their home-grown rice. Substitute an alien rice and, although the result may be quite palatable, it will bear scant resemblance to the real McCoy and is unlikely to taste anywhere near as good as it.

**Italian Risotto Rice**   There is absolutely no point whatsoever in attempting to make a risotto with anything other than proper Italian risotto rice, grown in the rice-fields of the Po valley. Risotto rice is a stubby plump long-grain, which swells and absorbs large quantities of liquid without collapsing to a mush. Its generous apportionment of starch is what makes risotto so creamy. Two grades of rice are used for risottos – *fino*, and better still, *superfino*. For star-rated risottos, choose arborio or carnaroli, both *superfino*.

**Valencia Rice**   The marshlands around Valencia are home to Spain's rice-growing industry. The rice produced is a short-grained variety and it may come as something of a surprise to learn that this is what should be used for a true paella. Abroad, paella is made, more often than not, with long-grain rice, which changes the nature of the dish. Of course, it is not just any old short-grain. Unlike cheap pudding rice, it holds its shape well, as long as it is cooked in a shallow layer, though it is not as sturdy as risotto rice.

**Basmati Rice**   The king of the long-grains, slender, curved Indian Basmati has a unique scent and flavour. Unappreciative souls describe it as "mousey", which is selling it short. This is the rice to use for biriani or pilau, but it is also one of the two best all-rounders (Thai fragrant rice is the other). It cooks to light, separate, fluffy grains, ideal rice as a side dish with stews of many kinds, or for rice salads.

**Thai Fragrant Rice** Thai fragrant rice is a long-grain with a delightful fragrance, as its name implies. This is the best "separate-grain" rice to partner South-East Asian foods, and a classic all-rounder, though a little stickier than Basmati. Most Oriental shops sell it.

**Chinese White Glutinous Rice** Although it does not actually contain any gluten, "glutinous" describes the texture of this rice well. The high starch content makes the cooked grains sticky and soft, so that they cling together in a mass. It is not the everyday Chinese rice, although for Westerners it is far easier to eat with chopsticks than straight long-grain. Its soothing blandness is a perfect backdrop to highly spiced Chinese and South-East Asian dishes. Glutinous rice is used to make congee, a rice porridge, and sweet dishes. It is also extremely useful for making rice fritters, or stuffed rice balls.

**Chinese Black Glutinous Rice** The grains look as if they had been charred and burnt in the fire. Although it can be eaten as a savoury rice, it is usually reserved for sweet or semi-sweet dishes. It has a malty flavour, and, when cooked, the colour changes to a dark blackberry purple. Overnight soaking speeds up cooking. Indonesians make a delicious black rice pudding with coconut milk. It is excellent cooked in more Western style, as well. Try cooking it in milk, with sugar and vanilla, then setting it in moulds, perhaps layered with white pudding rice.

**Wild Rice** Often described as the "caviar of grains", but not merely on account of its frighteningly high price! The long, glossy black needles split open to reveal a tan interior when cooked, and have a delicious nutty flavour and chewy texture. A little goes a long way, so do not let the price put you off. Botanically, wild rice is not a true rice, but it is a member of the same family.

Although wild rice is cultivated to some

degree in parts of America, in Canada it does indeed grow wild in the lakes and is still harvested by Indians in canoes. No chemicals, no fertilizers. Much of the grain falls back into the water, naturally reseeding itself, and providing food for the wild life. All in all, an ecologically sound crop.

Like brown rice, it takes a good 35–40 minutes to cook. It should never be boiled until soft and soggy. The point of wild rice is that it is chewy and substantial. It is best dressed with a large knob of butter, pepper and maybe a squeeze of orange juice.

## BUCKWHEAT
(Beechwheat, Saracen corn, Kasha)

Whole buckwheat is an Eastern European staple, with an almost meaty, smoky flavour. You can buy it in two forms, either plain and untampered with, or roasted, which enhances its naturally earthy flavour, and is, for my money, by far the better buy. Buckwheat is not a true grain. That is,

it is not the fruit of a cultivated grass. Buckwheat is the seed of a plant that belongs to the same family as rhubarb and sorrel.

Properly speaking, kasha means a cooked grain porridge, but buckwheat is often sold as kasha. Whole buckwheat can be simmered in salted water until tender, but it is improved by cooking as a pilaff, with stock. Mushrooms are a natural addition. Use either dried mushrooms, soaked and chopped, or a mixture of dried and fresh, cooking them first with onion and garlic, before adding the buckwheat. Use the soaking water as part of the cooking liquid. Served with a dollop (or more) of soured cream on top, it makes a meal in itself.

## WHOLE WHEAT
(Wheat berries)

Wheat does not have to be ground down to flour before it can be eaten. Wheat

CLOCKWISE FROM TOP LEFT: BUCKWHEAT, WHOLE WHEAT, BARLEY

berries, plump and golden, have a rich, sweet nutty flavour and make delicious eating. Unless freshly picked, they take a while to cook, an hour or longer before they become tender, and even then they retain a chewy texture. Timing can be reduced by overnight soaking, always a good idea with dried wheat. As the wheat cooks, the outer bran layer bursts open to reveal the white inner grain. If you carry on simmering, the wheat eventually softens to a soft, gelatinous texture, lovely in sweet dishes, such as the old English frumenty.

Besides making a good pilaff, whole wheat is a welcome addition to slow-cooking soups and casseroles. A favourite of mine is the Egyptian "ferique", a tumeric-scented chicken stew with whole wheat and eggs, which I discovered in Claudia Roden's *Book of Middle Eastern Food*. Well-soaked wheat berries can also be used whole in bread doughs.

MILLET, QUINOA

## BARLEY

If there was nothing else that could possibly be made with whole barley other than Lemon Barley Water, then that alone would justify its existence. Home-made lemon barley water is quite marvellous on a hot summer's day, and puts the commercial junk totally in the shade.

But, of course, there are other uses. Pot barley is barley with its tough outer husk removed, but a thin layer of bran still adhering to the inner grain. Pearl barley has had the bran layer polished off, too. Even with an over-night soak, pot barley still takes at least an hour to cook until tender. Allow at least 45 minutes when cooking pearl barley.

Using barley in lengthily cooked stews and soups is common practice (for instance in Scotch Broth), and, like other grains, it can be used alone as a pilaff. The flavour of barley merges well into sweet dishes, too. Barley can be substituted for wheat in frumenty, or pre-cooked and finished by simmering in a scented syrup.

## MILLET

A grain that is often unfairly overlooked. Millet has a mild flavour which is never going to make headline news, but it is the texture that really appeals to me, creamy and knobbly at the same time. It makes an ideal accompaniment to spicy stews. Cook it as a pilaff, using 2½–3 times its volume of water, stock or milk (you may even find that it takes a little more, since it puffs up dramatically, sucking in liquid like nobody's business), with generous seasonings. Like quinoa, it makes a warming breakfast cereal, or can be baked in the oven with milk and cream, sugar and vanilla for pud.

## QUINOA

Quinoa is to the grain world what superman is to us mere mortals. Well, that is the impression I got from all the elegiac blurb on the back of the first packet I bought. The prose has become more subdued since then, a good deal more fitting for a grain that is pleasant to eat but

hardly a mind-blowing gastronomic experience.

This "supergrain of the future" is more a supergrain of the past, dating back to the Incas. It is still grown high in the Andes in Bolivia and Peru. It gets the "super" prefix from the fact that it is immensely high in proteins and, what is more, complete proteins, rather than the usual incomplete protein of most grains, i.e. it is ideal for vegetarians.

It has a mild taste, and a firm, bobbly texture, much less "worthy" than, say, brown rice. When cooked, the tiny round grains become translucent, ringed with a band of white – polka-dot Uranuses. It makes a fine pilaff, absorbing about double its volume of water, improved by the presence of more demonstrative additions, tomatoes, chillies, garlic, and so on. A good basis for stuffings, too. Try it as a breakfast cereal, adding a chopped apple and a handful of raisins or other chopped dried fruit to the pan as it cooks. Sweeten to taste when done, and serve hot or cold with extra milk, yoghurt or cream.

# FRUMENTY

*An old English pudding of whole grains cooked long and slowly until they burst and soften. If you use barley, save the water from the initial cooking to make a glass or two of lemon barley water.*

**Serves 8**

**225 g (8 oz) whole wheat or barley,
    soaked for 8 hours and drained**
**pinch of salt**
**600 ml (1 pint) milk**
**300 ml (½ pint) single cream**
**50 g (2 oz) raisins**
**40 g (1½ oz) vanilla sugar or plain caster
    sugar and 1 vanilla pod**
**generous pinch of saffron threads,
    crushed**
**3 egg yolks, beaten**
**freshly grated nutmeg**

Place the wheat or barley and salt in a pan and add enough water to cover generously. Bring up to the boil, and simmer until the grains are tender and bursting open. Drain well and rinse out the pan. Return the grains to the pan with the milk, cream, raisins, sugar, vanilla pod, if using, and saffron. Bring up to the boil, stirring. Cover and simmer gently for 20–25 minutes. Draw off the heat and let the bubbles subside. Whisk 3 tablespoons of the cooking liquid into the egg yolks, then tip them into the pan and stir well. Add the nutmeg and return to a very low heat for a minutes or so, stirring constantly, until it thickens. Serve hot or cold.

# HAZELNUT YOGHURT CAKE

*Serve this cake on its own, or with fresh fruit and whipped cream.*

**Serves 8**

**75 g (3 oz) self-raising flour**
**pinch of salt**
**1 teaspoon baking powder**
**225 g (8 oz) semolina**
**150 g (5 oz) vanilla sugar or caster sugar
    and 1 teaspoon vanilla essence**
**150 ml (¼ pint) oil**
**1 × 225 g (8 oz) tub Greek yoghurt**
**1 tablespoon orange flower water**
**2 eggs, beaten**
**50 g (2 oz) lightly toasted hazelnuts, very
    finely chopped**
SYRUP:
**175 g (6 oz) sugar**
**juice of 1 lemon**
**300 ml (½ pint) water**

Sift the flour with salt and baking powder, and mix with the semolina and sugar. Make a well in the centre and add the oil, yoghurt, vanilla essence if using, orange flower water and eggs. Mix until smooth. Pour into a buttered 20 cm (8 inch) cake tin. Sprinkle over the hazelnuts.

Bake in a moderately hot oven (190°C, 375°F, Gas Mark 5) for 35–40 minutes, until a skewer put into the centre comes out clean.

Meanwhile, make the syrup. Place the sugar, lemon juice and water in a pan and stir over a moderate heat until the sugar has dissolved. Bring to the boil and simmer for 5 minutes.

Turn out the cake, and set in a shallow dish, hazelnut crust upwards. Pierce in about a dozen places with a skewer, and pour over the syrup. Leave to cool, basting frequently with the syrup seeping out around the cake. Once the cake is cold, cover it and leave it for at least an hour, preferably 24 hours, to really soak the stuff in.

# KADAIF MOUNDS

*Rounded mounds of kadaif, filled with nuts, are known as "young girls' breasts" in Turkey, the resemblance is obvious. At the heart of these "breasts" is a moist green filling of angelica and pistachio nuts, a beautiful discovery as you cut into them.*

**Makes 8**

SYRUP:
**225 g (8 oz) sugar**
**1 tablespoon lemon juice**
**250 ml (8 fl oz) water**
**50 g (2 oz) clear honey**
FILLING:
**50 g (2 oz) pistachios, finely chopped**
**50 g (2 oz) almonds, finely chopped**
**50 g (2 oz) angelica, finely chopped**

**200 g (7 oz) unsalted butter, melted**
**350 g (12 oz) kadaif pastry**
**8 almond halves**

To make the syrup, place the sugar and lemon juice in a pan with the water. Stir over a moderate heat until the sugar has completely dissolved, then bring to the boil. Boil for 5 minutes, stir in the honey, bring back to the boil, then leave to cool.

Mix the finely chopped nuts and angelica for the filling.

Grease 2 baking trays with a little of the melted butter. Pour all except for about 1 tablespoon of the remaining butter over the kadaif. Gently turn and squeeze the pastry, until each strand is buttery and supple. Divide into 8 portions. Keep the buttered kadaif covered while you work.

Find a small teacup or a ladle, about 6–7.5 cm (2½–3 inches) in diameter. Brush with some of the reserved butter. Place an almond half in the bottom. Pack in a rough two-thirds of one portion of kadaif. With your finger, make a

depression in the centre, pressing the pastry firmly up around the sides of the mould. Fill with one-eighth of the nut mixture. Cover with the remaining third of the portion of pastry, pressing down firmly to compact. Place your fingers or a saucer over the mould, invert, and let the pastry slide out, giving it a few taps to loosen it if it sticks. Transfer carefully to a buttered baking sheet. Repeat until all the pastry is used up (8 mounds).

Bake in a moderately hot oven (190°C, 375°F, Gas Mark 5) for 30 minutes until browned. Remove from the oven and pour the syrup evenly over. Leave to cool, basting occasionally with any stray syrup.

FROM THE LEFT, KADAIF MOUNDS, HAZLENUT YOGHURT CAKE, FRUMENTY

Fortunately, the range and availability of good dairy products is on the increase, I can whizz down to the supermarket on the corner and get thick Greek yoghurt, French fromage frais or Russian-style smatana, all made on a commercial scale to be sure, but still delicious. An excellent wholefood shop provides similar products and more, made with care and enthusiasm by small-scale producers.

The bulk of the dairy products I have included in this selection fall broadly into two groups as far as the cook is concerned: thick but runny or, at least, spoonable types, including creams and fromage frais (although technically a cheese), and fresh unripened cheeses, firm enough to hold their shape, milky and moist. In addition, there is a brace of singletons, far too interesting to omit – plain goat's milk, and goat's milk butter.

### Cultured products

It is such a charming term, isn't it? I can just see that little gaggle of cultured yoghurt pots trooping off to the opera. However, we are not dealing with that kind of culture here. Cultured milk products, such as yoghurt, buttermilk, or crème fraîche are milk (and/or cream) thickened by the introduction of bacterial cultures. Nurtured under the right conditions, the bacteria feast on the milk's lactose, transforming it into lactic acid, and other by-products. It is the acid, rather than the bacteria themselves, which coagulates the milk, as well as sharpening the flavour. The other by-products are what give each cultured product its individual characteristics.

### Fresh Cheeses

The first step in cheesemaking is the introduction to the milk of a bacterial culture, the starter, to develop a degree of acidity. Step two is the addition of rennet, a coagulant extracted from the stomach of calves or lambs, or from certain plants. This is what forms the curds, which are then cut and drained or pressed into shape.

Fresh cheeses are simply unripened, immature cheeses in the first flush of existence. The curds are then drained to a greater or lesser extent, and may be beaten to smooth them out, or moulded into shape. At this point, the flavour of the cheese will have begun to develop but will still be mild and understated. The cheese will be moist and malleable with no suggestion of a crust.

Elementary fresh cheeses can be made at home. Strained yoghurt cheeses (see Greek Sheep's Milk Yoghurt, page 179), are rich and tartly flavoured. The easiest curd cheese is made by heating milk to blood temperature (37°C/98°F), or, as a rough guide, when you can hold your finger in the milk for 10 seconds but no longer), and stirring in lemon juice (1 tablespoon to a pint of milk). This is set aside for an hour or two, allowing the curds to form, and then drained through a muslin-lined sieve. Mix the drained curds with a little cream and salt, and Bob's your uncle. A second method is to make an unflavoured junket with rennet (instructions are always given on the bottle or packet), then to cut and drain the curds. Fresh cheeses should be eaten within a day or two of purchase, unless they arrive sealed in an airtight packet. Once the packet has been breached the time limit is the same. Commercial fromage frais has a more protracted life expectancy, a good week or so in the refrigerator, as long as you are not overstepping the use-by date.

### Heating Dairy Products

Heating the runny types of dairy product is fraught with problems. Most of them are happy enough in mixtures that contain flour and/or eggs, to be baked or fried until set (e.g. fillings for quiches, cakes or pancakes), but can be most temperamental in more liquid preparations, such as sauces and soups. Take them up anywhere near boiling point and they have an unpleasant tendency to curdle, leaving you with a most unseemly-looking sauce.

Exceptions are those creams with a generous provision of butterfats – double cream, crème fraîche, and clotted cream. You can whisk these into a hot sauce (off the heat to be on the safe side), then bring the whole lot back to the boil and simmer down to an unctuous thickness.

The less fatty cultured products are the difficult ones. You are faced with two alternatives (apart from abandoning the project altogether):

1. Either stir into the sauce, at the end of the cooking period, with the pan off the heat, all bubbling well and truly at an end. Add a spoonful at a time – if the sauce is still too hot, the first couple of spoonfuls may curdle, but at least they will cool things down. As long as the bulk of the matter does not curdle, nobody will notice anything amiss.

2. The medium-fat cultured range can be stabilized – i.e. those with at least 8 per cent fat content, which includes some yoghurts and a smatana, but not buttermilk or low-fat fromage frais. To be honest, I am not convinced that this is worth the bother. During the process the yogurt or whatever does curdle, but the added cornflour thickens to hold the tiny grains together, giving the appearance of a smooth cream. It still feels grainy to the tongue, however, even if it looks okay. If you do want to give it a try, here is what you do: mix your product with a cornflour solution – 1 tablespoon cornflour dissolved in 1½ tablespoons of water to every pint – then heat gently to a simmer, and simmer for 10 minutes, stirring occasionally.

Fresh cheeses, with the exception of fromage frais, are much easier to deal with. Heat them up, in a cheesecake mixture say, or a filling for ravioli, and they will keep their form without mishap. It is unlikely that you will be using them for making hot sauces, but if the occasion arises, treat them gently, and avoid boiling.

### A Note on Fat Content

The more health-conscious travellers amongst us may have noticed, probably with horror, that in France dairy products seem to have a remarkably high fat content in comparison with very similar products bought in Britain. Actually, the difference is not truly so marked. It has more to do with number-crunching than cholesterol overkill. In France, the fat content, *matière grasse*, is calculated as a percentage of "dry matter", in other words solids, or what would be left if all the watery matter were sucked out. In Britain, it is calculated as a percentage of the total mass; solids and liquids lumped in all together, which seems a great deal more logical to me, but I dare say the French have their reasons.

### Approximate Butterfat Content for Dairy Products

|  | % BUTTERFAT |
| --- | --- |
| Buttermilk | 0.1% |
| Fromage frais | 0.1-8% |
| Greek sheep's milk yoghurt | 8% |
| Strained yoghurt | 10% |
| Smatana | 10% |
| Half cream | 12% |
| Ricotta | 15-20% |
| Single cream | 18% |
| Soured cream | 20% |
| Whipping cream | 35% |
| Crème fraîche | minimum 35% |
| Double cream | 48% |
| Clotted cream | minimum 55% |
| Mascarpone | 90% |

CLOTTED CREAM

## CLOTTED CREAM

Fresh strawberries and clotted cream in the summer, warm scones, home-made strawberry jam, and clotted cream in the winter. Clotted cream is one of the gems of Britain's culinary heritage, made from the rich milk of Devon and Cornwall, and so thick that you can literally stand your spoon up in it. In winter, when the milk is richer, the cream for those scones is, or should be, thicker than summer cream for soft fruit.

Traditionally, it is made by slowly heating great bowls of creamy milk to a temperature of 80-85°C/176-185°F, holding it at that temperature for 30 minutes or so, then cooling it. The cream rises and forms a thick golden crust on top of the milk, begging to be skimmed off and slathered on warm scones. The heating gives the cream its "cooked" flavour, and prolongs shelf-life. Clotted cream has a butterfat content of 55% or more.

## KAYMAK
(Kaimaki, Eishta)

The British are not the only makers of clotted cream. Middle Eastern kaymak or eishta is another "cooked" cream, made not from cow's milk, but from sheep's or water buffalo's milk, both of which have very high fat contents, perfect for cream-making. Though the method is similar, the end result has a distinctive flavour and can be even thicker than Cornish clotted cream. In an Athenian dairy, I ate kaimaki solid enough to be dished up in curls, like butter, blissful, with soft white rolls and Hymettus honey.

## GOAT'S MILK

Goat's milk is richer than cow's milk and, though the taste is similar in character, it is stronger with a hint of the muskiness of goat's cheese. I would not splash it into a cup of tea or coffee, but it gives a good flavour to sauces and, perhaps more surprisingly, many a milk-based pudding. Goat's milk fudge is a treat, but the ultimate is the wickedly sticky Cajeta from Mexico, the grown-up's version of boiled condensed milk toffee. Full instructions are given on page 183.

## GOAT'S CREAM BUTTER

It looks like lard but do not let that put you off. If you like goat's cheese and yoghurt, then try goat's cream butter if you get the chance. It has the kind of taste you would expect, buttery, but with an unmistakably goaty flavour. It is good enough to eat neat, slathered on to bread, toast or water biscuits. I would hesitate to add a layer of jam or any other sweet spread; the taste of goat's cream butter is geared to savoury embellishment.

## FRESH GOAT'S CHEESE

(Chèvre frais; Chèvre frais en faisselle

This is goat's cheese at its youngest, the precursor to ripened firm goat's cheese with a drier, sandy texture. The curds are ladled into "faisselles", perforated moulds that would once have been made of earthenware, but are more likely to be of plastic these days. The filled faisselles are left to drain until the curds will hold together when turned out. That is it. The cheese is now ready to be eaten, still moist

TOP: FRESH GOAT'S CHEESE, GOAT'S MILK; BOTTOM: GOAT'S CREAM BUTTER

and soft. Just enough time has elapsed for the cheese to develop a trace of goaty cheesiness, but only a trace. If little or no salt is added, it can still be eaten with sugar for a pudding, like fromage frais or blanc.

I love this mild young cheese and use it in many ways. Beaten with crème fraîche, it is excellent with crudités, and on occasions I have used the same combination to make

"chèvre chantilly", sweetened and scented with vanilla. I toss it in with pasta, or use it as a filling for pastries (sweet and savoury), vegetables, and strudels.

Fresh goat's cheese is often sold sealed in plastic tubs. Once opened, the cheese must be eaten within 48 hours. Unless kept in perfect cheese-ripening conditions, it soon goes off.

# TAGLIATELLE WITH BEANS & GOAT'S CHEESE

*An inspired shopping trip invention. The fresh broad beans caught my eye first. En route to a pint of milk, I noticed tubs of fresh goat's cheese and remembered the tagliatelle waiting at home. What a feast of a supper we had that night!*

*Removing the tough grey skins of cooked broad beans makes a huge difference. Since the quantity here is small it won't take too much time, and can be done well in advance.*

**Serves 2 as a main course, 4 as a first course**

**225 g (8 oz) shelled broad beans**
**225 g (8 oz) tagliatelle**
**150-175 g (5-6 oz) young, soft goat's cheese**
**1 tablespoon chopped mint**
**2 tablespoons olive oil**
**salt and pepper**

Cook the broad beans in lightly salted water. Drain and cool for a few minutes. Slit the tough outer skins and slip out the tender green beans inside. Finish cooling, cover and set aside until needed.

Bring a large pan of lightly salted water to the boil, and add the tagliatelle. Cook until just *al dente*. Beat the goat's cheese with the mint, 1 ½ tablespoons of the olive oil, salt and pepper. When the tagliatelle is almost done, reheat the broad beans in the remaining oil in a small pan.

Drain the tagliatelle, return to the warm pan and mix with the goat's cheese mixture. Tip into a warm serving dish, scatter the beans over the top and eat immediately.

# CAJETA ENVINADA
## (DULCE DE LECHE)

*Dulce de Leche is made throughout Latin America. Cajeta Envinada is the Mexican version, a gloriously sticky confection of caramelized, concentrated goat's milk, spiked with a splash of alcohol. It is used as a topping for ice cream and a filling for pancakes with chopped nuts. I have also used it as a pancake filling with slices of apple sautéed in butter, or pieces of orange, and as a filling for cakes and tartlets. The possibilities are endless. I even like it spread on toast for breakfast.*

**Serves 6**

**1.2 litres (2 pints) goat's milk**
**350 g (12 oz) granulated sugar**
**1 cinnamon stick**
**level ½ teaspoon bicarbonate of soda**
**2-3 tablespoons dry sherry, brandy or moscatel wine**

Pour the milk into a very large, heavy-based saucepan and stir in the sugar and cinnamon stick. Slowly bring up to the boil, stirring until the sugar has completely dissolved. Draw off the heat. Mix the bicarbonate of soda with a tablespoon of water. Pour into the milk syrup, stirring constantly as it bubbles up (that is why you need such a big pan).

Put the pan back on the hob and simmer for around an hour, stirring occasionally for the first 30 minutes. As the mixture begins to thicken, keep a careful eye on it, reducing the heat if necessary, and stir frequently to prevent burning. Keep going until it is thick and caramel-coloured and the base of the pan can be seen when a spoon is dragged across it. Strain the mixture through a fine sieve, and mix in the sherry, brandy or moscatel. Cool and store, tightly covered, in the refrigerator for up to 3 months, if needs be.

# TURNIP WITH FROMAGE FRAIS & CAPERS

*Grated turnip and capers may not sound too enticing, but I promise you, it turns out to be quite delicious. I have also made this dish with beetroot, another winner.*

**Serves 4**

**450 g (1 lb) turnips**
**2 tablespoons olive oil**
**salt and pepper**
**2 teaspoons lemon juice**
**1 tablespoon capers**
**1 tablespoon finely chopped parsley**
**6 tablespoons fromage frais**

Peel the turnips and grate them coarsely. Heat the oil in a frying pan and add the turnips, stirring to coat well. Season with salt and pepper, and add the lemon juice, and 4 tablespoons of water. Cover and cook over a moderate heat for 10 minutes or so, stirring occasionally, until most of the liquid has evaporated and the turnip is tender. If necessary, add a little extra water.

Draw off the heat, and add the capers and parsley. Let the mixture cool for a minute or so, then stir in the fromage frais, a tablespoon at a time. Taste and adjust the seasonings before serving.

# SHRIKAND

*My first taste of Shrikand came in an Indian vegetarian restaurant in Manchester. Love at first mouthful. Sweetly perfumed, thick and rich, it is hard to believe that it started life as homely yoghurt. Serve in small bowls – a little goes a long way.*

**Serves 4**

**600 ml (1 pint) Greek sheep's milk or strained yoghurt**
**generous pinch of saffron threads**
**2 teaspoons rosewater**
**3 cardamom pods**
**icing sugar**
**1 tablespoon toasted slivered almonds or pistachio nuts**

Line a large sieve with a double layer of butter muslin. Pour the yoghurt into the lined sieve, and gather up the edges of the muslin. Tie a knot to form a bag, and hang it up to drip. Leave for four hours, or until it is good and thick.

Scrape all the strained yoghurt into a bowl. Dry-fry the saffron for a few seconds to crisp up, cool and pound to a powder. Mix with the rosewater and let it stand for 10 minutes to dissolve. Split the cardamom pods, and crush the seeds inside as finely as possible. Stir the rosewater and cardamom into the yoghurt with sugar to taste. Divide among four small bowls and scatter the almonds or pistachio nuts over the top.

# CHICKPEA & HAZELNUT CREAM

*Though the consistency of this cream is similar to hummus, the toasted hazelnut and yoghurt give a new balance of flavours. Serve as a first course, or part of a mixed hors d'oeuvres, with warm pitta bread and raw salad vegetables.*

**Serves 8-12**

**50 g (2 oz) hazelnuts**
**½ tablespoon cumin seeds**
**350 g (12 oz) cooked chickpeas**
**2 garlic cloves, chopped**
**225 g (8 oz) Greek sheep's milk yoghurt or strained yoghurt**
**2 tablespoons olive oil, plus a little extra to serve**
**1 tablespoon chopped fresh mint, plus a whole sprig to serve**
**juice of 1-1½ lemons**
**salt**
**cayenne pepper**

Spread the hazelnuts out on a baking sheet and toast in a hot oven (200°C, 400°F, Gas Mark 6), for 5-10 minutes, until lightly browned. Roll in a wire sieve to remove the skins. Cool and chop roughly. In a small heavy frying pan, dry-fry the cumin seeds until they give off an intense aromatic smell. Cool.

Place the hazelnuts, cumin seeds, chickpeas, garlic, sheep's milk or yoghurt and oil in a blender and whizz briefly to give a grainy cream. Stir in the mint, and add the lemon juice, salt and cayenne pepper to taste. Leave for 30 minutes before serving.

To serve, spoon the cream into a bowl. Spiral a thin trickle of olive oil over the top, dust with cayenne pepper and top with the reserved sprig of mint.

# HERRING & CREME FRAICHE SALAD

*Matjes herrings are cured in a sugared brine, giving a gentle sweet flavour. The sharp fruitiness of apple, soft bite of red onion, and mild acidity of crème fraîche set them off admirably in this first-course salad. Swedish pickled herrings could be used instead, but, please, not vinegar-vicious rollmops.*

**Serves 4-6**

**225 g (8 oz) matjes herring fillets**
**1 tart eating apple (e.g. Granny Smith)**
**juice of ½ lemon**
**1 red onion**
**150 ml (¼ pint) crème fraîche**
**salt and pepper**
**1½ tablespoons chopped chives**

Cut the herring into pieces about 2.5 cm (1 inch) square. Core the apple, but do not peel it, then dice it into 1 cm (½ inch) cubes. Toss in the lemon juice. Slice the onion thinly. Set aside one of the thin slices, separating it into rings, and chop the rest. Mix the herring, apples, chopped onion, crème fraîche, salt and pepper and 1 tablespoon of the chopped chives. Taste and adjust the seasonings. Pile into a shallow serving dish, arrange the reserved onion rings on top and scatter over the remaining chives.

FROM THE LEFT: SMATANA PANCAKES, HERRING AND CREME FRAICHE SALAD, CHICKPEA AND HAZELNUT CREAM SERVED WITH RAW VEGETABLES

# SMATANA
# PANCAKES

*Serve these light little pancakes on their own, or
make more of a song and dance of it and
embellish them with extra smatana and salmon
caviar, smoked salmon, fried mushrooms, or
sweet and sour Swedish pickled herring. For
dessert pancakes, omit the dill, pepper and all
but a small pinch of salt. Use caster or vanilla
sugar, and increase the amount to 1 tablespoon.*

**Serves 4-6**

**75 g (3 oz) self-raising flour, sifted**
**¼ teaspoon bicarbonate of soda**
**salt and pepper**
**1 teaspoon caster sugar**
**nutmeg**
**300 ml (½ pint) smatana**
**1 egg, lightly beaten**
**1 tablespoon chopped fresh dill**
**oil or oil and butter, for frying**

Sift the flour with the bicarbonate of soda and
½ teaspoon salt. Stir in the pepper, sugar and a
grating of fresh nutmeg. Make a well in the
centre and add the smatana and egg. Mix to a
smooth batter. Fold in the dill. Rest for 30
minutes before using.

Grease a heavy frying pan or griddle and heat
it thoroughly. Drop tablespoonfuls of the
mixture into the pan and cook until browned
underneath, with small holes appearing in the
upper surface. Turn them over and cook until
browned. The pancakes are best eaten as they
come out of the pan; otherwise keep them
warm, piled up on absorbent kitchen paper,
while you fry the rest of the pancakes.

# GOAT'S CHEESE CHEESECAKE

*This American-style baked cheesecake can be made with a biscuit-crumb base.*

**Serves 6-8**

**225 g (8 oz) shortcrust pastry**
FILLING:
**200 g (7 oz) fresh goat's cheese**
**75 g (3 oz) cream cheese**
**2 eggs**
**75 g (3 oz) vanilla sugar**
**finely grated zest of I lemon**
**I tablespoon lemon juice**
THE CROWNING GLORY:
**300 ml (½ pint) crème fraîche**
**I tablespoon vanilla sugar**
**pinch of salt**

Line a 20cm (8 inch) tart or shallow cake tin, 5 cm (2 inches) deep, with a removable base, with the pastry. Prick the base with a fork and rest in the fridge for 30 minutes. Line with foil or greaseproof paper, and fill with baking beans. Bake blind in a moderately hot oven (200°C, 400°F, Gas Mark 6) for 10 minutes, remove the paper and beans and return to the oven for 3 or 4 minutes to dry out.

Beat the goat's cheese with the cream cheese to soften. Beat in the eggs, then the remaining filling ingredients to give a smooth cream. Pour into the pastry case. Bake in a moderate oven (180°C, 350°F, Gas Mark 4) for 25 minutes. Take the cheesecake out of the oven, and raise the oven temperature to hot (220°C, 425°F, Gas Mark 7). Cool the cheesecake for 10 minutes.

While it cools, beat the crème fraîche with the vanilla sugar and salt, then pour over the cheesecake, spreading evenly. Return to the oven for 5 minutes. Cool, then chill for at least 4 hours, but preferably for 12-24 hours. As the cake cools, the layer of crème fraîche thickens, then sets in the cold of the refrigerator.

# CARROT & HAM STRUDEL

*Ricotta makes a good base for the filling in this savoury strudel. Butter gives a better sheen to the pastry but olive oil provides as good a flavour.*

**Serves 6-8**

FILLING:
**350 g (12 oz) carrots, coarsely grated**
**I onion, chopped**
**2 garlic cloves, chopped**
**I bay leaf**
**2 sprigs thyme**
**25 g (I oz) butter, or 2 tablespoons olive oil**
**225 g (8 oz) cooked ham, diced**
**1½ tablespoons chopped parsley**
**225 g (8 oz) ricotta**
**2 eggs**
**salt and pepper**
**nutmeg**

**6 × 30 cm × 45 cm (12 × 18 inch) sheets filo pastry**
**50-75 g (2-3 oz) melted butter or 4-6 tablespoons olive oil**
**2 tablespoons dried breadcrumbs**

To make the filling, sweat the carrots, onion, garlic, bay leaf and thyme in the butter or oil in a covered pan over a low heat for 10 minutes. Cool, then mix with the remaining filling ingredients.

Lay one sheet of filo pastry out on a large sheet of greaseproof paper. Brush with melted butter or oil. Lay a second sheet on the paper, overlapping the first by a quarter of its width, so that you get a larger rectangle, almost a square. Brush the second sheet with butter or oil. Repeat with the remaining pastry, laying it sheet by sheet on top of the other two in the same way. Sprinkle the breadcrumbs evenly over a 10 cm (4 inch) band at one end of the pastry,

parallel to the overlap. Place the filling on top, moulding it gently to give a tubby sausage shape, leaving a 7.5 cm (3 inch) border down either side. Flip the border up to cover the ends of the filling, then, using the greaseproof paper to help you, roll up the strudel loosely, so that you get a fat roll of pastry, edges neatly tucked in.

Lift on to an oiled or buttered baking sheet, with the join underneath. Brush with butter or oil. Bake in a moderate oven (180°C, 350°F, Gas Mark 4) for 35-40 minutes, until golden brown. Serve hot or warm.

# BIBLIOGRAPHY

JANE GRIGSON'S FRUIT BOOK
Jane Grigson
(Michael Joseph, 1982)

JANE GRIGSON'S VEGETABLE BOOK
Jane Grigson
(Michael Joseph, 1978)

QUEER GEAR
Carolyn Heal & Michael Allsop
(Century, 1986)

COOKING WITH SPICES
Carolyn Heal & Michael Allsop
(Panther Books, 1985)

THE COMPLETE BOOK OF FRUIT
Leslie Johns & Violet Stevenson
(Angus & Robertson, 1979)

UNCOMMON FRUITS & VEGETABLES
Elizabeth Schneider
(Harper & Row, 1986)

EXOTIC FRUIT & VEGETABLES
Jane Grigson & Charlotte Knox
(Jonathan Cape, 1986)

THE COOK'S ENCYCLOPAEDIA
Tom Stobart
(B. T. Batsford, 1980)

HERBS, SPICES AND FLAVOURINGS
Tom Stobart
(Penguin Books, 1987)

A MODERN HERBAL
Mrs. M. Grieve
(Penguin Books, 1988)

PEPPERS
Jean Andrews
(University of Texas Press, 1984)

THE COMPLETE GUIDE TO EXOTIC FRUITS
& VEGETABLES
Josephine Bacon
(Xanadu, 1988)

ON FOOD AND COOKING
Harold McGee
George Allen & Unwin, 1986

SAINSBURY'S BOOK OF FOOD
Frances Bissell
(J. Sainsbury, 1989)

READER'S DIGEST COMPLETE GUIDE TO
COOKERY
Anne Willan
(Dorling Kindersley, 1989)

NEW LAROUSSE GASTRONOMIQUE
(Hamlyn, 1977)

GLYNN CHRISTIAN'S DELICATESSEN
FOOD HANDBOOK
Glynn Christian
(MacDonald, 1982)

CLASSIC INDIAN VEGETARIAN COOKING
Julie Sahni
(Dorling Kindersley, 1987)

INDONESIAN FOOD & COOKERY
Sri Owen
(Prospect Books, 1976)

SOUTH-EAST ASIAN COOKERY
Sallie Morris
(Grafton Books, 1989)

THE CHINESE KITCHEN
Yong Yap Cotterell
(Weidenfeld & Nicolson, 1986)

A POPULAR GUIDE TO CHINESE
VEGETABLES
Karen Phillips & Martha Dahlen
(Frederick Muller Limited, 1983)

JAPANESE COOKERY, A SIMPLE ART
Shizuo Tsuji
(Kodansha International, 1985)

A NEW BOOK OF MIDDLE EASTERN FOOD
Claudia Roden (Viking, 1985)

GOOD FOOD FROM MOROCCO
Paula Wolfert
(John Murray, 1989)

NEVIN HALICI'S TURKISH COOKBOOK
Nevin Halici
(Dorling Kindersley, 1989)

GASTRONOMY OF ITALY
Anna del Conte
(Bantam Press, 1987)

GASTRONOMY OF SPAIN & PORTUGAL
Maite Manjon
(Garamond, 1990)

CATALAN CUISINE
Colman Andrews
(Headline, 1989)

THE BOOK OF LATIN AMERICAN
COOKING
Elizabeth Lambert Ortiz
(Robert Hale, 1984)

AUTHENTIC MEXICAN COOKING
Rick Bayless with Deann Groen Bayless
(Headline, 1989)

THE ART OF MEXICAN COOKING
Diana Kennedy (Bantam, 1989)